GENOA

NICHOLAS WALTON

Genoa, 'La Superba'

The Rise and Fall of a Merchant Pirate Superpower

HURST & COMPANY, LONDON

Published in the United Kingdom in paperback in 2015 by
C. Hurst & Co. (Publishers) Ltd.,
41 Great Russell Street, London, WC1B 3PL
© Nicholas Walton, 2015
All rights reserved.
Printed in India

Distributed in the United States, Canada and Latin America by
Oxford University Press, 198 Madison Avenue, New York, NY 10016,United
States of America

A Cataloguing-in-Publication data record for this book
is available from the British Library.

ISBN: 978-1-84904-512-4

www.hurstpublishers.com

To Ilaria, for showing Genoa to her two boys

CONTENTS

ACKNOWLEDGEMENTS

Thanks for helping me write this book are due to a startling array of people, starting off with my wife's family – Franca Milazzo, Armando Ida, and Valentina Ida – who showed me so much of the city and plied me with endless focaccia. My wife Ilaria threw herself into the project like the best of fixers and translators. Thanks are due to Michael Dwyer at Hurst, and the curiosity that a visit to Genoa fired in him, along with his colleagues (many of whom, like Daisy and Georgie I am only just beginning to know). Many, many others in Genoa and Liguria were recruited to the cause, and here's a list of some of them – Luciano 'Zeffirino' Belloni, Rosella Bianchi, Alessandro Boccardo, Fabio Caffarena and Graziano Mamone at L'Archivio Ligure della Scrittura Popolare di Genova, Pierangelo Campodonico, Augusto Cosulich, Anna D'Albertis, Maria Camilla De Palma, Laura Di Bisceglie, Mark Ebury, Francesco from la tripperia di vico della Casana, Gregorio Gavarone, Mattia Giachino, Michele Lilley, Mario Macchiavelli, Chiara Martinoli, Susanna Millo, Niranga and Rodrigo from Genoa Cricket 1893, Mauro Olivieri, Giorgio Panni, Diane Prahl, Don Rapallo and Carlos, Rashid the fruttivendolo, Nicola and Bianca Rocca, Pietro Romanengo and Paolo, Alberto Sacco, and Ignazio Venzano.

Thanks also to almost everybody I met in Genoa (even the grumpy ones). Others helped in different ways – Dick Oosting gave me the time off from the European Council on Foreign Relations, little realising that I'd never return, and Hans Kundnani introduced me to

ACKNOWLEDGEMENTS

Michael Dwyer. I owe a terrific debt of gratitude to my own parents, Stuart and Jennifer: without them I'd barely have got beyond page 1 of life. Finally, it all came together thanks to my son, Luca, and Ilaria, and those months that we spent as a family living several floors up a sheer marble staircase in a palazzo in Genoa's dark and enchanting *centro storico*.

TIMELINE

TIMELINE

1202-4	The Fourth Crusade, including the Venice-inspired sacking of Constantinople
Early 13th century	A Genoese sailor and pirate, Enrico Pescatore (Henry the Fisherman), sets himself up as Count of Malta, treading a thin line between piracy and legality
1261	The Greeks recapture Constantinople with Genoese help, toppling the regime left in place by the Venetians
1266	Genoa gains trading posts in the Black Sea, including Caffa and Tana
1275	Branca Doria gains immortal infamy by murdering his father in law
1271–95	Marco Polo's travels in Asia
1284	The Battle of Meloria, with Pisa defeated by Genoa under Oberto Doria
1291	The last Crusader fortress in the Holy Land, Acre, falls to the Mamluks
1297	Francesco Grimaldi (Il Malizio) leaves Genoa and seizes the Rock of Monaco
1298	The Battle of Curzola, with Genoa under Lamba Doria defeating Venice. Marco Polo is thrown into a Genoese prison and begins to relate his adventures to fellow prisoner Rustichello da Pisa
1343	Zanibek, the Kipchak Khan, converts to Islam and tries to throw the Genoese and Venetians out of their Black Sea trading stations
1346	Genoese mercenaries (and heavy rain) are blamed for France's defeat by England at the Battle of Crécy
1347	Genoese sailors fleeing the siege of Caffa in Crimea introduce the Black Death to Europe, leading to the deaths of maybe one third of the European population

TIMELINE

1348	The Galata tower is built in the centre of the Genoese colony in Constantinople
1354	The Ottoman army is ferried across from Asia to Europe by Genoese sailors for 1 ducat per soldier
1379-80	The Chioggia campaign sees Genoa defeated right on Venice's doorstep
1407	The Casa San Giorgio is set up to manage Genoa's finances
1453	The Byzantine Empire comes to an end after the Ottomans sack Constantinople (despite the assistance of Giovanni Giustiniani, and with the help of Genoese artillery expertise)
1456	Lancelotto Malocello reaches the Canaries
1470s	Christopher Columbus leaves Genoa
1492	The Moors are expelled from Spain, ultimately contributing to the Barbary Corsair problem; Columbus "discovers" the New World
1497	John Cabot (Giovanni Caboto) reaches North America
1504	Aruj Barbarossa's first major haul as a pirate
1527	Andrea Doria marches into Genoa in the employment of the French
1528	Andrea Doria ends his contract with the French and begins working for France's rival Spain. He marches into Genoa once again and expels the French. Admiral Doria also sacks Savona and fills in its port
1533	Khizr Barbarossa is summoned to Constantinople to build the Ottoman fleet
1535	Andrea Doria recaptures Tunis at the head of a Christian fleet aimed at Khizr's destruction
1543	La Lanterna is built in its current form
1560	Andrea Doria dies at the remarkable age of 93

TIMELINE

TIMELINE

1815	After the final defeat of Napoleon, the Congress of Vienna makes Liguria part of the Piedmont-dominated Kingdom of Sardinia
1822	Percy Bysshe Shelley drowns off the coast of Liguria
1831	Mazzini founds La Giovine Italia while in exile
1844	Charles Dickens adds his name to the other prominent visitors to Genoa and Liguria, with an extended stay in Albaro
1849	The short-lived Rome Republic is headed by Giuseppe Mazzini
1854	The railway between Genoa and Turin opens
1857	Herman Melville describes Genoa as "the capital and fortified camp of Satan"
1860	Garibaldi's Thousand set sail from the Genoese suburb of Quarto to liberate Southern Italy
1861	The Kingdom of Italy is founded, inadvertently sparking off the great migration of many Italians across the Atlantic (largely through Genoa)
1866	The first official mention of Romeo Viganotti chocolate factory
1867	James Richardson Spensley is born in Stoke Newington
1869	The Suez Canal opens and the Mediterranean once again finds itself on trade routes heading east. The British start to establish maritime service companies in Genoa
1872	Giuseppe Mazzini dies, and 100,000 (including Garibaldi) attend his funeral in Genoa; Luigi D'Albertis reaches the Arfak mountains in New Guinea

TIMELINE

1880s	Friedrich Nietzsche is inspired by the Promontorio Portofino during the writing of *Thus spoke Zarathustra*
1893	Genoa Cricket and Athletic Club is founded, and the Italians begin to discover calcio
1901	Laws are passed to protect vulnerable emigrants passing through Genoa
1904	Amadeo P Giannini sets up what would become the Bank of America in San Francisco to provide finance to the local Ligurian community
1912	William Garbutt is appointed coach of Genoa CFC and Italy learns the word *mister*
1919	Second Lieutenant Giuseppe Chioni returns to Genoa after time as a prisoner of war, and starts work on *Arte culinaria*
1922	Benito Mussolini comes to power
1924	Genoa CFC win their ninth (and possibly last) Scudetto title
1933	The Rex captures the Blue Riband and confirms Italy's arrival as a modern industrial nation
1940	The Torre Piacentini becomes the tallest building in Europe
1942	More than 300 Genoese are crushed to death in the Galeria delle Grazie during an air raid
1944-5	Friedrich Engel is the SS Commander in Genoa
1946	The La Spezia Affair sees two boatloads of Jews win their standoff over emigration to Palestine
1947-51	Genoa is used as a key part of the Rat Run by escaping Nazi war criminals
1956	51 people die after the Andrea Doria collides with the Stockholm in the Atlantic and sinks

TIMELINE

1963	Giorgio Carbone begins his quest for Seborga's independence from Italy to be recognised
1965	The *sopraelevata* is opened
1971	Sampdoria fans begin the modern ultrà movement
1986	The *sorpasso* sees Italy overtake Britain as the world's fifth largest economy
1990	Italy hosts the World Cup at the height of its post-War rebuilding
1991	Sampdoria win Serie A
1992	The Pesto Confraternity is founded; the 400th anniversary of Columbus' arrival in the New World is marked by an extensive rebuilding project in Genoa's rundown and dangerous port area
2001	Carlo Guiliani is killed as Genoa hosts a notoriously violent G8 meeting
2002	The Villa Bernada, which inspired DH Lawrence's Lady Chatterley's lover, is demolished
2007	Genoa's interest in cricket is rekindled
2008	Wayne Rooney weds Coleen McLoughlin in Portofino
2009	Giorgio Carbone dies after a life transforming himself from a humble flower seller to His Tremendousness Prince Giorgio I of Seborga
2011	Several die during apocalyptic flooding in the Cinque Terre and Genoa
2012	Don Andrea Gallo, friend of transsexuals and Genoa's downtrodden, dies; the last residents of the Albergo dei Poveri move out
2013	The 5 Star Movement of Genoese comedian, Beppe Grillo, wins more than a quarter of the vote in a general election; the Pitchfork protest movement spreads across Italy

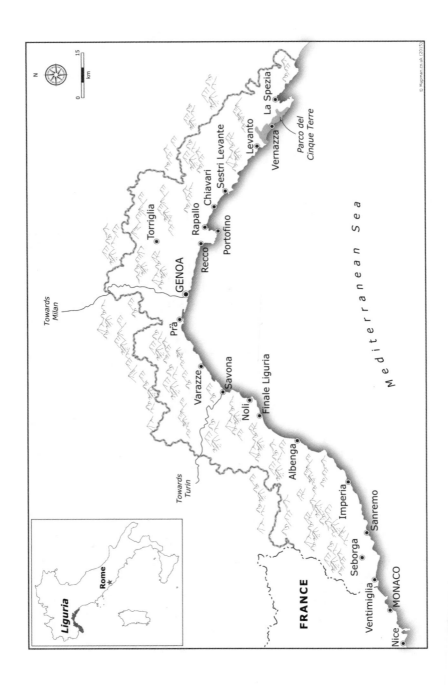

INTRODUCTION

How can some people be so blasé about air travel, nabbing an aisle seat in the hope of shaving off two minutes between touchdown and the arrivals lounge? Wouldn't a Leonardo da Vinci or Isaac Newton hand over a slice of their accumulated lifetime earnings for the chance of a window seat on a budget airline flight between Manchester and Malaga? It is one of the modern world's great opportunities to catch a remarkable but undervalued experience. Blasting through the air in a pressurised aluminium tube is the ticket to an astonishing panorama that brings together the geography, history and economics of the world that we live in and fly over.

A humble flight from London Gatwick to Genoa gave me the best glimpse of how this particular port city was able to catapult itself from nothingness to superpower status in a matter of decades. Liguria – roughly the historical Genoese Republic – consists of little more than a rocky wall of mountains and the deep blue Mediterranean. As that humble flight came in to land, a window seat on the right-hand side of the plane provided a grandstand view of this spectacular but unpromising launch pad for greatness. The secret ingredient was the desire of those who lived there to make something out of resources that were so meagre. The rest, as they say, is history. Genoa was the merchant pirate superpower that rivalled Venice and changed the world – and kept doing so, even after it began its long, punctuated decline.

While most people are well aware of just how incredible Italy is, very little of the limelight has fallen towards Genoa. Faced with the competition from destinations as celebrated as Rome, Florence and Venice, perhaps this is not surprising. It is not an *obvious* place. This book is an attempt to redress that balance: not in the hope of funnelling hordes of tourists into the city's labyrinthine *vicoli* (many of them might end up disappointed – or simply lost), but of telling a story that is too often skirted over in favour of more familiar names and places.

This book is also a deeply personal one for me, thanks to my wife having been born there, and – after frequent visits – the chance we then had to live in the *centro storico* for several precious months. We made our home at the top of an old *palazzo*, we climbed up and down well-worn slate steps, and we ate enough pesto to turn our complexions green. A measure of how much Genoa got into my blood was how much I bridled at its relative anonymity after visits to Florence and Venice. Those tourists, what did they know?

Finally, as the father of a little Anglo-Italian boy, I wondered whether this should also be a book about Genoa's future. Should it be an investigation into whether Luca might one day be able to make his home on the Italian Riviera, in the city they used to call *La Superba*? In the end I have touched on this, but steered clear of real engagement with those weighty and troubling questions that face Genoa and Italy (indeed the whole of Europe). There is simply too much in flux, and too much complexity in those questions. For one thing, trying to wrestle with them might obscure the story I want to tell about Genoa; for another, other books already exist to do that job.

A word also needs to be said about how I have arranged a book about something as fiendishly complicated as Genoese history. Perhaps that word is "sorry". Alas, with Genoa a simple chronological narration does not necessarily make most sense. Instead, I have tried to pick out themes and run with them, even if it means occasionally leaping decades or even centuries ahead of what I relate a chapter or two afterwards. To help, I have constructed a rough and slightly eccentric time line, which should help readers slot things into whatever chronological order makes most sense to them. I hope this works as history, but I also feel hamstrung by my background in journalism, which makes me want to tell the stories that matter, even if they end up in slightly disjointed sequence.

THE MEDIEVAL HEART OF GENOA

"A bewildering phantasmagoria" *Charles Dickens*

"If it's only for fifteen or twenty minutes, come during the day," was the message. "But if you need more time it'll have to be the evening." I thought twenty minutes would be enough, but Rossella was not an easy woman to find in the maze of tiny alleyways that make up the largest medieval quarter in Europe. It was a Friday, and several Algerians were standing around the entrance to a basement mosque, joking among themselves, as a tall Senegalese man bent over to pull his shoes back on. Twenty metres up Vico Della Croce Bianca a tall woman with a padded jacket and long black hair was loitering at a crossroads: obviously a prostitute, but better dressed than most. Did she know where Rossella was? She smiled. She spoke in a soft, creamy voice. She was transsexual.

"That chair over there. That's where her *magazzino* is." The word indicated a storeroom rather than an office or flat. She pointed another twenty metres away, down the *vico* that cut across Vico Della Croce Bianca. A couple of unmarked little doorways had chairs parked outside them, with cushions laid across them. Both were empty, but the door behind one of them was open.

"Excuse me?" Inside was a small, homely room with a pot on a gas flame. A toy poodle with well-trimmed white fur popped out into the street to investigate.

"Yes?" An older woman, again transsexual, followed the dog. She had blonde hair and a leather jacket. Yes, Rossella's place was the door behind the other seat, she said. "That light over there." But, she said, glancing at the closed door, Rossella was busy at the moment. Thank you, we will wait.

The small *piazza* just beyond the woman's door was an ideal place for killing time. There were shutters on the faded pastel buildings, and scaffolding climbed its way up the walls in one corner. The sun found an angular patch of old cobbles to warm, fighting for space against the irregular shadows of the tall, jumbled roofline. Clothes hung on lines slung beneath windows, drying in the November air, while a flag in the familiar Sampdoria colours of blue, white, red and black flapped idly in the breeze. Tiny *vicoli* darted off from the *piazza* into the stony darkness, where life bubbled away as it had done in the medieval heart of the city for century after bloody, salt-tinged century. Prostitutes and tripe sellers, hawkers and tailors: they all had a place down one *vico* or another, even if you had to navigate using a compass and a ball of string to find your way back again.

A man stepped out of the door that we had identified as Rossella's, followed by a notably tall woman with a mop of curly strawberry blonde hair. She spotted us, waved hello, and opened the door to her *magazzino*. Inside I could see two rooms. A photo of Marilyn Monroe hung on the wall, and the same image was magnified across a three-piece screen just in front. A television was on in the corner, perched on a shelving unit topped by a couple of lipsticks. A small sofa settled under an Indian patterned throw, and there was a bed just visible in the room beyond.

Rossella said a few words in what seemed like good English, but then excused herself and reverted to Italian. Her voice was warm, and when she coughed it was clearly a woman's cough. She wore a leopard-print blouse and a shimmering dark red parka with a hood trimmed in fur of the same strawberry blonde colour as her hair.

Rossella is the president of an organisation called Princesse, a self-help organisation that the transsexual prostitutes in this small part of the *vicoli* formed a few years ago. "We are part of the social fabric of Genoa," she said. "We've been here for many years."

Back in the sixties nobody would employ transsexuals in normal jobs, so many turned to prostitution. The transsexual scene was based around several bars in the port, and they started attracting quite a few foreigners, from the US, Norway, Germany. In the seventies there was a lot of heroin-dealing in Genoa's labyrinthine *vicoli*, and drug use spread quickly through the community. Many died, and their numbers gradually shrank from around 100 to the 25 or so who work the area today. Most are older; younger transsexual prostitutes tend to do their marketing through the internet.

Their trade revolves around the *magazzini*, the little homes that open directly onto the alleyways through tiny doors. The *vicoli* can be so tight that there is sometimes barely enough room outside for a comfortable seat from which to solicit trade and say hello to friends. The ladies elsewhere in Genoa's medieval *centro storico* have to rent their *magazzini* for as much as €50 to €100 a day, and work in shifts to cover the costs. But the transsexual prostitutes are owner-occupiers. They have lived and worked in this area, the old Jewish quarter, for decades, and the cosiness of the *magazzini* used by Rossella and her poodle-owning neighbour is the result.

A few years ago the authorities moved against prostitution in the city, part of a gradual clean-up of the port area that had become out of bounds to many Genoese. It was backed by shopkeepers who complained that the prostitutes attracted crime and drug use. But in Rossella's area, despite it being a hop and a skip from streets that Rubens and Dickens fawned over, there are few shops. So the transsexuals fought back. Local residents agreed to sign a petition to let them continue operating out of their *magazzini*. Rossella explained that the prostitutes helped look after the neighbouring streets. They were, after all, long-standing residents of the area. And they don't harass people, she said; they simply sit on the chairs that guard the blameless little doors leading off the *vico* and into their workplaces.

The war still had to be won. On the advice of Don Andrea Gallo, a Genoese priest who was well known for his charitable work, the women formed Princesse (it was named after a Brazilian transsexual who died in prison). In response to threats from the authorities to close the *magazzini*, they uncovered alleged evidence that certain politicians might profit from property deals connected to the closures, and sent it to the newspapers. They were then given leave to continue working out of their little hobbit homes, just as they have for decades.

Rossella held up a contract and told us that she was soon to publish her autobiography. It will be called *In Via del Campo nascono i fiori*, which can translate as "flowers grow on the Via del Campo". Rossella is evidently a very intelligent woman. After all, she is not a prostitute because she fell through the holes in society; she is one because she grew up believing she should have been born female, and prostitution offered her a way to earn a living.

Rossella said that Genoa used to be the only city in Italy to have a transsexual community like theirs, working out of *magazzini* in the medieval centre. There was another in Sicily, she said, in Catania. But she added that it had been *bonificata* by the local authorities – meaning it had been cleaned up, or even sanitised. It is not a compliment. Some other cities have developed their own small transsexual districts, and that means her business is now mostly local. She got up and stuck her head out of the door. It seemed the twenty-minute window was up, and a client was waiting. Rossella did not make a fuss about her time; employees in other Italian service industries might learn from her.

One last question: prostitutes are ubiquitous in some parts of Genoa's medieval centre, but are they really accepted by the local community, or does their presence cause friction? There are no social tensions, said Rossella. I suspect she is correct, at least when drugs are not involved. A Brazilian transvestite lives and works around the corner from my in-laws, and seems to be known and welcomed by everybody, as part of what makes Genoa the city it is. What about with the mosque, just around the corner? Oh no, said Rossella, they have a relationship of mutual respect. Her smile was like a full stop on the conversation. It was time to let her go about her business.

After shaking her hand I stepped out into the street and noticed an older gentleman entering the door quietly as soon as my back was turned. Rossella's neighbour was outside her own door, with her toy poodle. *Grazie, ciao.* Around a corner, just outside the Palazzo Spinola, a tall Senegalese woman in a thong that was clearly visible under a skin-tight neon dress continued her working day. Two of her friends were a few metres down the old street, half hidden by shadow. On other streets small clutches of Ecuadorian and Colombian women stood and talked among themselves, waiting for business. They are all part of life in Genoa, a city that has seen too much of the world to be shocked or judgemental. Just as there always has been in these tiny, narrow *vicoli*, there is room for you, however you want to make your living.

THE MEDIEVAL HEART OF GENOA

***

To understand the history of Genoa and Liguria, you must first understand their geography. Liguria is a mountainous slug that sits over the lid of the Mediterranean like the moustache on the cruel top lip of a South American dictator. In a lazy crescent stretching from Ventimiglia to La Spezia, rocks rise steeply out of the sea with a sense of purpose and barely a thought of giving ground to houses or cultivation. They hit the watershed within a few miles of the coast and start falling off again into the foggy, mosquito-plagued Po basin and the economic might of Milan and Turin.

This unforgiving geography forced its inhabitants to scratch a living from the sea, and this they did in grand, if ruthless, style. Genoa became a merchant pirate superpower that traded punches and goods with the rest of the Mediterranean and the world. It brought the Black Death to Europe, changed the world of finance, bred explorers and slave dealers, and built *palazzos* that were admired across the known world. Even as it declined it still demanded attention, giving the gift of unity to the peninsula, football to the Italians, and pesto to the world.

Genoa is not part of the easily digestible theme-park Italy of tourist menus, fancy dress centurions, and obvious photo opportunities. Its heart lies in those teeming *vicoli* that fill Genoa's medieval centre like bronchioles filling a lung. But just as the narrowest *vico* can suddenly burst open without warning into the echoing glories of a medieval church, Genoa is about the grand canvas of its seaside amphitheatre as much as the intimacy of its *centro storico*. And that grand canvas is best understood by mounting the four-lane beast of a 1960s eyesore that erupts from the rock of the Riviera and sweeps through the city without blinking.

The *sopraelevata* is the shameless concrete serpent that winds its way between the medieval port city and the waters that allowed it to draw breath and find fortunes. You climb the ramp at the western end of Genoa's amphitheatre, with the angular La Lanterna, the city's landmark lighthouse, on your right and the sweep of the city rising on the left. The massive side of a modern cruise liner may rear its eighteen decks directly in front, or a ferry lining its belly with cars and articulated trucks, readying itself for the voyage to Tunis. You veer left and skirt the ferry port, the Stazione Marittima and the docks from where so many millions have set off for a new life across the ocean.

As you drive, Genoa's houses, churches, towers, castles jostle for a view of the Mediterranean from their allotted parts of the mountainside. You can spy the turreted folly of the Castello D'Albertis in its eyrie, and then the tight coil of the port opens out on the right, with its oligarchs' yachts, its cranes and oriental behemoths stacked with shipping containers. On the left the closest buildings jam together into a centuries-old multi-coloured pastel wall, like the jumbled interlocking shields of ancient warriors. The mass of the medieval centre starts to tumble out behind them, and on the other side the port starts to show itself: maybe a ludicrous galleon from a film set, a whale-watching pleasure boat, gaggles of schoolchildren, and old couples just looking out to sea and letting their worries vanish. Palm trees reach up and tickle the concrete edge of the *sopraelevata* with their fronds, and the octopus arms of a strange machine used to hoist tourists into the air sprout up from the redeveloped docklands. Standing proud just outside the medieval centre on the left is the Palazzo di San Giorgio. Although it looks for all the world like a giant frescoed musical box, there can be no doubt that it lives in a city happy to sacrifice nostalgia for pragmatism. Even the Palazzo, one of the most important buildings in the Western world, has to duck to avoid the mighty *sopraelevata* taking off its nose. Other *palazzi* are not so lucky. The *sopraelevata* slices straight through several of them, starts to turn, and disappears in a blaze of options: to Piazza di Ferrari, the *molo vecchio*, or the Corso Italia and the Riviera beyond.

The *sopraelevata* is the perfect way to encounter Genoa. Few cities give such a defiant account of themselves to visitors as this elevated dual carriageway that cuts through the heart of one of Europe's most extraordinary cities. The *sopraelevata* is undeniably ugly in itself, but it also affords a grandstand introduction. It sets the perfect tone for a city that forced itself upon the world from nothing, working its way up to become a superpower through sweat, willpower and the blood of enemies and neighbours alike. That was many centuries ago, but Genoa's dotage has been long and influential. It has continued to change the world we live in while refusing to settle down and join that theme-park Italy of ice cream and jostling umbrella-led tour groups.

The *sopraelevata* is also a nod to the power of geography, that driving force behind Genoa's reason for being. When it was opened in 1965 it was the 1.75 billion lire answer to the question of how modern traffic could exist in a city squeezed between the mountains that protected it and the sea that gave it life. A total of 15,000 tonnes of steel were used to build more than 200 supporting columns which heedlessly smashed their way through *palazzi* dating back to the seventeenth century. In one case the corner of a building has simply disappeared, replaced by a neat, angular hole through which buzzing scooters and honking cars tear along the path of the *sopraelevata*.

Without that geography, Genoa would have had a very different life. It would never have flowered into such an unlikely superpower and then kept its toehold in history as the world started growing up without it. It would never have been the birthplace of admirals and explorers, or nurtured its special identity within the peninsula that it did so much to help unite. Instead it would have filled itself with pretty buildings and flitted in and out of other people's histories, without demanding its own unlikely place at the top table, whacking its fork against its plate and bellowing its demands.

This geography means that every approach to Genoa is packed with drama. The writer Tobias Smollet wrote in 1765 that "there is no other way of going from hence to Genoa, unless you take a mule, and clamber along the mountains at the rate of two miles an hour, and at the risque of breaking your neck every minute". In the twenty-first century things are better, but despite being close to the great cities of northern Italy, the prominence of sea and mountains make Liguria the country's most peculiarly remote region for everything but a flying crow.

The traditional way to arrive in Genoa is of course by sea, with the wall of mountains appearing on the horizon, then gradually stretching out in both directions like long spindly arms welcoming you in, until you pull into a berth that despatched Columbus, Garibaldi and Andrea Doria. Driving in from either end of Liguria is a glorious, heart-stopping race along mountain crests and coastal valleys. The sun blinds you from every second bend, then threatens to disappear forever as you are shunted into the dark of yet another tunnel before being flung out onto a viaduct suspended high above a rocky valley. There are seventy-something tunnels if you approach Genoa on the *autostrada* from La Spezia, near the salt marshes and marble quarries of the Tuscan borderland. From the French frontier there are more than a hundred. The steep passes that lead down through the mountains to Genoa from the agricultural and industrial riches of the Po turn into two- or three-lane toboggan runs, as cars hurtle around yet another tight bend, scarcely sticking to one lane or the next. In truth they are just hedging their bets: on any of Liguria's *autostrade*, they might tell you, it doesn't pay to fence yourself in (the lorries do that for you). In Genoa they are fond of blaming Milanese holidaymakers, heading for the coast at German speeds with Italian recklessness.

The trains are safer. They chug along, in and out of tunnels, occasionally blinding passengers with the sun and the sea in one heady jolt, before all goes dark once again as you trundle under thousands of tonnes of rock. The tracks scarcely top the waves as they thread between the hillslopes, the rocks and the salt water. The trains to Milan and Turin head up through even more tunnels, following the line of rivers that alternate through the year between arid and torrential.

Air passengers have the best view, especially if they are wise enough to sit on the right-hand side of the plane. From the north the plane descends after the Alps, crossing the featureless plains of northern Italy, and then rises over the peaks of Liguria's own Alps. It usually heads for a strange lump of rock jutting into the Mediterranean, then describes a long loop in the sky until it is facing just past due east. From the Promontorio Portofino the pilot simply has to stay on the line of the coast, losing height above the waves, with the house-speckled cliffs and terraced slopes watching carefully as the plane descends: Camogli, Recco, Nervi, Quinto, Quarto, Boccadasse, Albaro, then over a lip and the port is below. The final approach skims over cranes, container ships and La Lanterna itself, with Genoa spread out over the mountainsides to the right like a smear. The runway occupies an artificial island – thanks to the demands of geography once again. With the gathering mass of Monte Beigua looming directly in front, there is no final approach from the west, although the pilot may swing around from the eastern approach in the last couple of minutes to land in that direction if the sea breezes demand it.

***

After the spectacular geography and remarkable history of Genoa, the *vicoli* are its most striking feature. They fill the heart of the city, the *centro storico*, and they have pulsated with life ever since the city's medieval glories. This is not a *bonificata* photo opportunity or a frenetic modern city; this is Italy as it was centuries ago, whores and all. It is busy with people, arguments, laughter, sweat; it is a cramped medieval version of the Richard Scarry children's book, *What Do People Do All Day?*

"There seems to be always something to find out in it," wrote Charles Dickens after staying in the city. "There are the most extraordinary alleys and by-ways to walk about in. [...] It abounds in the strangest contrasts; things that are picturesque, ugly, mean, magnificent, delightful, and offensive, break upon the view at every turn." It is not a planned city, but an organic jumble of stone and life, shops and prostitutes, reckless scooter riders and those odd little motorised tricycles that Italians use to deliver things to inaccessible places. There are fishmongers lounging out on the street, workshops where violins are made by hand, and neatly manicured shop windows showcasing the type of beautiful dispensable trinket that stylish women sell to other stylish women who carry tiny dogs in their arms. Indian immigrants selling flashing Chinese toys jostle for space with dignified old men in their scarves and moustaches, and of course my father-in-law, bumping into yet another friend with a friendly *salute*. Go back a few decades and only the jobs might have changed: there would be knife sharpeners, lotto sellers on street corners, rag merchants, exotic bagpipers down from the mountains, and men up from Abruzzo carrying metal containers full of skewers of cooked pears.

Perspectives are always surprising you. Tiny alleys will twist between walls before opening out suddenly into *piazze* where old women complain about prices and old men about football. Liquorice-striped churches will appear without the grand entrance demanded elsewhere in Italy, and beckon you into calm, cool interiors that defy the congestion and claustrophobia surrounding them. Through one door you might find an austere eleventh-century interior, decorated only with a glass case containing the bones of some desiccated saint. Through another will burst a feast of eye-watering rococo, contrasted with sombre inlays of grotesque skulls and crossbones in the flagstones beneath your feet. "Wherever it has been possible to cram a tumble-down tenement into a crack or corner, in it has gone," wrote Dickens. "If there be a nook or angle in the wall of a church, or a crevice in any other dead wall, of any sort, there you are sure to find some kind of habitation: looking as if it had grown there, like a fungus." The constant in-fighting between the grand families of Genoa led to each establishing a stronghold in the city, and any new building had to be squeezed into their territory. A walk through the medieval city is like a walk between the scent-marked territories of wolf packs.

Rashid, the Moroccan *fruttivendolo* (or *bezagnin* in Genoese dialect) who turns each bag of tangerines into a mini-performance, told us that he once tried to live outside the *centro storico*, but had to return because nowhere else reminded him so much of the tumbling medieval cities of his home: Meknes, Fes and Marrakesh. But for every Moroccan *fruttivendolo* or transsexual prostitute there is a bewildered tourist, looking for the very obvious qualities that Italy is famed for. They will not find it in Genoa. It has more in common with Marseilles, Naples and Palermo than with Florence, Milan or Rome. It has a heedless authenticity that accepts the dog dirt on the cobblestones, the muck that has accumulated on the marble, and the shameless intrusion of the *sopraelevata*. That is life. If you want to catch a glimpse of Italy as it has been lived for centuries, rather than simply something that looks good on postcards, come to Genoa.

2

NOWHERE TO TURN BUT THE SEA

"Speak to the Genoese about the sea" *Leonardo da Vinci*

The baseline of Genoese history is that its people had few other options than to turn to the sea and take what they could from it. It is a glorious history but not always a pleasant one. The Genoese themselves were often less than attractive: their reputation as merchants and traders came with a warning that they would sometimes sell their own mothers for a profit. Human flesh, in fact, was a Genoese speciality, as was piracy, and when they engaged against the Muslim corsairs conducting slave raids it was often in the spirit of competition as much as protection. They were renowned for infighting, and much blood was shed both in violence between families and factions within the city and between Genoa and the other aspirant cities of the Ligurian coast.

The character of the people owes a lot to the harshness of the landscape. In Liguria flat areas are so rare they are often known as islands. Agriculture was as much about hewing terraces out of the rocky mountainsides as harnessing the power of the soil and the sun. The chestnut groves are such a feature of the mountains between 500 and 800 metres altitude that they provided the staple crop for many Ligurians, and until recently the local bread could be made with chestnut flour. Above the chestnuts grow beech trees, and below there are maritime pines, but the timber has not been an easy resource to fell because the slopes rise so precipitously from the coast. The largest river is the Trebbia, which flows north-east into the verdant, fertile plains of the Po basin; more meagre rivers like the Bisagno and Polcevera have failed to provide either transport or reliable fresh water. There are also no minerals of note; and because the mountains plunge into a tideless sea and keep on going down into the blue depths, there has been no rich fishery to be harvested and no shallow water for salt manufacture. For centuries, Liguria's beauty has disguised its poverty.

What Liguria has always had is a useful position on the way to other places. Despite the height of its mountains, they form a relatively narrow strip between the seaways of the Mediterranean and the bounty of the northern Italian plains. Liguria was also positioned on the shortest route between the Italian peninsula and the Roman territories in Spain and Provence. Rome built the Via Aurelia to connect the ancient capital to those territories, and the Via Postumia to link the plains to the Tyrrhenian Sea. Genoa became the port for Placentia (Piacenza), Ticinum (Pavia) and Mediolanum (Milan). The winds were also favourable for both entering and leaving Genoa, which offered the best natural harbour between La Spezia and Barcelona. The city was not a particularly important one for the Roman Empire, but it began to understand that its future lay in developing its use of the sea, especially after the collapse of Rome led to its roads falling into disrepair.

***

The history of Genoa in the murky centuries after Rome fell is difficult to piece together. The Ostrogoths were there, and evidence of a Jewish synagogue suggests that it was plugged into trade routes to the East. The Byzantines turned up and ran the place from 537 for just over a century, but little is known about what happened in those years. The Lombards and the Carolingians played a role in Genoa after that, but it was still small and relatively insignificant.

This started to change with the violent expansion of the Islamic world into the Western Mediterranean. When Muslim raiders established a settlement at Fraxinetum in Provence they seemed to ignore Liguria entirely, but in around 930 a Muslim squadron heading for Genoa was defeated by a Byzantine fleet. In 934 a Fatimid fleet attacked Liguria, and shortly afterwards Genoa itself was sacked. Many residents were killed, and the attackers sailed away with a thousand female slaves, linen and raw silk. As David Abulafia notes, "Whereas Roman naval power had been based on the extinction of piracy, Muslim naval power was based on the exercise of piracy."

This Muslim threat was the catalyst for the process that eventually made Genoa into a medieval superpower. The Genoese were confronted with a choice: they could retreat into the mountains or they could engage with the sea and the raiders, developing their military capabilities and defining themselves as devoted Christian warriors. They chose the latter course.

By the turn of the millennium a powerful new Genoa was starting to take shape, and looking across the Tyrrhenian Sea for what it did not have at home. Its first target was Sardinia, which gave access to salt, grain, sheep and slaves. Although many Sardinians would live to regret the interest in their island from the Genoese, the first named slave that we can find in Genoese records was not from there, but from Burgundy. In 1005 a woman named Erkendtruda was sold by a man called Armano to a couple, Benedetto and Benedetta, for ten *solidi*. She came with a warranty: Armano promised that she was neither stolen property nor a fugitive, and that she had a healthy body and mind. Genoa was to become the Western Mediterranean's pre-eminent slave market.

At around the same time other Italian maritime powers were on the rise. The closest of these was Pisa, which had access to grain from its hinterland and was less vulnerable to raids from the sea. There was some cooperation: the two chased a Muslim warlord called Mujahid out of his base in Sardinia in 1016, and in 1087 they cooperated in an attack on Al-Mahdiyya, a Muslim state in what is now Tunisia.[1] But Genoa and Pisa were also developing a rivalry that began to spill over into warfare, often centred on control of Sardinia or trade routes.

These trade routes took the Genoese to the Eastern Mediterranean and also forced them to be both enterprising and avaricious. They had little to trade from Liguria itself, and so made use of the silver they could get from Sardinia to sail to the east. They were merchant pirates, as interested in any Muslim vessels that they encountered as with trading. Slaving was another opportunity, and humans became the largest commodity passing from the mainly rural Western Mediterranean to the East, with Genoa plugged in and making profits. As well as continuing Muslim raids on coastal communities, established slave trading routes grew up across both sea and land; the land route often went from Eastern Europe, through castration centres in Flanders run by monks, before heading to the wealthy, slave-hungry Islamic lands.

One factor in the rise of Pisa and Genoa was their relative success in clearing the seas of pirates, which then allowed them to open up lucrative trade routes to Byzantium, Egypt and the Mediterranean end-points of the Silk Road. Meanwhile, two other Italian maritime states were also emerging. The first seems unlikely: Amalfi was really just a scattering of small hamlets in neighbouring coves, and even though its time of prosperity was brief, it is remarkable how it was able to eclipse Naples just to its north.

The second of these states was to prove far more formidable, and although it was to establish itself as the great superpower rival to Genoa, its beginnings were similar to the Ligurian port's. Venice was just a series of small communities on little islands in a lagoon ("conjured out of marsh", in Roger Crowley's words). Like the Genoese the Venetians had no agriculture, so they had little choice but to turn to the sea and take what advantage they could from their position on trade routes linking Europe and the East through the Adriatic Sea. Venice and Genoa became warring twins, medieval maritime superpowers blinded to their similarities by their mutual animosity.

By the end of the eleventh century Genoa was prominent enough in the medieval world to be a notable contributor to the First Crusade. Nine of the city's nobles were part of the fleet that sailed for the Holy Land in 1097, and the Genoese played an important role in both the blockade of Antioch and the siege of Jerusalem itself. The Embriaci family used the wood from their ships to fashion siege engines for the campaign. Some Genoese returned to Liguria with relics, including the remains of John the Baptist, and others stayed to enjoy new trading privileges and property, such as the Church of San Giovanni in Antioch. Another fleet in 1100 picked targets along the coast of the Holy Land. An attack on Caesarea in 1101 produced another valuable relic: a shallow hexagonal green bowl thought to be the Holy Grail, used by Christ at the Last Supper. The *Sacro Catino* was also thought to be made of solid emerald, until Napoleon's troops managed to drop it in 1806 and demonstrate conclusively that it was really made of glass.

That bowl is now part of a spectacular collection of sacred oddments that fill a museum underneath the Catedral San Lorenzo. The relics are testimony to the role that Genoa played in those Christian ventures to the Holy Land and affirmation of the city's role in the medieval world. A large crucifix, the *Croce degli Zaccaria*, incorporates several fragments of the true cross in its centre, surrounded by gold, gems and pearls. A spectacular plate made of chalcedony, with gilt edging and an enamelled, bearded face at its centre, is called the *Platto di San Giovanni*, which was thought to be the plate upon which John the Baptist's head was served to Herod. If you search hard enough you'll also see a silver reliquary that is supposed to contain cuttings from the hair of the Virgin Mary, and a silver and gilt casket containing the remains of John the Baptist. The collection includes a couple of gilded hands that are attached to what seem to be handles positioned like forearms; glass panels in those handles reveal that they are elaborate holders for the bones of St Anne and St James.

That First Crusade turned Genoa from a small port city in the Western Mediterranean to a true naval power. As well as the relics and booty, the Genoese fleet brought back commodities such as pepper, giving it a sniff of the world of trade that was opening up to the East. It also picked up more territories: acknowledging the Crusaders' heavy reliance on Genoese seafaring and military assistance, King Baldwin of Jerusalem gave the city piazzas in the Holy City and Jaffa, and a third of both Acre and Caesarea. He promised a third of Cairo too, should Genoa help to conquer that city next. For any Genoese merchant with an eye for a deal, a sharp sword and a ruthless nature, these were boom years.

***

The early twelfth century produced a commercial revolution in Genoa, following a governmental one. Central authority in northern Italy was collapsing, and local elites and patricians were taking on governing duties. The cities were becoming *communes* and republics. In Genoa the new authority was a *compagna*, literally those who break bread together, and its main purpose was to provide for specific public goods within a limited period, for instance building a fleet of ships or dealing with the latest outbreak of brawling on the streets. Bodies such as monasteries gradually fell under their control. Their most powerful offices, the *consuls*, came to be controlled by the city's main families, such as the

Spinola and Doria. There was fierce rivalry, violence on the streets, and lots of opportunities to make money.

A new medieval economy was being created across much of Europe, cross-fed by markets and traders. Venice extended its tentacles into Southern Germany, and Genoa up the Rhone valley, linking with the trade for Flemish woollen cloths. (This in turn generated demand for alum, which was used as a fixative and cleansing agent by textile manufacturers. The alum trade led to the Genoese adventurer Benedetto Zaccaria claiming territories for Genoa along the coast of Asia Minor, including the island of Chios.) The maritime powers connected this trade with the Eastern Mediterranean, to Byzantine and the growing Muslim world, and then via the Silk Road across Central Asia to China and the Orient.

Genoa's role in this new world grew, and the shrewd business brains in the city looked for novel ways to finance it. The Church kept its eye out for any signs of usury, so mechanisms were developed to hide devilish concepts like profits and losses. Luckily our archives are blessed with a treasure trove of diligent book-keeping from the middle of the twelfth century onwards. The oldest to survive (in Europe as well as Genoa) came from the notary Giovanni Scriba in 1154, using paper imported from Alexandria. Three types of contracts appeared that allowed for different levels of investment, physical participation and reward.

In 1158 Bongiovanni Malfigliastro invested in a venture bound for Sicily under the terms of a *commenda* contract. The travelling merchant, also called Bongiovanni, did not invest beforehand, but received a quarter of the profits as the reward for his labour and physical risk. A year earlier Guglielmo Vento had put up two-thirds of the capital in a *societas* contract, with the merchant Guglielmo Visconte contributing a third and risking being shipwrecked or enslaved. When Visconte returned they split the profits down the middle. The third type of contract was a *sea loan*, which would then be repaid as a set amount should the borrower return from a trading voyage.[2] Scriba's *cartulary* is a sophisticated record that documents just how commonplace such contracts were: it contains 1,306 acts in its 163 pages, and 335 of those acts involved overseas commerce. Investing in trade was not just something for the rich – many sums were modest enough to be within the reach of the city's middling classes.

The *compagna* became the guarantor of a system of trust that extended into regularised weights and measurements, and the law. Notaries found guilty of falsifying documents would lose a hand, and the very act of giving false testimony could result in public beatings or having one's nose sliced right off. As the basis for a trading state the system worked: wealth began to spread through Genoese society, which became hungrier for more trade, and more profits. The Dark Ages were being replaced by a dynamic new world. A new, integrated European medieval economy was taking shape, and Genoa was in the middle of it, counting its cash, and linking Western Europe to the riches and luxuries of the East.

***

In these boom years for the merchant-pirate city state of Genoa, many fortunes were being made, although the trading life was a hard and fiercely contested one. In Genoa itself great patrician families started to prosper from the profits they made, using their influence to direct foreign policy (which naturally they tried to align with their trading interests). Society became increasingly clannish, creating the patchwork of densely packed fiefdoms that visitors to the city's *centro storico* will still find. With policy following the interests of the powerful, Genoa was gaining its notorious reputation for factional strife and the ability to place a knife in the back of an enemy caught escaping along one of the city's dark and gloomy *vicoli*.

Towers were now erected at the centre of each fiefdom, used to dominate the surrounding area from above. The towers themselves became targets of fighting on the streets. There is even a description of siege warfare taking place within the city of Genoa itself, between Genoese factions, from a chronicler in 1194: "Then [they] came and set up a 'machine' in the orchard of St Syrus with which they propelled many stones against the houses and towers of Oberto Grimaldi and the Spinola family. They later erected other machines and the other side also constructed many machines and shot many stones at the houses and towers of the court party." The destruction of towers became an official punishment, and in 1196 a height limit was imposed to try to control the various violent feuds and squabbles. The only tower to escape this imposition was the Embriaci tower, thanks to the leading role its members had played in the siege of Jerusalem. That tower still stands today, in a fairly seedy part of the *centro storico* above the Molo district, full of *vicoli* that are steep, twisted and dark.

The violence was not just the product of rivalries between great families. A notary called Martino paints a vivid picture of the kind of crime that was endemic at the time. He writes of a woman called Berta Mazalina who went to court in the city of Savona to complain that another woman, Bonanata, had assaulted her with a rock. The two women then filed claims and counter-claims, and flung insults back and forth: one is called a *prencessa* (or "princess", meaning a prostitute) and a *bagassa* (again a prostitute – the word *bagascia* is still used in Genoese). Jewellery was stolen, and by the end of Martino's account one of the women had been attacked with a lump of stone pulled from a sewer.[3]

Life was similarly dangerous for those who left the city behind to seek their fortunes at sea. Some of the best accounts come not from the merchants but the passengers they carried. A rabbi from Navarre called Benjamin of Tudela set off to travel the Mediterranean in around 1160, hoping to describe it in Hebrew. He wrote that Genoa was "surrounded by a wall, and the inhabitants are not governed by any king, but by judges whom they appoint at their pleasure". He also noted that the Genoese made effective pirates as well as traders, raiding both Christian and Muslim lands.

Pilgrims also used Genoese ships for transport, and the captains were always happy to take on passengers who could add to the profit of a voyage. One was Muhammad ibn Ahmad ibn Jubayr, the secretary to the governor of Gibraltar. The story goes that when the governor tried to force him to drink wine he refused, and the governor gave him seven cups of gold coins by way of either apology or reward. He used the coins to fund a journey to Mecca, setting out in February 1183 in a Genoese ship. Unsurprisingly, given the time of year, they ran into a great storm near Sardinia, and when they made it into harbour he saw eighty Muslim men and women for sale as slaves. Ibn Jubayr then followed the established route via Sicily and Egypt to Mecca, before returning to the Mediterranean at Acre. He was not enamoured with the place, describing it as a place of pigs and crosses: "It stinks and is filthy, being full of refuse and excrement." Again he finds a Genoese sailor ("perspicacious in his art and skilled in the duties of a sea-captain") willing to help him continue his journey. His account notes that anybody who died at sea, whatever their religion, was buried at sea, and that their belongings went to the captain. There were very few stops for supplies, so the passenger was forced to buy fresh food from the crew ("in this ship they were as if in a city filled with all commodities" – he lists everything from bread, water and figs to cheese, quinces and pomegranates). The ship, alas, ran into storms as it was passing Crete, and ibn Jubayr rued that "all modes of transport have their proper season, and travel by sea should be at the propitious time and the recognised period. There should not be a reckless venturing forth in the months of winter as we did." By the time they were shipwrecked off Messina they were living on a pound of moistened ship's biscuit a day.[4]

Such hardship at sea was justified by the money that could be made: especially welcome in a city that relied upon drive and graft, with so few natural resources to fall back on. The city had exploded in decades from almost nothing to a major power that played a vital role in an extraordinary interlinked new economy. Slaves and woollens went east; sugar and other delights came west, and Genoa ran its enviable empire of trading posts across the Mediterranean and to the Levantine shores. Scuffles continued with pirates and with Pisa, and the real rivalry with the Adriatic town of Venice was only just taking shape. But despite its riches Genoa still had grim poverty, and some of its more virtuous residents began to help those who were left behind by the city's miraculous rise.

3

THE DOWNTRODDEN

"From diamonds nothing was born, from dung flowers bloom"
Don Andrea Gallo

Genoa's startling rise had taken it from nothing to the status of leading player in the medieval Mediterranean. Western Europe was finding its feet after centuries of post-Roman dithering, and Genoa was a vital step on the trade routes that led to more dynamic places in the East. The narrow streets where the Genoese squabbled, stabbed backs and counted their profits were now filled with foreigners: slaves and merchants, sailors and pilgrims.

On the edge of the *centro storico*, at a slight angle to the *sopraelevata* that roars by at lamp-post height just a few metres away, is a splendid old structure that was built to cater for some of these new visitors. Like much of Genoa, the Ospitale della Commenda di San Giovanni di Prè has little of the symmetrical beauty of postcard Italy. Instead, it looks as if it was assembled in layers by a seven-year-old experimenting with building blocks. Different configurations of pillars and arches feature on different floors, and at its end, above a *vico* that disappears into the darkness of medieval Genoa, are two separate churches, one built unceremoniously on top of the other.

The Commenda's location, however, is no accident. It sits directly on the old harbour front, in full view of the pilgrims who boarded ships on their way from or to the Holy Land.[1] The only entrance fee was a confession and taking the Eucharist. Inside, there are two main floors: the sick headed upstairs, to be prodded and leeched by the best medieval doctors, for better or worse; healthier pilgrims and crusaders bunked down on the ground floor. But after long journeys to the Holy Land it could be hard to sort the sick from the healthy, as most people stepped off those long, stormy voyages with more than a hint of malnourishment and worm-eaten illness.

In the late twelfth century the Commenda was just one beneficiary of an evident charitable impulse among the Genoese. This went hand-in-hand with the city's strong Christian ethic. They gave money to paupers and lepers, donated directly to churches and monasteries, or helped raise money to pay off ransoms for soldiers who had been captured and thrown into some foreign rat-infested cell. This raising of ransoms tended to be the preserve of richer Genoese, in effect looking after their own; but records show that even those on modest incomes gave to the Commenda so that it could look after pilgrims (and women were more likely to donate than men). Their charity might have been galvanised by Ugo, the commander of the Hospitallers, who died in 1233 and was canonised soon after. He was a small and pious man, who wore a hairshirt and washed the diseased with his own hands. Among the miracles attributed to him are causing a fountain to spring up during a water shortage, and (presumably once water was more freely found) turning water into wine.

Throughout the centuries Genoa has never been short of those in desperate need in the darkest days of their lives. And despite the city's persistent eye on the bottom line, Genoa has also never been short of those with a firm Christian impulse to help those less fortunate. Perhaps the most striking example can be found in a remarkable institution that was housed in a vast building, a short walk up the hill from the centre of the old city itself.

***

In August 1698, Signora Paola Spinola was desperate. Her husband, Angelo, had died at the age of 65, leaving her in charge of a daughter, Laura, and a niece, also Paola, and in a state of utter misery. She was literate, which marked her out as originally from a relatively respectable background. But it was an era without a safety net, and life was precarious: the untimely death of an impecunious husband could easily tip an entire family into poverty. Signora Spinola gathered up the courage to write a letter to the Magistrato dei Poveri (Magistrate of the Poor), asking for bread and noting that – if necessary – she was willing to collect it if they wished. In other words, her situation was so bad she was willing to face the shame and loss of face of accepting charity in public. At the bottom of the letter is a scrawl in a different hand, confirming that Signora Spinola and her family was indeed entitled to bread; and no, there was no obligation for her to collect it in person.

This letter is just one of a brick-sized sheaf of requests for bread from a few years around the end of the seventeenth century; they were bound with a single length of cord threaded through a hole in the centre of each letter. Other stories are similar to that of Signora Paola Spinola: there is one from Anna Maria Vedona, the widow of Giacomo Guasco Genovese; she was a librarian, but had been forced by widowhood to sell her furniture and books, and remained in such a calamitous state that she too was forced to apply for bread from the Magistrato dei Poveri.

The letters are kept in a vast archive on an upper floor of the Palazzo Ducale, just above where modern Genoa holds its antiques fairs and farmers' markets. Mustard-yellow girders support four dizzying floors of documents that stretch high above up into the roof of the Palazzo, where air-conditioning pipes a metre across pump out their measured air. Rule-conscious clerks keep their wary, officious eyes on a couple of researchers; cabinets are full of curiosities, like a selection of olive oil measuring pots; and a display sets out the whys and wherefores of Genoese trading colonies in the Crimea. All around are shelves of fastidious archives documenting the speedy rise and slow decline of a merchant pirate superpower all those hundreds of years ago.

Even when Genoa was at the height of its wealth and power, it combined utter misery in the gutters alongside the most splendid of *palazzi*. As the cases of Paola Spinola and Anna Maria Vedona show, even a moderately comfortable life could be overturned by a death, an illness or a run of bad luck. A single broken leg could condemn a working family to a slow end through starvation; a sudden squall at sea could mean a fisherman's wife being left to fend for her family in an uncaring world.

One man's solution to this kind of misery can still be seen from the Corso that traces a meandering contour through the middle-class districts above the chaotic medieval heart of Genoa. Just below the stretch known as Corso Firenze is an enormous semi-derelict building, consisting of four sides, each as big as a palace. The central space between these sides is divided into four large courtyards by halls that converge on a central chapel. Under the collapsing roof of this giant edifice, in those crumbling and decaying rooms is one man's answer to the human suffering that he saw around him, a monumental agglomeration of stone and pious goodwill. The Albergo dei Poveri was the brainchild of Emanuele Brignole, and a landmark in the way the Western world treated the less fortunate: it was a workhouse.

In 1652 a serious outbreak of plague swept along the Ligurian coast till it reached Genoa, killing around 700 people every day. The Genoese were used to digging mass graves in the region's rocky terrain, and on this occasion they used a gully in Carbonara, just outside the city walls. The broken, splitting and putrid bodies of an estimated 10,000 victims were laid there.

As well as killing thousands, the plague caused widespread suffering for many who survived. Families lost their wage earners, economic life was disrupted, and charitable institutions were closed down. That particular outbreak of plague in 1652 spurred one of the city's richer (and more virtuous) residents, Emanuele Brignole, to find a way to help the suffering. Work began on the Albergo dei Poveri in 1658, building directly on the site of the mass grave in the gully. The idea behind building the Albergo was to offer work to the poor and the destitute to pay for their food and shelter: getting them off the streets and into the four walls of an institution, with good works and Christian charity at its heart.

Brignole himself died in 1678, leaving much of his estate to the project. He asked for a plain burial within the chapel of the Albergo, and ended up entombed under a marble slab. A statue of the founder, quite against the spirit of his wishes, was added later.

The Albergo itself evolved in stages, with gradual additions until the grand entrance was completed in 1834, damming the steep walls of the gully with self-conscious neo-classical elegance. When finished, the Albergo's sides were each 175 metres long, and the six-storey building covered 19,000 square metres. Men and women had separate food halls, infirmaries and chapel seating, and the four courtyards were enhanced with hundreds of plants and trees.

By the early years of the twentieth century the Albergo boasted facilities like a bronze foundry, a room for war widows, a women's theatre, and a room for training residents in the use of radio sets. Smartly dressed slight young men sat at individual desks, concentrating as they listened to their Bakelite headsets. They could also study carpentry and mechanics, shoe-making and tailoring. Their apprenticeships were often organised by private companies. For the women it was all about domestic economics, and skills like sewing. The diet at the time was not bad: 100g of bread and a cafe latte for breakfast; soup, 100ml of wine and another chunk of bread for lunch; and then more of the same for dinner, but this time with meat of some sort in the soup. At weekends the wine ration was doubled.

The Albergo was occasionally turned over to the military, as in 1746 when the residents were turfed out and 4,000 soldiers bunked down instead. It never had less than a thousand inmates, who each had to have lived in Genoa for five years to qualify. It was also usually financially self-sufficient.

This being Genoa, where almost anything worth its salt (or capable of turning a profit) was written down and recorded, there are files, files and more files dedicated to it in that echoing old archive room in the Palazzo Ducale. Every line and every entry tells a story and sheds a benevolent light on how the city's poor lived, worked and died over the centuries.

As well as the neat brick of dusty and heartbreakingly businesslike requests for bread, there are seemingly endless accounts kept by those running the Albergo itself. One embossed leather cover holds hundreds of tattered and fragile pages of accounts, comings and goings, credits and debts, from 1779 and 1780. The accounts are held together with a flattened knot of cord that can be untied in a tiny puff of dust: *"Detto dove a spese D li Poveri dell' Albergo L700..." "Eugenio Ervino Conte di Schönbrunn..." "Compagnia d'Indie L1256..." "Banco Giro in Venezia Conto..."*

There is also the *Rolli di Poveri*, scrolling down pages of carefully ruled lines and columns, listing all who passed between those huge and forgiving walls. In the lists covering 1790-91 there was Giacomo Garribaldo, who moved in on 19 February 1791 but managed to be thrown out only two days into March; Giacomo Ghiglione, who secured what was probably a cushy deal by moving to the Albergo's bread-making department; and poor old Gió Batta Cantagrillo, who promptly died.

***

Genoa's charitable instinct continues to this day, under the banner of a personality just as remarkable as Saint Ugo and Emanuele Brignole. Heading on around the curve of the old port beyond the Ospitale della Commenda di San Giovanni di Prè, past insalubrious districts flavoured by Senegal and Equador and spliced by access roads to the ferry port, comes the tastiest legacy of this man's work. Several decades before Jamie Oliver established the London restaurant *Fifteen* to help unemployed youngsters find a better future through food, a small Genoese *trattoria* was busy pioneering the same idea, under the guidance of a priest on a mission to help the unfortunate (and annoy the Church hierarchy).

From the outside, the Osteria Marinara A'Lanterna does not look particular, especially on a dismal December day of damp puddles and barely controllable umbrellas. Inside however, the Osteria is smartly nautical, a place where local workers can rely on a couple of lunchtime courses and a cheeky quarter litre of *vermentino*. The food is just as you would expect: inexpensive, simple, maritime – and good. A coatstand in the corner balances on the blades of an old steel propeller, with the prongs of a ship's wheel on top providing the pegs for sodden coats and dripping hats. A rope ladder is strung out over the diners in one room; a string of flags in the next. Model ships decorate the walls, and a trip to the bathroom gives you all the dark wood and brass that you would expect on a tea clipper tacking its way to China. If ever the Osteria needed to raise more money, it could sell its fittings to a themed lobster restaurant in a good suburb of Boston.

On the wall just above the seat where my soggy wife tucked into a plate of crisply battered mermaidy morsels was a small reminder that this was no ordinary *osteria marinara*. Inside a slightly gaudy polished metal frame is a certificate that reads: "*A Don Gallo – un amico che si è impegnato per i diritti delle transessuali e non solo...*" Underneath are affirmations of support from "Miss transitalia" and "Miss transitalia sudamerica". Don Gallo, the mastermind of the operation (and many other initiatives in Genoa), is the same Don Gallo who helped Rosella set up her self-help group for transsexual prostitutes back in Chapter 1.

The idea of the Osteria Marinara A'Lanterna was to teach the city's unemployed a proper trade, giving them a leg up into the world of work while also acting as a first-class local seafood *trattoria* in a fairly benighted part of town. Youngsters could apply for work directly through the local job centre, and if they were successful they started as trainees, learning the ways of the kitchen and front of house, gaining experience, skills and self-confidence. The city's restaurants are full of Osteria Marinara A'Lanterna alumni.

Don Gallo himself died in 2012, after many years in Genoa's toughest district ministering (as he put it) as a "priest of the sidewalk". His long career saw him steer the Comunita' San Benedetto al Porto di Genoa in the direction of the city's poor and dispossessed, and he was outspoken in his support of the LGBT community. He was fined after smoking a joint in support of legalising soft drugs; but no matter what the Genoese thought of his leftish views, most miss him and his megaphone, posing in front of a rainbow flag bearing the letters P-E-A-C-E, or helping to launch a fundraising transsexual calendar.

Just a bit further along the road from the Osteria Marinara A'Lanterna is the ultimate symbol of Genoa, the splendid Lanterna itself. The lighthouse looks like a 76-metre Art Deco space rocket, plastered with the cross of St George and helpfully positioned to the west of the main harbour, both to keep shipping (and aircraft) safe and to embellish tourist photos of the Genoese sunset.[2] It is one of the world's tallest lighthouses, which is an amazing achievement given that it was built in 1543.

The San Benigno district that surrounds it is now quite a forbidding area, dominated by a massive power station (where my father-in-law worked for many years) and the container port, stretching out to the east. However, the views for anybody who makes it up the tightly winding stairs to the public viewing gallery, halfway up in the world of the seagulls, are stunning. They are a reminder of the sculpted geography that shaped Liguria and made Genoa into the vital port it has been for a millennium. The chunk of rock where La Lanterna stands used to be the end point of a peninsula, punctuating the line of hills stretching out in both directions along the coast; but dynamite and a desire to link the main harbour to the burgeoning industrial suburb of Sampierdarena just to the west put a stop to that.[3]

***

The last eighty or so ageing residents of the Albergo dei Poveri moved out in 2012, to find homes in the five hospitals that are run by the Azienda Pubblica di Servizi alla Persona (ASP) Emanuele Brignole. In their stead – at least in one tiny corner of the Albergo – are now knots of university students who cluster and flirt around a doorway that seems like a tradesman's entrance, given the scale and grandeur of the rest of the building. Inside that doorway, the stone is freshly plastered and painted, and echoing corridors stretch off along one side of one of the four courtyard gardens. It feels like a spruced-up monastery, until a glance out of the window reminds you of the scale of the whole building. There are spaces for lectures, for seminars, for computer work. Displays tacked to the walls show computer-generated images of further planned developments, including one surprising scene of a couple of randy computer-generated students enjoying each other in a distinctly pre-marital way. The grand plan for this remarkable and vast piece of Genoese history is for the university to take charge, redeveloping the decaying Albergo and laying the foundations for more good to come out of the vision of Emanuele Brignole, all these centuries after he found his mission in life. I am not so certain that the plan will succeed.

I was surprised to find that it is still possible to go through the main doorway into the echoing main entrance hall of the Albergo. It looks very different to the corner of the building that the university has already colonised. The smell is different too: dust, damp and neglect. Solid wooden doors lead off into the forgotten and the unknown, their decorative inlays frosted by ridges of white dust undisturbed other than by gravity. On the left through one door there is a small, incongruous and possibly under-visited branch of Banca Carige. Busts of benefactors from across the centuries stare down with sympathetic expressions of concern etched across their brows. A set of iron gates directly ahead is padlocked, but a sad stony corridor lit by neon strips leads off beyond them into the depths of the great building. Massive marble staircases run up to a second grand entrance hall, where doors are wired shut and more dust has dulled the black and white chessboard floor into tones of washed-out grey. There is the statue of Emanuele Brignole himself, looking not unlike a stylised Jesus with his long rock-star hair and shapely beard.[4] The only colours disturbing the muted monochrome are a red cross of St George, a green *Uscita di emergenza* sign, and a green and gilt lamp that hangs down, sullen and unloved, from the 8-metre-high ceiling.

I was there to see Mattia Giachino from the ASP Emanuele Brignole. The organisation's offices, just like those last ageing patients, were being moved out to more suitable accommodation. The offices had been in the rooms off one side of a long corridor, leading off that upstairs entrance along the front of the building. Marble slabs lined the walls of the corridor, between large windows that looked down on a forlorn courtyard dominated by a solitary palm tree and the sloshing of water from faulty guttering. More benefactors were listed on each of those marble slabs along with the amount they gave: *Vanoli Francesco e Alfredo – 1925 – Oblazione 1000; Palau Carlo – 1907 – Oblazione 9375; Gandolofo Raffaele – 1934 – Legato 10,000.*[5] In one office twenty-two chairs were ranged round a long, oval table, and dark paintings of monks hung on the walls. There was an old grandfather clock, and large wood and glass cabinets stuffed full of innumerable box files. Mattia was trying to work out what they could take to their new offices, and regretting every minute of leaving these grand premises.

Around the corner and along the side of the Albergo was a storeroom, full of forgotten items that could be defined as junk or equipment; I spotted a few tired old Christmas decorations. Beyond that was a long room stacked with ancient documents like those I had leafed through among the mustard-coloured girders of the Palazzo Ducale. Dozens of letters from Genoese citizens leaving sums of money to the Albergo were strung into paper bricks like the requests for bread from Paola Spinola and Anna Maria Vedona. The documents in this room had all been catalogued; many more from across the centuries lay elsewhere, unopened but fertile fodder for PhDs in social history or anybody with time to work them out.

Another door led off to the right, into what was the male part of the central chapel. The chapel itself formed the centre of the cross that divided the internal space of the Albergo into four courtyards, and this male part linked that central chapel with the left-hand, western side of the building. It was an enormous space, somewhere between a bombsite and a treasure trove, full of rubble and dust, shards of glass and the occasional cigarette butt. There were stacks of old paintings, a gloriously painted alcove hidden away behind a life-size crucifix and surprisingly a grand piano. An alleyway had been cleared between the glorious piles of dusty objects and the chapel itself, where a monumental marble altarpiece was framed by rusting scaffolding poles under the grand cupola that I had first spotted from up on the hill outside. A plain, unmarked marble slab lay on the floor where the male chapel met the main chapel. This was the resting place of Emanuele Brignole himself, just as he wished – without adornment, and constantly trampled under the feet of those whom he sought to help.

Mattia led the way up a tiny winding staircase. At the first exit there was a balcony for the organ, high up above the marble altarpiece, and further up there was a bell tower. I inspected a pile of rusting cogs that in a former life had mechanised the ringing of the chapel bells, and felt the uneven floor boards for signs of rot. "The first time I came here I had a walking tour of the building," said Mattia. "After three hours of walking we still had not finished."

Genoa's Albergo dei Poveri is an extraordinary building, and a monument to how this great and unequal city tried to care for those who could not thrust their way to the top of the food chain. Genoa's history is often red in tooth and claw, but thanks to the legacy of Emanuele Brignole and many of its less celebrated citizens it also retained a social conscience that was ahead of its time. Seeing the grand old building in such a state of disrepair, and yet with such potential, the question is whether this entire chapter of Genoese history is now under mortal threat.

The ASP Emanuele Brignole is not in a position to do much: its priority is the 400 or so old people it still cares for, and as the property market is fairly flat it is not a good time to raise money by selling any other assets. Much rests with the university, which has taken control of the actual building on a fifty-year lease. There is ambition, as those computer-generated graphics suggest, but it is a massive and expensive building to deal with on a tight budget. One estimate has suggested that even with those smart, newly-painted university corridors, 87 per cent of the Albergo will still be derelict.

I was surprised to hear that the large green space behind the Albergo, a half-valley where the city council grows its municipal plants in rundown greenhouses, is also owned by the ASP Emanuele Brignole and is rented for what seems like a scandalously small sum. Again, my fresh but perhaps naive mind considers the opportunities that such an area could afford in a city as devoid of space and greenery as Genoa, and I wonder how and why it is being wasted in such a miserable way. It seems like ripe territory for some intrepid journalist from the redoubtable local press, although both they and the council are probably as cash-strapped as both the university and the ASP Emanuele Brignole itself. But, as Emanuele Brignole showed all those decades ago, when he dared to consider the fate of those with less fortunate lives than his: fortune favours the bold. The fate of one of Europe's most remarkable buildings, institutions and landmarks in social history now lies in the balance.

4

THE LIGURIAN MENU

"I'm no expert on cooking." *Giuseppe Mazzini*

"Sometimes in mushroom season," said Mario as we clambered out of his asthmatic Lancia on a switchback curve, "you can't find any space for parking up here. It's as busy as Via Settembre in the centre of Genoa." It was just before dawn on 3 October and there were already four other cars on the side of the road, next to where a path led off up a ridge into the trees. I had woken up at five, all the way back down in the centre of the city, and driven up to Torriglia with my father-in-law. Armando had that peculiar Italian combination of impatience and lack of urgency, cursing merrily whenever a traffic light turned against us but showing no great need for speed otherwise. We met Mario outside a bar in the centre of Torriglia, and the two of them had a slow, thoughtful cigarette together as though we were waiting for somebody else to turn up. We were not, and as soon as they stubbed them out there was an unexpected change of pace as we threw back our espressos and climbed into that tiny Lancia.

When the sun started to rise we were already high up on the footpath, the Alta Via that runs all the way along the crest of Liguria's coastal mountain chain. The valleys below us to our left began lighting up with the sun's rays, field by field, and in the distance we had an occasional glimpse of the sea itself, cutting its way into the slopes to the south-east.

We passed dense clumps of hazelnut, climbing higher still until we were surrounded by grand beech trees and the occasional chestnut. The coast may be beautiful, but for me this early morning clamber up the wooded crests of those steep slopes that barricade Liguria from the north is a match for anything at sea level.

At first I thought Armando and Mario were carrying sticks for stability on the steep, muddy slopes, but when I saw how they used them to scrape away thick layers of beech leaves around anything vaguely mushroom-like, I grabbed one myself and joined in. Mario showed me the two types that we were looking for: stout, swollen porcinis, and another type that came in a variety of colours from battleship grey to beech-leaf ochre to muted muddy red. I spotted around a dozen other varieties, including enormous red ones covered in white spots that Mario warned were *quasi fatali*, almost fatal. One type of delicate dark purple mushroom looked as if it had been made from badly bruised human skin, and another fungus lay directly across the forest floor like a pale filigree mesh.

Mario pointed to where clumps of trunks stood together. "Look there, push the leaves around and you might find one growing, one of these miracles." I tried, and it worked. With a bit of practice the plump, round caps started to stand out from the surrounding leaf litter, and a swoosh of my stick revealed the thick white stems underneath. A deeply satisfying firm tug plucked them from the dark soil.

Compared with my struggles when I pick up a rod and try to tempt fish into my frying pan, I was rather surprised to see how briskly my basket filled up with meaty mushrooms. But any self-satisfaction was always cut short by Mario's ruthless policing, peering into my basket and chucking away what I thought were prime specimens. "Too old... You can eat these but... No..." I was grateful for only one of Mario's stern *quasi fatale* comments.

The three hours that we spent mushrooming were hypnotic, one fifth of my attention absorbed by the need to stay upright, and four-fifths studying the patterns of the leaf litter. I stayed in touch with the other two through periodic whistles, but just after one particularly fruitful patch of half rotten leaves I looked up, whistled, and heard nothing.

At least, I thought, I'm on the ridge that we walked up. New arrivals appeared every few minutes, clutching hopeful looking baskets, looking at my own bumper crop, and asking *"Trovati?"* ("Did you find any?")

Each time I nodded, I only confirmed what they were already thinking: for some, optimism that there were mushrooms to be found; for others, pessimism that they were already too late. A bit further down the ridge the track petered out, but a large man who was more sweat than T-shirt confirmed that the Alta Via was just ahead, while ogling my basket.

The large, sweaty man was wrong. Very wrong. I was on a 45-degree slope, surrounded by dense brush, and the muddy excuse for a track was covered in hoof prints rather than the neat outline of shoes and boots. I had got lost among the ridges of Liguria's mountains thanks to the bewitching power of a mushroom hunt, so I did the sensible thing and phoned my wife. She told me off, then phoned her dad, who realised he was lost too. She told him off. He phoned Mario, and then my wife, who then phoned me. After another chastening telling off I was sent back up the slope from where I had stumbled, basket in hand. An hour later I was back at the asthmatic Lancia with Mario merrily throwing most of the contents of my basket into the bushes, leaving me with a few dozen mushrooms of various sizes and shapes. Despite my wife's anger and the loss of three-quarters of my basket, my first ever mushroom hunt had to be seen as a resounding success.

By noon we had trundled back down half a mountain and were sat in La Locanda da Becassa, a roadside *trattoria* that served as a shrine to two things: Genoa CFC and the mushroom.[1] On a couple of tables by the door, baskets full of *funghi* were being decanted into piles according to size, type and quality. The men worked the tables (and presumably were responsible for all the red and blue Genoa CFC memorabilia that covered every inch of wall space) while the women worked the kitchen, shouting hellos to locals in Genoese dialect and attending to a great vat of creamy tripe. Some of the mushrooms would be dried and some cooked up that very evening, so the lunchtime menu was disappointingly mushroom-free. Instead, we started with ravioli in a succulent meaty sauce, and then rabbit and tripe (the rabbit was mine – I left the tripe to Mario and Armando), all washed down with a bottle of rosé that could have been used to strip paint. Armando used a lump of bread in his left hand like an extra limb, shovelling jellied strips of cow stomach onto his fork. A dozen middle-aged men at the table behind me occasionally burst out into finely arranged songs (Armando said they were part of a famous male voice choir), as though we had blundered onto the set of a musical. I may be wrong, but I saw no pesto on the menu – something so rare in Liguria that it is worth remarking on.

I did not mind missing the chance to round off a morning's mushroom hunting with a few dishes featuring the things. A week before I had met Mario at a mushroom-themed meal that featured porcini slices fried in breadcrumbs; porcini lasagne; stuffed and baked porcini; and a pudding of baked peach halves topped with *amaretti* biscuits, designed to look like mushrooms again. And there would be mushrooms still to come: Armando and I had enough in our baskets to provoke admiring glances from men and women, old and young, as we walked back home through the centre of Genoa later that afternoon. Even the most urban of Genoese could appreciate that tramping through forests at dawn in search of tasty things to eat was an unreservedly good thing.

Ligurian cooking has two basic origins, and the mushrooming experience was firmly part of one of them: the mountains. The other side is easy to guess: the sea. Pesto almost seems worth a category of its own, but it is clearly of the mountains as it relies on ingredients like herbs and pine nuts.[2] Unlike bountiful regions such as Emilia Romagna, Liguria has never been able to cultivate its way to culinary glory. The mountains have been too sheer, and there has been precious little flat space for much else. The waters off the Riviera have also been too deep and too salty (and non-tidal) to be particularly productive as fisheries. Ligurians have had to be both tenacious and inventive to get anything on their plates, but the results have been way out of proportion to their basic resources.

***

Not only have Ligurians had to pull together a cuisine from an unpromising geographical backdrop; they have also had to put up with their two best-known dishes being misrepresented and bastardised into inferior products that bear little relationship to the original. While the pesto on the typical supermarket shelf bears little relationship to the true green hydrogen bomb from Genoa, something calling itself *focaccia* has spread across the globe, but it owes more to anti-heat tiles on a space shuttle than the lunchtime snack they eat with gusto across Liguria.

Focaccia is a Ligurian picnic in one handy slice. Wherever a Ligurian is hungry but has no access to a proper sit-down meal (with wine and bread, as Armando would demand), there is always a paper bag and a slice of *focaccia*. The outward appearance of the real thing is not too different to the global supermarket version: it is a golden, flattish bread, full of dimples. But while the global supermarket bread has an inconsequential crust above a body as white as trench foot and as thick and friable as loam, the original is a hymn to olive oil and salt, below a crust worthy of the name and with a thinner body that is the texture of an English cloud. There is crunch and oiliness, and then there is chewiness and succulence. A *focacceria* will produce rectangular sheet of it after rectangular sheet, cutting them up into slices the size of iPads and selling them by weight. A good *focacceria* will have a loyal customer base that winces at the thought of having to go anywhere else; what if we buy it and it's not as good and we spend the whole meal regretting not having the real stuff? A terrible prospect. The real stuff is not there to make sandwiches out of; it is there to munch on until you feel slightly nauseous from the oil. Every time we have either flown in to Genoa or had the in-laws come to visit us elsewhere, the first thing is the proud announcement that they have *focaccia*; the second thing is the noise of munching. I am told that in the dark, distant, pre-Greenpeace past, melted whale blubber was used instead of olive oil – probable, given Genoa's seafaring tradition, although I wonder what the smell would have been like. The smell of a neighbourhood *focacceria* is one of the glories of Genoa, and an invaluable aid to navigating the *vicoli*.

Focaccia has its variants, and in Liguria the most notable one is from the town of Recco, just along the coast from Genoa. The town was a victim of bombing by the Allies in the Second World War, and it sits slightly uneasily alongside the Riviera's gemlike fishing villages and pastel-coloured resort towns. What it does have, however, is a reputation for *focaccia* that makes many divert their journeys as they hunt for the perfect beachside picnic. Recco is particularly famous for a type of *focaccia* that bears little resemblance to standard *focaccia* at all. *Focaccia al formaggio* is made with a type of light, sour cheese called *crescenza*. The story is that locals hiding in the mountains from Muslim raiders had only flour, olive oil and cheese, and put their minds together to come up with this splendid dish that resembles a delicate pie as much as a traditional *focaccia*. I firmly believe that it is no longer true that you cannot find good *focaccia alla formaggio* outside Recco – I sat and watched it being made in a new restaurant just opening near Genoa's

Porta Soprana. The chef stretched a thin disc of dough until it was the size of an umbrella and as translucent as an Edwardian virgin's skin, and threw it over a tray where blobs of white cheese sat on another layer of dough. He then cut holes in the top, sprinkled some olive oil, and threw it into a pizza oven for a couple of minutes. Recco now has some serious competition, on this stretch of coastline at least.

The local *focacceria* will almost certainly sell *focaccia* topped with onions, or olives, or tomatoes, along with another one of Liguria's signature dishes: *farinata*, in effect a salty pancake made from chickpea flour. *Farinata* tends to be made in large circular trays, in the same oven that is used for the *focaccia,* and eating it gives me that virtuous feeling that you ought to eat it rather than want to. *Farinata* was a staple for mariners as it was easy to make at sea – simply take a load of chickpea flour, mix with sea water, and cook it over a fire or in an oven on a flat metal tray.

Street food gets a good hearing in Genoa, beyond the slices of *focaccia* and *farinata* eaten hot out of a paper bag while staring at the sea. The port is full of small shops that will fry up all sorts of seashore bits and pieces to go with their *farinata*, from salt cod fritters to squid and suspiciously small fish.

For those grazers with a more robust hold on their stomachs, Genoa is also home to a number of tripe shops. Just down one of the *vicoli* from where my in-laws live is the Antica Tripperia La Casana, which has been in the records as having existed since 1811, although the owner thinks it was there well before that. If the wind is in the wrong direction the smell of cooking tripe wafts out along the *vicoli,* and judging by its popularity the aroma might boost business even further. School kids as well as pensioners drop in to buy a few strips of rubbery tripe doused with oil and salt, and eat them on the move off trays, just like ice cream.

From the street the *tripperia* displays itself with a glass front full of variously textured shimmering chunks of tripe, hanging from hooks. Inside, there is a marble counter with a set of scales and a mechanical slicer (like a machine used for shredding office documents). Two copper pots, each a metre across, fill the fitted stove. There's more marble, brass, yet more marble, and at the end of the *tripperia* a small statue of Jesus in an alcove, lit by a single clear light bulb. This particular *tripperia* is flourishing, but it is only one of four that survives in Genoa itself. There used to be 150 across the wider area, and even half a century ago there were 70, but it is a time-consuming business for both the *trippaio* and the customer. Preparing tripe for sale takes up seven days a week, with the work continuing even when the shop is closed. If you buy the tripe to prepare at home, you are still looking at two hours of cooking if you do it properly, and the owner reckons that only old people have any time for that these days. However, there is money to be made, and this *tripperia* provides two good salaries as a reward for all the hard work. The current owner learned the trade from a man (he refers to him as his tripe master) who was able to buy up several flats in Genoa's historical centre with his profits. Who knew there were such riches in cows' stomachs?

Is tripe of the sea or the mountains? In a sense it is of the sea, thanks to its role in providing the cheap sustenance to power the working class of a heroic industrial port city. With another of Genoa's more pungent specialities, the answer is more obvious. To find salted, dried cod on Genoese menus is no surprise. It has long been a staple of seafarers, and is a cheap, transportable form of protein for those with limited access to a bountiful larder. In Genoa it is known as *stoccafisso*, and is found in its hard form or pre-soaked, ready for cooking. I had a bowl of the stuff, its firm texture and salty flavour a great addition to a very Ligurian combination of broth, *taggiasca* olives and a few chunks of tomato, in the legendary Da Maria trattoria. Da Maria is a city institution, the place to eat a very typical two-course lunch with wine and bread in exchange for a single 10 euro note. You may need to share your table, and paying at busy times can mean tackling a scrum of shouting Italians, but it is worth it.

The *stoccafisso* trade may be the reason behind the small Icelandic flag halfway up the Salita di San Francesco, my favourite alleyway in Genoa (although there are very many still to discover). The Salita heads up from the very heart of Genoa's glorious district of *palazzi*, from the end of Via Garibaldi, up a steep path interspersed with steps. Tiles that look like half bricks provide some grip for shoe soles, and the sides of the path are stepped so that those coming down can descend at their own pace rather than at a speed chosen by gravity. The Salita turns a sharp left, past the Icelandic flag (above an abandoned, graffitied doorway), bears right, then branches off to the right up a sharp lactic-acid-friendly incline, before reaching Castelletto and several of the best views in Genoa (as ever, lifts are available).

Despite the relative poverty of the sea harvest, many of the gorgeous tumbling multi-coloured villages strung along the coast nevertheless owe their existence to fishing. Camogli, nestling in the morning shadow of the Promontario Portofino just after Recco, is a perfect example. Its houses were apparently painted in different colours so that they were recognisable to each of the fishermen while they were out at sea. The name means "wife's house", suggesting that the women of Camogli were used to having to look after things while their men were away at sea, or gone forever beneath the waves. Despite its undoubted beauty, my first impressions of the place were mixed. Camogli managed to combine picture-perfect looks on a sunny winter's day with teeming crowds of ice-cream-guzzling Italians in expensive sunglasses and designer padded jackets, walking in a kind of Brownian motion, below zigzagging switchbacks with more cars than parking spots. Goodness knows how crowded it gets on the second Sunday in May, when it hosts the Sagra del Pesce, at which a 4-metre-diameter frying pan is used to cook up a suitably vast amount of fish. This commemorates a bountiful catch by the village's fishing boats during the Second World War. German mines had prevented them from setting sail for so long that the villagers had become desperate with hunger. They offered their prayers to San Fortunato and the men set sail anyway, returning with bulging nets.

Even if it is not prime fishing territory, Liguria and Genoa are indelibly associated with seafood in the minds of most Italians. In 1938 a Fascist-sponsored exhibition of regional foods was set up in Rome, in the Circus Maximus. Benito Mussolini himself inaugurated this theme-park embodiment of the rural Fascist ideal, which featured seven different regional *trattorie*. In the Ligurian *trattoria* the men were all dressed as sailors and fishermen, and dockside props were scattered around in theme-restaurant style. A sycophantic journalist in Mussolini's entourage gushed, "You can really breathe the air of sea and ships. It's just as if you are down in Genoa's little alleys by the docks."

A favourite dish in the house of my wife's family is *polpo alla tellarese* (from Tellaro near La Spezia), which is purple-tinged rubbery white chunks of octopus served with boiled potatoes, parsley, garlic, lemon and olives. Although the sea off Liguria is not a great fishery, its saltiness is very good for anchovies, which used to form an important export (cured in salt and oil, and packed into barrels in layers). In Imperia anchovies are even used in a special type of *focaccia* called *pisslandrea*, which is dedicated to Genoa's great mercenary hero, Andrea Doria (who was born in Oneglia, one of the two towns that form modern Imperia). The fishy specialities change almost from village to village along the Ligurian coast, from tiny shrimps to mussels to sardines, and most are delicious. I am far less certain about another one of the region's specialities: *capon magro* sounds sinister and looks forbidding, as a pyramid built up from a base of sea biscuits, involving vegetables, eggs, tuna and cheap fish like gurnard. The posh versions are then decorated with large pink crustaceans, and the whole affair looks as if it's straight out of a 1970s hotel buffet. The places that sell *capon magro* also seem to do an inexplicable roaring trade in thick, gloopy Russian salad.

Up in the mountains the favoured ingredients are herbs, game (especially rabbit and boar), and of course mushrooms. In this historically poor land chestnuts were a staple, and chestnut-flour bread was often associated with hard times. Getting hold of adequate wheat supplies was a constant imperial priority for the Genoese, and as well as allowing it to develop its heavenly *focaccia,* Liguria was able to build a reputation for its pasta.

Before arriving in Genoa for the first time I had never encountered those little twists called *trofie* which go so well with pesto – but then I had never eaten pesto like the stuff they make in this corner of the Mediterranean. On the eastern side of Liguria they make little discs of pasta called *corzetti*, which are stamped with a cross. This posh pasta, properly packaged, is often given as presents, so all kinds of other logos and patterns can be stamped on the discs in place of the cross. One other type of pasta that deserves a mention is *pansotti*, thick little *ravioli* stuffed full of greens like chard, and served with a slightly cloying but distinctive walnut sauce. The walnuts are part of the heritage of Genoa's empire – in this case the Black Sea coast.

Genoa being in southern Europe, olives play an important role in cooking. The *taggiasca* olives that are thrown into stews of everything from *stoccafissa* to rabbit are phenomenally tasty – low in acidity and extremely fragrant. (I tried a superb and surprising desert of olive parfait in a *trattoria* just off Piazza di Ferrari, where the quality of food made up for six successive power failures.) The olive oil (especially from the western end of the Riviera, where the *taggiasca* olives are grown) is right up there with the best in Italy.

The wine, however, is a mixed bag. Some of the whites are great, like the terrifically zesty *vermentino* (it is not too dissimilar from sauvignon blanc, especially with something fishy in the pot on a hot summer's evening). Liguria does not lend itself to growing particularly beefy red grapes, and sometimes a glass of local red arrives both cold and slightly fizzy: not something I have ever relished. But the Genoese and Ligurians have shown such a genius for making a lot out of a meagre inheritance that I am sure there will be a local winemaker who can crack the secret of good red wine from a couple of rocky terraces and a bit of ingenuity. In the meantime I can recommend a wine bar in a little passageway just off the Piazza Matteotti where a happy evening can be spent getting delightfully sloshed on an ever-changing menu of generous single glasses of the best that Italy has to offer.

***

In a city of unlikely alleyways there are few alleyways that you are less likely to wander up than the Vico delle Carabaghe which becomes a dead end just 20 metres after branching off the Vico dei Castagna. Barred windows to the right open onto stuffy living rooms filled with old furniture, and a doorway leads off to the left. The door is utterly unassuming, except for the single word *Viganotti* written on it in small letters. If Roald Dahl had set *Charlie and the Chocolate Factory* in Genoa, this is where the action would take place. The interior looks as if it was lifted from the fantasies of a nineteenth-century child, with little piles of chocolates of every description and hue sitting under hand-written labels, arranged in glass and wood counters and cabinets. Baskets contain marrons glacés and crystallised violets, and behind it all, through a doorway, is the chocolate factory itself. Belts and shafts crowd the ceiling, all connected (eventually) to a small engine squatting in the corner of the room. These in turn power an array of resolutely old-fashioned machines, built by venerable companies such as J. M. Lehmann of Dresden (they switched to manufacturing guns rather than sweets during the Second World War). A belt turns two enormous marble wheels that trundle round in a tight circle, smashing up almonds and other ingredients. The next machine is a hopper-fed three-cylinder industrial mangle, polished despite the layer of sugar dust that seems to coat everything else. Dotted around are stoves and marble tables, similar to those found in any Genoese kitchen.

Alessandro Boccardo is no eccentric Willy Wonka figure, but the personification of sober passion hiding behind wire-framed glasses. His face might belong to a diligent priest in medieval times. He wears a white chef's smock, with a little hat of white netting, finely chequered trousers, and kitchen clogs. His hands are large, expressive and well-scrubbed, and when he speaks the noise rises from the back of his throat, becoming more enthusiastic with every sentence.

"It's the teeth on the cogs that wear out first," says Boccardo, but the previous owners were typically Genoese in wanting to keep the old machinery going as long as possible. Boccardo bought Romeo Viganotti from those owners (a brother and sister) back in 1999, on condition that the old ways continued. They stuck around for six months after the sale to make sure he knew what he was doing, and, he thinks, to make sure he was worthy of taking on the project. The *fabbrica del cioccolato* dates back to at least 1866, but some digging through the church archives of San Vincenzo reveals that the father of the original Romeo Viganotti (born in 1866) was called Domenico and was already listed as a chocolatier.

"Nothing had changed since the company's early days, so of course I couldn't come in and change everything," says Boccardo. "I just tiptoe around and find things to tweak." The Viganotti recipes came with the business, along with the factory fittings, and the brother and sister kept the building themselves until 2010, when they handed it over with an insistence that the whole thing continues to run in the same way that it always had. Luckily, they had sold it to the right man.

Changing everything would be self-defeating in a business like Romeo Viganotti. Genoa would not be an Italian city if the people were not fond of two things: sweets and entertaining guests. Instead of a bottle of plonk from the local off licence, guests in Genoa turn up with lovingly packaged little trays of something sweet and fancy. That is good news for local confectioners and excellent news for a company as traditional as this one.

The Genoese are quite conservative, and Boccardo had some complaints when he dared to switch round a couple of baskets. But after the Joanne Harris book of *Chocolat* and the Juliette Binoche film came out, some started asking for unusual and exotic flavours. Boccardo was happy to oblige, and tried adding spices and different grades of salt to his mixtures. Some flavours work best depending on the season – cool minty ones in summertime for example. The core ingredients – including the chocolate itself – are bought in, because of the lack of space. So Boccardo spends his time examining flavours and supply chains, blending and formulating them into the best chocolates possible. He says that he thinks of himself as a chocolate alchemist, with a light dancing in his eyes just as it would in the eyes of Willy Wonka.

Some of the results of the alchemy are astonishing: red tea with lemon and vanilla, rose, or plain Genoese basil. Others have been less successful (his attempt to make an onion cream was one notable failure). Viganotti chocolates have been ordered by Genoese around the world. He has sent them to an embassy worker in Kabul, and to NASA over in the US. When he sent a couple of Easter eggs to NASA, to the grandsons of a local Genoese, one of them shattered in transit. The NASA rocket scientists pieced together the fragments, and realised that it had shattered through changes in air pressure; now any Easter eggs sent by air get a hole drilled in the bottom to prevent this happening again.

"For me the reward is what we do and how we do it. I get pleasure from the passion people exhibit when they find this tiny shop, and are amazed at the types of chocolate we sell and the old machinery we make them with. It's not just about money." Romeo Viganotti is one of those businesses that Italy does so well. If it was in Britain or the US the equipment might just be there for display, and the chocolates might now be made in some soulless light industrial estate on the edge of the city. As Alessandro Boccardo says, it is not just about the money. There may be nothing particularly Genoese about chocolate, but the presence of this funny little chocolate shop, stuck down a dead-end *vico* and unchanging from decade to decade, century to century, feels absolutely right for this city.[3]

5

LA SUPERBA AGAINST LA SERENISSIMA

"Our city, thanks to God, outshines others in strength, wealth
and agreeable qualities. If therefore we wish to preserve praise,
nobility and quiet and to destroy utterly our hostile neighbours,
it would be wise and most useful to begin to create native-born
knights in our city..."
Caffaro di Rustico da Caschifellone

Despite being from Venice, Marco Polo was not treated like an ordinary
prisoner. He was allowed out of his cell for fresh air, and received visitors
keen to meet a man already known as a great traveller. He was moved to
a second cell, along with a prisoner from Genoa's other great rival, Pisa.
They had access to books and good food, and the new cell was better lit
and ventilated than the old one. The two men were working on a
project: Polo was relating the story of his travels from 1276 to 1291,
which had taken him beyond the trading posts of the Black Sea and as
far as China; and Rustichello da Pisa was writing it all down.

"The great khan, lord of lords, named Kublai, is a fine middle size... He has
four ladies, who always rank as his wives..."

"At the end of this journey is a kingdom named Tain-fu... It yields also
much silk, abounding in the trees on which the worms are fed..."

"But the riches and profit which the khan derives from the province of Manji is so great that no man could dare to mention it..."

"This place is visited by various merchants, who purchase slaves, make them eunuchs, and then either sell them or convey them to other places..."

Although the book became known as *Il Milione*, because it was believed by sceptics to contain a million lies, this was intoxicating stuff to anybody interested in trade at the turn of the fourteenth century. Since the early years of the First Crusade, when Genoa had first started to make its mark, the focus of trading interest had shifted from enclaves on the coast of the Holy Land and the Levant to the Black Sea. Venice had Tana on the Crimea coast, and specialised in higher value items, while Genoa used its base in Caffa for products like slaves, grain, wax, furs and dried fruits. Some of the produce came from the Black Sea area itself, and some from the lands along the Silk Road that led across the steppes and into Asia.

The trade was lucrative. The two Italian cities avoided fighting on the basis that this was bad for business, but their mutual animosity, the riches that were at stake, and the blurring of the lines between traders and pirates meant that a showdown was always a possibility. The Battle of Curzola that led to Marco Polo sitting in a Genoese prison, dictating his adventures, was a spectacular and cruel settling of accounts, but the bitter rivalry that lay behind it had grown up over many, many decades.

***

If Genoa was audacious and belligerent, Venice was wily and clever. Its Adriatic base was a fine location that plugged into trade through northern Italy into Germany and Central Europe, and gave it a natural orientation towards the Eastern Mediterranean. It also pushed Venice hard against the interests of the creaking Byzantine Empire, which was now on the front line of the struggle between Christendom and Islam. The Venetians had come to learn that courting (and threatening) Constantinople paid dividends. The Golden Bull of 1082 gave it the right to trade freely throughout the Byzantine realm, giving it a considerable advantage over Genoa, Amalfi and Pisa. Byzantium, however, realised that there was profit to be made in playing the rivals off against each other, and granted them trading rights too (Pisa in 1111 and Genoa in 1156). They developed trading posts in the towering streets of Constantinople itself (which were soon splattered with the blood of the brawling rivals). But the aggressive city states, face to face with the splendour of the Byzantine capital, also began to see it as a juicy target in its own right.

All the while, trade was growing. The population of Italy doubled between the tenth and fourteenth centuries, with an even larger proportional increase in the numbers of those living in towns and cities. Marshy land was cleared in areas like the Po valley, and irrigation systems established. The simple trade in commodities like grain and salt was accompanied by new products that required sea transport: spices, dyes and high quality textiles. Banking and credit arrangements, like those used by Genoese investors, became more complex. In Genoa itself the value of goods passing through the port doubled between 1214 and 1274 and kept on rising. Grain from the Black Sea, more profitable to the Genoese merchants than costlier supplies from places like Morocco, was snapped up by the growing population of Italy and Europe. Slaves also came from the Black Sea area, especially Circassians and Tartars, and were sold on to work in richer households in Italy and as soldiers for the Mamluks of Egypt (to the great displeasure of the Pope).

Byzantium itself was a puzzle to many Western Europeans. Avaricious Italians viewed it as the key to the riches of the East, while the pious saw Eastern Christianity as essentially decadent and ungodly. Despite its Christianity, some thought it was too eager to accommodate the Muslims who gathered around its borders. The embattled Byzantine Empire was familiar with having to strike deals with its enemies and rivals in an attempt to preserve Constantinople's position as the gateway to the Black Sea. Its various concessions to the Italian trading states can be seen as an attempt to buy them off, one by one. However this also caused friction within Byzantium, as some parts of society did not benefit from the presence of the Italians, and resented their presence. As a result there were periodic attacks against the Latin community. But most bloodshed, as ever, was caused by fighting between the Italians themselves; in 1171 the Venetians largely destroyed the Genoese quarter of Constantinople. The worst violence, however, occurred in 1182 when Andronikos I Komnenos came to power. His predecessor was close to the merchants and large landowners who had benefited from the presence of the Italians. The new emperor was supported by those who were angry about being excluded from this prosperity, and the celebrations when he entered the city to assume office soon spilled over into a vicious pogrom against all Latins: Genoese and Venetian; young and old; male and female. A community estimated at 60,000 was destroyed, with many of those who escaped death being sold into slavery. To some members of the Western Church, Constantinople was considered barely Christian – untrustworthy and vulnerable, with the memory of the bloody Massacro dei Latini of 1182 sitting heavily in Italian minds.

This then is the background to the notorious Fourth Crusade of 1202–4, which is remembered with infamy as a moment when bloodthirsty Christians fell upon other Christians under the initial pretext of fighting the Muslims in the Holy Land. In essence the Crusade was hijacked by the Venetians, under the ninety-year-old blind Doge, Enrico Dandolo. There had been intense competition between Venice and Genoa, and this competition inevitably involved the Byzantine Empire, which controlled much of the Eastern Mediterranean and was the gateway to the Black Sea. Venice had taken a leading role in preparing for the Crusade, and suspended its trading operations to fulfil a contract to build the fleet that would transport the Crusaders to their main target, Egypt. The Crusaders, however, were unable to pay the sum agreed for the fleet. This left Venice in a difficult financial position, given the sacrifices it had made to build it. Doge Dandolo managed to persuade the Crusaders to repay the debt by attacking various sites on the Dalmatian coastline, including the city of Zara (which had rebelled against Venetian rule).[1] The sack of Zara was suitably bloody, and the Venetians then ushered the Crusaders on to Constantinople itself. The Venetians were determined to put a Byzantine prince of their own choosing on the emperor's throne, thereby gaining favoured access to the empire's riches. It was cynical and audacious, but the move would give Venice the decisive upper hand against Genoa for decades to come.

When the great city finally fell, the Crusaders disgraced themselves. For three days they sacked Constantinople, destroying its famous library and violating its religious buildings. Pope Innocent III was outraged. The Crusaders, he said, "made their swords, which they were supposed to use against the pagans, drip with Christian blood, they have spared neither religion, nor age, nor sex. They have committed incest, adultery, and fornication before the eyes of men. They have exposed both matrons and virgins, even those dedicated to God, to the sordid lusts of boys." His foul mood improved, however, when he discovered that some of the plunder was on its way to him.

Venice, predictably, did rather well out of the whole nasty business. It was able to proclaim itself "lord of a quarter and half a quarter of the empire", gaining enough territory from the Byzantines to build up an empire of its own in the Eastern Mediterranean, centred on Crete.[2] The battle for trading stations and routes between Venice and Genoa became even fiercer. Genoese pirates continued to harass enemy shipping; the ongoing struggle for influence over Constantinople picked up again; and ships started to probe through the Bosphorus and up into the Black Sea, looking for new trading opportunities.

Unfortunately for Venice, their great advantage in Constantinople did not last. Genoa offered naval support to the Greeks when they recaptured the city in 1261 from a weak regime left in place after the Fourth Crusade. This gave them privileges including a trading colony in the Galata area, with the right to self-government (by the mid fourteenth century its trade revenues were around seven times as large as those earned by the main Greek part of Constantinople). Genoa also gained excellent access to the grain and wax, slaves and furs of the Black Sea. Muslim advances in the Levant had curtailed traditional trade routes to that coast, making the Black Sea routes even more important (Venice, meanwhile, concentrated on Egypt). When Pope Boniface VIII demanded a ban on trading with Muslims, some Genoese started looking further afield. (In a portent of later Genoese explorations, two galleys set sail to the west, hoping to find a new route to the Orient. Both ships disappeared.)

At home, meanwhile, Genoa remained riven by feuding and infighting. We know quite a lot about life in the city at the time. One poet, Fazio degli Aberti, noted that Genoese women had a reputation for beauty, and painted both their eyes and their teeth. Another poet said the men were clean-shaven, although the upper lip was always tricky to tackle. He said Genoa was a high-rise city, full of towers and five-storey apartment blocks, with some glass windows, and that it was wise to drink enough wine every morning "to comfort nature".

Another very visible feature of life on the streets of Genoa – not just at this time but over the centuries – was slavery. Human labour was one of the great commodities of the Mediterranean economy, and Genoa had therefore begun its path to greatness partly as a response to raids on the rocky Ligurian coast by Muslim slavers. Slavery was like piracy, in that almost everybody was at it in one way or another – but the Genoese were better able than most when it came to making it work as a business.

The slave market in the city was famous. Genoa's first imperial target, Sardinia, provided slaves as well as sheep and other goods. In the twelfth and thirteenth centuries an increasing number of the slaves were Muslims, but the extension of Genoese interests into Constantinople and the Black Sea led to the appearance of many Tartars, Circassians and Russians. Predictably, the lighter the skin colour, the more expensive the slave. By the 1420s the best slaves with the lightest skins could cost more than a house (around two years' worth of wages for a typical sailor), and acted as status symbols as much as captive muscle.

As well as trading slaves, the Genoese kept their own. In 1458 there were 2,059 in the city, but only 54 were men; Liguria simply did not have the type of large-scale agriculture that demanded extensive cheap labour. The women worked in domestic service, doing everything from the laundry to digging latrines. Many slave-owners inevitably ended up having sexual relations with their human property.

There was a hefty body of rules and laws governing the conduct of slaves. It was forbidden to sell slaves old keys or arsenic (for fear of escapes or poisoning), and, to deter theft, bankers and goldsmiths were not allowed to buy precious stones, gold or silver from them. Slaves could be freed by their owners or marry, but if three-quarters of residents in an area so wanted, they could expel an emancipated slave from their district. With so many female slaves in the city there were also rules governing pregnancy and childbirth, for instance stipulating that any child born to a slave could be kept by the mother's owner for a fee. Although rape in general was punishable by death, raping a slave incurred only a fine (half of the money went to the owner). Slaves could be beaten by their owner, provided they did not use a weapon, and they also faced curfews. They needed a permit to go beyond 10,000 paces outside of Genoa, and runaways were branded on the face.

As those very many thousands who had lost their liberty in the slave trade knew, this was a brutal and cruel age. The Genoa of that age may seem reprehensible to us now, but it was an expression of its time. It perhaps had a reputation for being more brutal and cruel than most cities, but this was really a reputation founded upon its success in business, and in turning an unpromising port on a rocky coast into an unlikely superpower. This rise was partly due to the fierce competition with rivals such as Pisa and especially Venice. Any advantage was taken to get ahead. And just as the Venetians had hoped to alter the balance between the two cities with their subversion of the Fourth Crusade, so the Genoese started planning for a military showdown that they hoped would secure a decisive victory to give them the upper hand for decades to come.

**

At first glance the site of the Battle of Curzola heavily favoured the Venetians: it was on their home territory, far up in the Adriatic, on the rocky and island-strewn Dalmatian coast. The Genoese strategy was audacious: the calculation was that sending a fleet into their enemy's lair would force a showdown that they thought they could win. Victory could then tip the scales of their rivalry with Venice decisively in Genoa's favour. If the Genoese triumphed they would have power and riches, and influence over Constantinople, and the Venetians would struggle to reassert themselves as a maritime superpower. The stakes were enormous.

The Genoese had raised a fleet of over eighty warships, and gathered them in the bay of La Spezia, at the far end of Liguria. The year was 1298, an era of flag-bedecked galleys descended from the warships of the Roman age we know from *Ben Hur*. They were long and shallow, banked with oars, and built for combat rather than resilience. When they met at sea, the galleys used archers and crossbowmen to rain missiles down on each other as they closed. The oarsmen, some chained slaves and some free men, built up speed, heaving the giant oars and aiming for the heart of the enemy vessels. They came together with a crash, a splintering of timbers, and the screams of men smashed by buckling oars. Older versions of the galleys had powerful rams built into their prows, to shatter the enemy's hull at the water line; but newer ones concentrated on getting men onto the enemy's deck, to settle things through hand-to-hand fighting. When a galley went down it took most of its crew with it, the slaves struggling in vain to free themselves from the iron chains that bound them to their oars. Galley warfare was both magnificent and grisly.

Despite the close-quarter potency of galleys, they were not brilliantly seaworthy. They had sails to complement the oars, but these could only be used for short stretches or for sudden accelerations when engaged in galley warfare. Their shallow drafts made them difficult craft to use in high seas, so they tended to stay close to land and to the supplies for their crews; their preferred campaigning season was when the seas were calmer.

The mighty Genoese fleet had just reached the Gates of Otranto, the entrance to the Adriatic, when a storm hit. The fleet scattered, every galley trying to stay afloat and find a harbour until it was safe to continue. The core of the fleet, under Admiral Lamba Doria, was able to regroup and continue up the Dalmation coastline, ravaging Venetian towns to undermine the hated Venetians. A second group of galleys was slower to regroup, and followed behind; it was to play a major part in the battle that followed.

In early September Doria reached the island of Korčula. Its fortified town lay across a small channel from the end of the Pelješac Peninsula, which stuck out from the harsh Dalmation mainland like a finger. Just as Doria was starting to sack the town, reports came through that the Venetian fleet was almost in sight.

Most of the fighting took place in or near the channel of clear blue water between the island and peninsula. The Venetians seemed to take the upper hand early on, but some of their galleys ran aground and were lost. The Genoese seized one and used it to confuse the Venetian fleet. Then the sixteen Genoese galleys that had been separated from their main fleet by the storm in Otranto reappeared and attacked the Venetian flank, so the battle was won.

It had been a daring and brave display by the Genoese fleet. Lamba Doria demonstrated his single-mindedness when his son was killed during the fighting; rather than be distracted for one moment from the battle, the admiral ordered the body to be thrown overboard without ceremony. For the Venetians the battle was a disaster. They lost eighty-three of their ninety-five galleys, and around 7,000 men. The rest of their force were taken back to Genoa and thrown into prison. Their Doge, Giovanni Dandolo, committed suicide.

Marco Polo was lucky to be treated well, as the Genoese were not noted for their hospitality. Following the Battle of Meloria in 1284 against that other rival, Pisa, 9,000 prisoners were chained up in what is now Campo Pisano.[3] Most died from ill-treatment and exposure, and on stormy nights in the city today some claim that you can still see the poor wretches in their chains, huddling together for protection against the rain and the brutality of their captors. Two years later Genoa captured Porto Pisano, which gave the Tuscan city its access to the sea, and filled up its harbour. Pisa's days as a major maritime power were finished, and Genoa was able to dominate the Tyrrhenian Sea. After the victory at Curzola, Genoa also had the upper hand across the whole Mediterranean and into the Black Sea. But on the shores of the Crimea the Genoese were soon to encounter an enemy more cruel and destructive than the Venetians, and they would unwittingly help that enemy devastate the whole of Europe.

6

THE PLAGUE

"In men and women alike it first betrayed itself by the emergence
of certain tumours in the groin or armpits, some of which grew
as large as a common apple, others as an egg."
Boccaccio

Genoa and Venice were quintessential maritime trading empires, linking
up bases and trading stations across the great expanse of blue that
represented their opportunity for commerce. Just as imperial Britain had
Singapore and Malta, Aden and Ascension Island, Genoa had Chios and
Pera, Famagosta and Sardinia. But where the mountains of Central
Europe gave way to the endless, wind-ravaged steppes of Eurasia, an
even greater land-based empire was on the rise. The Mongol conquests
of the early thirteenth century had united the Orient with Central Asia,
Persia and Southern Russia, encouraging the caravan routes reaching
from China to the shores of the Black Sea to flourish along the great Silk
Road. In 1266 the Mongol leaders of the Golden Horde ceded Caffa to
the Genoese, and Tana (on the Sea of Azov) to both the Genoese and
Venetians.[1] The Italians were given permission to build warehouses and
consulates, and to fortify their trading stations. Unsurprisingly, Caffa
was to host one of Europe's largest slave markets. Genoa was tapping
directly into major trade routes thousands of miles long, and linking

them with the rapidly developing European economy. It was the medieval invention of globalisation.

But just as the spread of Islam had disrupted trade through the Levant, its spread was to disrupt the Black Sea trade too. In the early fourteenth century the Kipchak Khanate converted to Islam, and in 1343 its Khan, Zanibeck, cut the caravan links to China and tried to evict the Christian Italians from their trading stations. He succeeded in throwing them out of Tana, but they held on in Caffa. The Mongols besieged the city twice, and during the second siege a virulent disease started to kill the attacking armies.

Bubonic plague had been known before in the West – it first swept in from Egypt in the Justinian pandemic of 541, followed by fourteen more waves through to 767. But the economy that Genoa and Venice had helped build was far more interconnected and urbanised than in previous centuries, and this was to have profound implications for the spread of infectious diseases. In fact, the hostility of newly-converted Muslims to trading with Christians and their severing of trade routes might have lessened the likelihood of the bubonic plague making it over to Europe. But through the Genoese trading port of Caffa, the Europeans had a toehold in Eurasia, and so the plague had its entrée to the Europeans.

The outbreak that eventually spread into Europe probably came from a "plague focus" that stretched from the north-western shores of the Caspian Sea, west into Southern Russia.[2] "In [1346], God's punishment struck the people in the eastern lands," says a contemporary Russian source.[3] "...the mortality was great among the Bessermens, and among the Tartars, and among the Armenians and the Abkhazians, and among the Jews, and among the European foreigners..."

The signs of the plague were grotesque swollen sores and an agonising, miserable death. The Mongols who were camped outside Caffa were among the first to suffer. Gabriele de Mussis of Piacenza wrote that "It seemed to the besieged Christians as if arrows were shot out of the sky to strike and humble the pride of the infidels who rapidly died with marks on their bodies and lumps in their joints and several parts, followed by putrid fever; all advice and help of the doctors being of no avail."[4]

According to legend, at this point, with the Mongol army in tatters, they devised a dastardly plan: "...the Tartars, worn out by this pestilential disease, and falling on all sides as if thunderstruck, and seeing that they were perishing hopelessly, ordered the corpses to be placed upon their engines and thrown into the city of Caffa. Accordingly were the bodies of the dead hurled over the walls, so that the Christians were not able to hide or protect themselves from this danger, although they carried away as many dead as possible and threw them into the sea. But soon the whole air became infected, and the water poisoned, and such a pestilence grew up that scarcely one out of a thousand was able to escape."

This horrible innovation in early biological warfare is likely to have taken place, but modern experts in infectious diseases say there is not a scientific basis for it spreading the plague to the Christians. The Christians were more likely to have been infected by rats burrowing under their fortifications, rather than by the grisly remains of dead Mongols, flung over the walls by the Kipchak Khan.[5] The story may have its roots in the Christian belief that the plague was God's punishment to the Muslims for besieging them; the catapult theory would explain how this holy punishment then came to infect the Christians too, despite their faith.

As the monstrous scourge of the plague wreaked havoc on both sides of the lines, the siege began to disintegrate. Some Genoese were able to flee across the Black Sea to the safety of Constantinople. Unfortunately these sailors were already infected, and carried the plague rats with them on their flight back to Europe, starting with the Byzantine capital. They sailed on, via Reggio di Calabria in the toe of the Italian peninsula, to their home port of Genoa. The Black Death, a transformative event in European history, from England to Iberia, Byzantium to Italy, had arrived.

The newly urbanised manufacturing centres that had been both the engines and the beneficiaries of medieval commerce were especially badly hit as the pestilence tracked its way along the trade routes of Europe. In Tuscany more than a quarter of the population was concentrated in towns and cities, compared to a European average of around a tenth, so Florence lost well over half its population. Marchionne di Coppo Stafani wrote an account of how the city dealt with the corpses: "At every church they dug deep pits down to the water table; and thus those who were poor who died during the night were bundled up quickly and thrown into the pit. In the morning when a large number of bodies were found in the pit, they took some earth and shovelled it down on top of them; and later others were placed on top of them and then another layer of earth, just as one makes lasagne with layers of pasta and cheese."

Families and communities were ripped apart. "Father abandoned child, wife husband, one brother another... And in many places in Siena great pits were dug and piled deep with the multitude of dead... And I, Agnolo di Tura, called the Fat, buried my five children with my own hands. And there were also those who were so sparsely covered with earth that the dogs dragged them forth and devoured many bodies throughout the city."

From Genoa, from Constantinople, and from ports like Venice, Reggio di Calabria and Pisa, the plague spread across Europe. Estimates vary, but some suggest that more than half the population of Europe died during the Black Death. The world's population fell from around 450 million to perhaps around 350 million. Such a sudden decrease was bound to have a huge impact. Genoa being a densely populated city at the centre of extended networks of trade suffered one of the highest death rates. However, the city's labour force was partly replenished by migration from the poor and much more sparsely populated (and therefore less badly hit) Ligurian hills. The fall in population also contributed to a longer-term rise in living standards – pressure on Liguria's meagre supply of farmland was relieved, and in the city itself records show that after the Black Death more people were able to afford wheat flour rather than chestnut flour.

This was a trend across Europe. Continuous population increases between 1150 and 1320 had led to rises in food prices and falls in income. But the massive mortality of the Black Death put population growth into reverse. The price of labour rose thanks to scarcity of manpower, while employers saw their incomes fall. Western Europe also witnessed an increase in social mobility and an undermining of traditional authority. Anti-Semitism flourished in German towns as people sought an explanation for the calamity. Attempts to restrict wage rises among labourers led to rebellions like the Peasants' Revolt of 1381 in England. Rises in the cost of labour also led to innovation and mechanisation, and a notable increase in productivity. So in some ways, it was the dawn of a new age. The globalisation of trading routes between East and West had produced a new interlinked economy of urbanised manufacturing centres, with the Genoese once again unwittingly in the vanguard.

***

Even in a changed world some things stayed the same: the Venetians could not abide the Genoese, and the Genoese hated the Venetians. In the 1370s, in the aftermath of the Black Death, Genoa once again found itself plotting a knock-out blow that would deal with *La Serenissima* once and for all.

The final great war between the two maritime superpowers began in a familiar way. Brawls broke out between groups of Venetians and Genoese in the port of Famagusta in Cyprus. There was also rival meddling in the Byzantine succession, and a focus on the island of Tenedos that controlled access through the Dardanelles. Genoa launched a fleet under the command of Luciano Doria, and decided, as in the Curzola campaign, to take the fight right to the home of its enemy.[6]

The Genoese advanced up the Adriatic and won an important victory at Pola in May 1379. Luciano Doria was killed, but Venice lost the fleet that it relied upon for protection. The Venetians blocked two entrances to their lagoon with chains and half sunken hulks, but the Genoese managed to get inside at Chioggia, right at the lagoon's southern end. This was not just a battle between rivals; it was an invasion.

Despite Genoa allying itself with the king of Hungary and the lord of nearby Padua, the Venetians held out, keeping the invaders at arm's length at the southern end of the lagoon. A second Genoese leader (another Doria – Pietro this time) was killed when a cannon ball caused a tower to collapse on top of him. The Venetians tried to starve the Genoese out of their positions, while Padua floated supplies on barges down the river to reach their allies.

Eventually in June 1380 the Genoese position collapsed, and Venice was able to claim victory. The cohesion of the Venetians had allowed them to pull together and outlast the perennially squabbling Genoese. They identified Genoese soldiers among the various enemy allies by asking them to say the word *goat*. If they said *capra* they were freed; the 4,000 Genoese could only manage *crapa* and were thrown into prison. But it was a bittersweet victory: although Venice had won, and resisted the catastrophe of a full-blown invasion, they were humiliated by the incursion of the Genoese right into the fastness of their lagoon. Much else remained as it was before the war, and the Genoese were even able to win some concessions. It was not a total victory for Venice.

In retrospect the war was the last crossing of swords between great powers that were now inexorably in decline. The great changes in the European economy had resulted in the formation of larger and more coherent states that were more than a match for small, buccaneering maritime city states like Venice and Genoa. The internal strife that permanently beset the Genoese now worsened, with ten doges holding office in the following five years, before it handed itself over to the French kings to prevent implosion. Neither Venice nor Genoa could ever count itself as a superpower again. Worse, their rivalry had been a real distraction from the rise of another great power to the east. The Ottoman Turks had gradually been building their powerbase in Asia Minor, threatening the teetering Byzantine Empire and the wider balance of power in the Mediterranean. The world was changing: would Genoa be able to find a new, diminished role, or would it be condemned to the history books?

7

FROM FRANCESCO THE SPITEFUL TO THE FLOWERSELLER OF SEBORGA

"The ARGE was created to recover the values of the glorious
Republic of Genova... Enough grumbling. Let's do this."
Website of the ARGE Genoese independence movement

"I defend the Prince in front of everything and everyone," said the man
in the blue beret and smart uniform. He flourished his hand like an
actor, then followed it up with a conspiratorial stage whisper: "Unless
they are really big, in which case I run away." He was, it appeared, both
the official security force of the independent principality of Seborga and
something of a performer. It was a fitting introduction to a village that
seemed to have found its own wormhole leading back centuries to a
time when borders and sovereignty were very much in flux. The
reputation that Genoa had developed for its infighting extended beyond
the families that contested power in its narrow streets, to various
enclaves and villages along the Ligurian coast, and this was a tradition
that the people of Seborga – and their one-man security force – seemed
determined to continue into the twenty-first century.

A few things set this hilltop village apart from other settlements that
encrust the mountaintops of Liguria like barnacles: that theatrical man
in the beret and uniform, loitering about ostentatiously; the ribbons and
flags that are tied to everything that is not moving; the slightly kitsch

references to the Knights Templar; and the sentry box positioned on the narrow road that winds its way up from the coast. Perhaps most striking, however, is the sense of order, of prosperity and of tidiness. The higgledy-piggledy alleys, crooked stone buildings and oddly shaped tiled roofs are all in good order, and the magnificent views to the Mediterranean far below are from smart, refurbished terraces. Even the communal areas, often neglected in Italy, are cared for and spruce, including the perfectly presented old prison. It is a strikingly good-looking spot in noticeably decent condition. As these farming villages go, Seborga is wealthy and jauntily prosperous, and that is mainly down to one man and his idiosyncratic interpretation of history.

"Giorgio was very charismatic," said Susanna Millo, a smartly dressed and helpful woman who looks after tourism for Seborga's council. "Women especially liked him. He used to wear a blue suit with a white and light blue sash, and on formal occasions he wore white trousers and a light blue tunic." A couple of uncharacteristically tatty flags flapped above Susanna's head. Giorgio, of course, designed them. "The flag has nine white and nine light blue stripes, to remind us of the first nine Knight Templars. He chose the colours because of his love for the Virgin Mary. The white symbolises her purity, and the light blue reminds us of the colour of the sky above Seborga." There was no trace of a smirk on Susanna's lips.

Giorgio Carbone did better out of life than most flower salesmen. For one thing, he was known as Prince Giorgio I, with the official addendum *Sua Tremendita* ("His Tremendousness"). He drove a black Mercedes that was kitted out with official flags, although at one point it was impounded by the Italian authorities for carrying Seborgan licence plates (his was number 0001). His privileges included helping himself to cheese and ham from the village shop, yet he did not draw a salary. His trade was growing mimosas for the flower merchants of nearby Sanremo, and he was also known as a poet and a songwriter. His most noteworthy composition was, of course, Seborga's national anthem. He also coined the motto *Sub umbra sede* – "sit in the shade" – and he claimed to secure some form of recognition from a handful of countries such as Burkina Faso and the Comoros.

The whole business started back in 1963, when Giorgio Carbone decided to take on the Herculean task of championing the independence of his village from the rest of Italy. One suggestion was that he was looking to create a tourist industry in Seborga, as the Sanremo flower business started shifting to the Netherlands. But his ambitions were also built upon a clear (if slightly dense) historical argument that reaches back to the years when the Republic of Genoa had as many internal as external rivals.

"The first time we can read about Seborga in official documents is in 954, when Count Guido of Ventimiglia donated Castrum Sepulcri to the monks of Lerino," said Susanna Millo, along with an apology for the complexity of what she was about to spell out. She rattled on through the dates, the names and the treaties, hardly missing a beat. The first plank of the argument was that Seborga, known as Castrum Sepulcri, was owned by monks for centuries, surrounded by (but not part of) the territory of the Republic of Genoa. By the fifteenth century the Abbot of Saint Honorat was signing documents using the title of Prince of Castrum Sepulcri, and in 1666 an abbot began to mint new coins called *Luigini* that formed Castrum Sepulcri's new currency.

Seborga, however, was a distinctly unprofitable territory for the monks. It was full of peasants and shepherds, and hardly anything worth taxing, so in 1729 they sold the place to the Savoys, and at that point it disappears from documents. This, said Susanna, was crucial, and the focus for Giorgio Carbone's heroic amateur research project. His contention was that the sale itself was never registered, so while the Savoys and their territories continued to march through history to their place in the nation-state we now call Italy, Seborga was in fact still independent. Forget about the *Risorgimento*: when Italy was forged into one country, this little village should really have been sitting it out.

This case of national exceptionalism was exactly what Giorgio Carbone set out to prove, and during his long and fruitful years wearing the prince's sash of office, *Sua Tremendita* became a diligent researcher. He ploughed assiduously through archives and files in search of the crucial evidence that an independent Seborga was fact, rather than a peculiar and increasingly lucrative joke. In the 1990s new documents turned up that apparently supported the argument that the village had fallen through a complex little hole in history. The European Court of Human Rights in Strasbourg is still in possession of an application to have independence recognised, based on these documents, but in the meantime the *Seborghini* continue with their double life. They hang those blue and white flags from their flagpoles, the man in the beret promises to protect the prince against anybody who is not too large, and in the meantime they carry on paying taxes to the Italian government and acting just like a small Ligurian village, just in case.

His tremendousness Giorgio Carbone died on 25 November 2009 at the age of 73, and it is testament to his efforts to put Seborga on the map (though not the Italian one) that the place is still living this double life quite happily. He was evidently a fairly popular chap, and when his self-assumed title was finally put to a public vote in 2006 he easily beat the challenger, an outsider calling herself Princess Yasmine von Hohenstaufen Anjou Plantagenet, who claimed to be the descendent of a thirteenth-century Holy Roman Emperor. Even those who thought Carbone's Quixotic quest for Seborgian independence was all a bit of an eccentric pantomime tolerated him for the visitors that he attracted.

Seborga is, after all, a small hillside village where tourist money comes in handy. Its territory only covers five square miles, and most of the villagers otherwise earn their corn through the flower trade, a bit of terraced agriculture, and working just over the border on the French Riviera. When they published Giorgio Carbone's obituary, the *Washington Post* came up with the figure of 2,000 tourists a day visiting Seborga, from the resorts of Bordighera, Sanremo and beyond. "Even the local police and *carabinieri* were saluting him," said Laura Di Bisceglie. "The stamps with his image are still sold, and visitors still put them on postcards – next to the Italian ones of course." Laura is Giorgio's daughter (although he never married, saying he loved all his female subjects equally) and used to be his secretary. She now runs a shop that is crammed full of Knights Templar paraphernalia and Seborga memorabilia, including stamps showing the bearded *Sua Tremendita,* along with various blue and white patterns of his own design.

There are also coins, or *Luigini* to be precise, just like the ones minted back in the second half of the seventeenth century. "Turkish women used to love the *Luigini* that the Genoese merchants brought over," said Susanna Millo. "They were small and perfect for earrings, bracelets and necklaces." There are, she said, only twelve of the original *Luigini* left, after Louis XIV closed the mint in 1669. One was found by a local a few years back and valued at almost €30,000.

When Prince Giorgio I died he lay in state in his house, with grand old newspapers like the *New York Times* taking a delighted interest in the story of a mimosa grower who became some ersatz minor European royalty. At the time, most observers might have been justified in thinking that the whole independence business would be buried with him. But the blue and white flags are still flying, and Seborga has a new prince, called Prince Marcello I Menegatto. The situation is not entirely happy, and some suggest that this "foreigner" – he is not even from Liguria, let alone Seborga – might not be right for them. Laura Di Bisceglie voiced concerns that the current Prince's ambitious plans were out of keeping for a humble village, no matter what its pretensions to statehood. She said she was thinking of putting herself forward as a candidate the next time the election for the sovereign comes up – a local candidate for local people.[1] It is also admittedly hard to follow in the footsteps of a political visionary – just ask those who emerged from the shadows of Gandhi or Emperor Marcus Aurelius. But as long as the tourist money keeps coming, even the most sceptical *Seborghini* will keep smiling while they take you through the tortuous historical twists and turns of an independent village state.

***

Despite the best efforts of Mazzini, Garibaldi, Cavour and Victor Emmanuel II, the territorial integrity of Italy has long been open to more serious questions than those posed by the *Seborghini*.[2] Italy hosts the maverick states of San Marino and the Vatican. Alto Adige continues to contain many Italian passport holders who speak German and would prefer to live in a place called Südtirol. And that is before asking the members of the *Lega Nord* (and many, many more who would not countenance voting for such a party) who cannot see the logic of making one country out of the north and the *Mezzogiorno*, just because they happen to share the same boot-shaped peninsula.

Genoa and Liguria have been dominated for centuries by foreign forces with whom they have had to reach compromises, so they are more inclined to separatist movements than most areas. Those movements have tended to be parochial rather than aimed at dismembering entire nation-states and empires. Despite Liguria's geographic cohesion as the moustache-shaped ridge of coastal mountains between France and Tuscany, there have been constant instances of places determined that the Republic of Genoa was not quite right for them.

Savona is a solid working port city that enjoys its own natural harbour, very much in the image of La Spezia and Genoa itself. However, like many ports on the Ligurian coast, it spent a good deal of its history in direct disagreement with its pushy and grand neighbour. For its pains it was sacked by Genoa a total of ten times, before Andrea Doria decided to destroy its livelihood by filling in the port in 1528. The Genoese razed Savona's castle and built the monstrous and forbidding Fortezza del Priamàr, which still broods between the city and the sea. Visitors to its battlements today will find that its one remaining cannon is trained over the city's rooftops rather than out to sea. Such was the nature of Genoese power. The city is also credited with giving its name to soap (through the French *savon*), after the wife of a fisherman made the fortuitous mistake of boiling olive oil together with soda.

Noli was another independently-minded place that dared to confront the ambitions of that neighbouring superpower. It was an important maritime republic in its own right, almost meriting a place alongside Genoa, Venice, Pisa and little Amalfi. Noli was involved in the First Crusade and benefited greatly from it, but before long it realised the direction that history was turning, and found itself a favourable position as an ally of Genoa in its scuffles with nearby Savona.

The most historically notable act of independence in Liguria, however, came not from a city or town, but from a noble family.

***

If you drive along the *autoroute* west of Seborga, above the resorts of Bordighera and Sanremo, just as the sun is coming down on another beautiful Riviera weekend, you will witness a remarkable migration. The migration does not involve whales, wildebeest or storks. It involves expensive pieces of metal that were assembled in Stuttgart and Maranello, and that make an astounding racket every time they enter one of the tunnels on those last few miles back into France. What you are witnessing is the setting sun calling the Porsche 911s and Ferrari 458s back to Monaco, like fruit bats flying back to their roosts in the trees of West Africa.

Monaco is a European version of a Gulf State, a destination for people who believe everything they read in Rolex and Patek Philippe adverts. I visited in mid-December, and was able to wander around a Christmas funfair full of locals searching out more shiny trinkets to add to their already bounteous collections. It was quite overwhelming to see the gaudy, the plastic, the tasteless and the over-decorated, and the funfair was ghastly as well. A couple of hundred yards away, on the edge of the marina, was a yacht dealer: €34.75 million for the *Parafin*; a whopping €69.9 million for the *Aquarius*; and for those men who doubtless have many more blades on their razors than is strictly necessary, there was the stealth-like *Proteksan Turquoise NB58*, coming in at a thoroughly reasonable €22.5 million. Few sights are more ridiculous than grown men revving their Ferraris, capable of near-supersonic speeds, in a frustratingly congested Monagasque downtown street.

Historically, Monaco is best understood as constructed on the ill-gotten gains of people that were so bad and so ruthless that even Genoa was unable to satisfy them. In 1297 a Genoese rebel faction, led by a member of the Grimaldi family (Francesco Grimaldi, known as *Il Malizia* or *The Spiteful*), grabbed the rock of Monaco (which at the time was just within the western side of the Republic of Genoa). This rebel faction was to become an enormous nuisance as pirates. In 1336 they seized two galleys returning to Genoa from Flanders, and this proved the last straw: that entire lucrative route to the rich woollen markets on the North Sea was suspended for twenty years. The Genoese continued their efforts to reclaim the rock of Monaco for the Republic for decades, but Monaco stood firm. To this day the Monagasque language is very closely related to the Genoese dialect.

The Grimaldis, of course, did not just branch out on their own as pirates. By the mid-fourteenth century they had strong links to the French crown, and one Carlo Grimaldi was able to use the profits from this alliance to buy up territory around Monaco itself, such as Menton and Ventimiglia. In 1345 he signed a contract to provide the French with 33 ships and 7,000 crossbowmen, showing a typically Genoese skill in mercenary activities to go with the piratical ones. Genoese crossbowmen were an elite force in the military world at the time, but in this case ended up being a fundamental part of one of the most celebrated French military defeats in history.

Genoese crossbowmen were the most recognised infantry component in the army assembled by Philip VI, who used them to address a known weakness in his archers. Crossbow practice was as familiar to the Italians as longbow practice was to the English and Welsh. Crossbowmen were a key part of the armoury of the great galleys that controlled the Mediterranean, firing upon the occupants of other ships as the oarsmen crashed their craft into them. They could also be hired out to other armies for a hefty fee, for use on sea or land: one document in the archives of the Clos des Galees naval arsenal in Normandy describes a galley called the *Sainte Marie*, captained by a Grimaldi, with a crew that included 205 sailors and crossbowmen. The galley was serving a 161-day contract for a total purse of 4,831 florins.

Philip VI was to deploy his crossbowmen against the English at what became known as the Battle of Crécy in 1346, with the specific aim of breaking up the enemy lines so they could be exploited by charging French knights. Grimaldi's contingent was added to another one led by Ottone Doria, who was also the overall commander of the Genoese crossbowmen. However, as the French army prepared for battle with the English, it was clear to Doria that certain things were not quite right.

The Genoese were used to fighting under the protection of large shields carried by *paversari* during the laborious process of reloading. When the final preparations for battle were being made, the shields were still buried in the baggage train, and the crossbowmen felt particularly vulnerable. They also complained that they did not have adequate ammunition, that their targets were both uphill and into the sun, and that they had just endured a long march. To crown it all, they faced something that frequently clears the streets of most Italian towns and cities to this day: rain.

To be fair, this rain shower was particularly heavy, and for the Genoese it was particularly destructive. The water worked its way into the strings on the crossbows, which stretched as a result, leading to a critical loss of power and range. The English longbowmen, by contrast, were simply able to dismantle their much simpler bows and keep the strings dry under their hats until the rain stopped.

Given these disadvantages, it is no surprise that the crossbowmen were in trouble from the start. Arrows and cannonballs rained down on them. Not long after the battle, Giovanni Villani remembered that "The English guns cast iron balls by means of fire... They made a noise like thunder and caused much loss in men and horses... The Genoese were continually hit by the archers and the gunners... the whole plain was covered by men struck down by arrows and cannonballs."

It was carnage, but what made it worse was that when the survivors tried to escape they were attacked by French knights who suspected betrayal or cowardice. Given the close association in most contemporary minds between the Genoese, piracy and mercenary activities, this is not a surprise.

The Monaco of today feels too ordered and antiseptic to acknowledge its grubby but fascinating beginnings, beyond a statue of *Il Malizia* in a monk's cloak carrying a concealed dagger. You will search in vain for any decent museum that extends the Principality's heritage beyond Grace Kelly, tax avoidance and Formula One racing. This is a crying shame, as what Monaco really needs is some kind of reckoning with its past, just as the Gulf States still celebrated their roots in desert tribes, before somebody turned the money tap on.

***

Given all this history of separatism, it is no surprise to learn that some Genoese are still at it. Not that Ligurian independence movements share much in common with their violent counterparts in Northern Ireland or the Basque country. The quaintly outdated website of the MIL (Movimento Indipendentista Ligure) is studiously level-headed, listing sensible points in a variety of curious fonts against a background of digital clouds. It talks of a tolerant land of free people of different races and colours, and achieving statehood through firm but non-violent action. So far so reasonable (if slightly bloodless, given Genoese history).

The MIL delves deep into the region's complex past to make its case. It notes that the Republic of Genoa had its roots in anti-pirate operations, and the golden age when it put the Pisans and Venetians to the sword, before becoming the world's leading financial power. The Republic existed from 1005 to 1797 before Napoleon marched in.[3] It then resurfaced for a brief moment, gasping for air, before the Congress of Vienna of 1815 pushed it back under the murky depths of history by making it part of the Kingdom of Sardinia.[4] The Congress marked the re-ordering of the post-Napoleonic world, and the Kingdom was in effect the Piedmont-based House of Savoy, the island of Sardinia, and now Liguria.

This was extremely vexing for the Genoese, who thought they had succeeded in getting their venerable old Republic back up and running.

To be fair, for centuries they had been forced into ever-more humiliating compromises with various foreign powers, but they had succeeded in keeping things going in one way or another for a remarkably long period, before Napoleon's ambitions got the better of them. This air of grievance – and the links to Piedmont and the House of Savoy – also helps to explain the prominence of Ligurians like Mazzini and Garibaldi in so many conspiracies during the nineteenth century. In 1849 it even led to an uprising in favour of restoring autonomy, which was put down with great brutality by King Victor Emmanuel's forces. Yet again the city was bombarded from the sea, this time for a remorseless thirty-six hours, before soldiers entered the city, raping and murdering their way back to order. (The MIL says that Savoy was born "on the tips of bayonets", destroying Genoa's mercantile and financial culture through its Jacobin centralism.)

The MIL's website lists the calamities that Genoa and Liguria have since been dragged through: the disaster of the First World War, which in turn led to the birth of national hatreds, Fascism and Nazism; the Second World War; and then modern Italy. Their grievances about the state of modern Italy are shared by MIL with other northern Italian groupings, including the *Liga Nord*. The list of calamities includes organised crime groups, the massacres of the *anni di piombo* (the "years of lead", when left- and right-wing terrorists bombed, shot and kidnapped their way to precisely nowhere), and more recent corruption scandals such as *tangentopoli*.

The MIL separatists conclude that the only solution for Genoa and Liguria is to go back to that moustache-shaped Republic of Genoa, with a federal structure able to take into account the differing needs of everybody from Genoa to Savona to Noli (and no doubt, if they want it, Seborga). They want it to join the list of vibrant small states that they see making waves elsewhere in the world, including Singapore, Luxembourg, Monaco and Ireland. Alas, the web manifesto ends with a list of *Strategic objectives for the year 2001*, and although the fire of an independent Genoa still burns in the souls of some, the MIL could no doubt learn a few lessons in sticking power from that Mimosa seller up in Seborga, the late *Sua Tremendita* Prince Giorgio I.

Another separatist grouping, the ARGE (Associazone Repubblica di Genova), has a more modern website and is more up to date. It was founded in 1994, but as I write this there is a blog post from just yesterday, bemoaning the amount spent on the Italian president's palace (more than Buckingham Palace and the Elysée, the writer notes sarcastically). The blog's targets and issues range from the transport system to education to basil (a Genoese obsession). Under the flag of St George and the motto *Il nostro cuore dice la verità* ("our hearts speak the truth") there is a genuine feeling of coherence and determination about *ARGE*, reflected in the anger that is once again starting to spill over onto the streets of Genoa. More of that later in the final chapter of this book, but before we leave the ARGE, it deserves respect for its accurate diagnosis of exactly what the Genoese need to do if they are to lift their current malaise: "Enough grumbling. Let's do it."

8

WHEN IS A PIRATE NOT A PIRATE?

"Ah Genoese – to every accustomed good
Strangers; with every corruption amply crowned:
Why hasn't the world expunged you as it should?"
Dante Alighieri

Piracy was always part of the common currency in the Mediterranean, from Roman and Phoenician times (including the memorably hapless pirates of the *Asterix* books, falling into the waves with a philosophical *alea iacta est*) through to the nineteenth century. Sometimes it was official, and sometimes it was not. When it was official, of course, it was not necessarily called piracy: it was the protection of one's own trading interests by other means (with a little bit of freelance instant profiteering thrown in). English readers will be familiar with the privateers of Elizabethan times, when heroes such as Francis Drake and Richard Hawkins trod a thin line between serving the crown and using the crown's protection while indulging in piratical mischief.

The Genoese were of course adept at combining the worlds of trade and piracy, even when telling the world with straight faces that they were clearing the seas of pirates for the good of all. Although there were harsh sentences for piracy (the leader was to be hung in chains; the crew would have their right hands chopped off), in at least one case in 1230 violent public protests led to two leaders being released. Stephen Epstein argues that this was because piracy was so ingrained in Genoese society that the punishments were seen as over-harsh, especially for the crewmen who would never be able to work again.[1]

For a few, piracy became the route to serious wealth and status, especially when plunder was combined with furthering state interests. Back in the early thirteenth century an ambitious Genoese called Enrico Pescatore ("Henry the fisherman") set himself up as Count of Malta. In 1205 he seized a couple of Venetian ships on the way to Constantinople before conducting a raid on what is now the Lebanese coast. As a result of this raid, the Count of Tripoli promised Genoa trading rights from his port, confirming piracy's role in the foreign policy toolkit. "He is generous and intrepid and chivalrous, the star of the Genoese, and makes all his enemies tremble throughout the land and the sea," sang a troubadour, celebrating Enrico Pescatore's exploits. "And my dear son Count Henry has destroyed all his enemies and is so safe a shelter to his friends that whosoever wishes may come or go without doubt or fear." As this suggests, there was a fine line to be trodden between what was acceptable on the part of a state, and true piracy. One key factor was the nature of the interests that were being furthered by piracy, and for Christians that line was crossed in the sixteenth century. A new and menacing chapter in Mediterranean piracy was beginning that could not simply be ignored as duplicitous business as usual.

Two things lay behind this new development. Firstly, the expulsion of the Moors from Spain in 1492 flooded the coasts of the Mediterranean with desperate Muslims, looking, like the early Genoese, for any way to make a living from the sea. Secondly, the rise of the Ottoman Empire gave the Muslims of North Africa an influential sponsor. These two factors aided the rise of the infamous Barbary Corsairs.

The two most famous Corsairs were brothers, and together they went under the single name Barbarossa.[2] The older brother, Aruj, began his career inauspiciously, in an unsuccessful expedition against the Knights of St John. He ended up captured and in chains, sweating on one of the Knights' galleys. At some point he was ransomed and not long afterwards appeared again in Tunisia, working with his brother as a privateer. In 1504 Aruj secured his first major haul off the Italian coast near Elba: two papal galleys, rich in Genoese cargo, which were then brought back to Tunis. The following years saw the brothers prey on more and more Christian shipping, until in 1509 a Spanish fleet of 90 ships and 11,000 men under Don Pedro Navarro was despatched to bring the North

African coast to order. The fleet enjoyed some success, for instance in its capture of Oran: 4,000 of its inhabitants were massacred and 5,000 were taken into captivity (along with half a million gold ducats). Other cities fell too, but Aruj was firmly ensconced in his base on the island of Djerba and survived (although in 1512 an abortive mission against the Spanish garrison at Bougie led to his left arm being shot off).

Genoa, naturally, also wanted to deal with the Barbary menace, and sent twelve galleys to attack Tunis, under the command of a *condottiero* from one of their most esteemed families, the admiral Andrea Doria.[3] The city's fortress was sacked, and considerable damage was done to the pirates who sought refuge there. The one-armed older brother, however, survived once again. (Andrea Doria was to remain a thorn in the sides of the pirates for decades, and breathe new life into Genoa's relationship with the sea – more of him in the next chapter.)

From 1516 Aruj's influence started spreading west, by turns facing off both local strongmen and Spanish forces. His capture of Algiers confirmed what Spain, Genoa and other Christian states had feared: a sometimes wild stretch of North African coastline was quickly turning into something of an elemental risk for the hub of globalised trade that was the western Mediterranean. The Spanish had little option but to raise the stakes, and began assembling a more formidable force to deal with Barbarossa. This time Aruj could see that the scales were tipping against him, and despite gathering more forces together to fight the Spanish he eventually fled Algiers with the Christians hot on his tail. He was caught on the banks of a mountain river, made his stand, and perished. For the Spanish, however, there was only a brief respite: the younger brother assumed the Barbarossa mantle, and continued Aruj's Barbary Coast piracy with gusto.

Khizr matched his brother in many ways – audacity, brutality, bravery – but in one key area he was an upgrade on Barbarossa I. The younger Barbarossa was a natural politician and diplomat, and understood that a pirate king with the official stamp of the Ottoman Empire had far wider horizons than a lone wolf. As well as forging a series of alliances with the tribes of the interior and other pirate chiefs along the coast, Khizr began to court the support of the Ottomans.

This was a canny move, as the Ottoman Empire was firmly in the ascendant, and looking to establish its naval capacity to complement its undoubted prowess in land warfare. Its capture of Constantinople several decades before had been the final nail in the coffin of the Byzantine Empire, and had given it a strategic hold on the Eastern Mediterranean and Black Sea that could – with the right investment in naval forces – turn into dominance. As ever, the Genoese role in the downfall of the Byzantine Empire had been equivocal, even morally questionable. For Genoa, Constantinople was seen in functional terms, viewed through the lens of its rivalry with Venice and the opportunities and obstacles it afforded its merchants in the Black Sea and the Eastern Mediterranean. These were already under pressure thanks to the collapse of the Mongol Empire in the mid-fourteenth century (an opportunity the Ottomans made the most of in Asia Minor) and the severing of the great trading routes from the Orient to Genoese Black Sea ports like Tana and Trebizond.

Genoa had played a small but important part in the rise of the Ottoman Empire: in 1354 in a tawdry piece of short-termism Genoese sailors had ferried the Ottoman army across the Dardanelles for one ducat per person, allowing them to establish themselves on European soil. By 1450 the Byzantine Empire consisted of little more than the area around their capital, and the Peloponnese. The last direct inheritors of Classical Rome were surrounded. When the Ottomans prepared their final siege of Constantinople, the Byzantines received scant help from the Genoese. Worse, the Genoese had contributed heavily (and profitably, of course) to the Ottomans' crucial siege artillery, and helped train the Turks how to use their cannons. The Byzantines tried to get Genoese and Venetian merchants to help supply the city by making imports duty free, but the Genoese persisted with a policy of profitable neutrality.

As the Ottomans drew up around the city walls, some of the Venetians and Genoese in the city decided not to make their escape, and threw in their lot with the Christian defenders against the Muslims. Curiously, perhaps the most important figure in the defence of the city was a Genoese soldier: Giovanni Giustiniani Longo, who was a famous kinsman to the Doria family and was based in the Eastern Mediterranean. He arrived in January 1453 with 700 well-armed soldiers (400 from Genoa itself, and 300 from Chios and Rhodes), all paid for out of his own pocket. His speciality was a valuable one: the defence of walled cities. A measure of how well he was thought of is that even the Venetians who were preparing to defend Constantinople against the Turks agreed to work with him.

Giustiniani was placed in charge of the city's land defences by Emperor Constantine XI Palaiologus. This meant that he was responsible for maintaining the walls and defences despite continuous damage from the Ottoman artillery. He deliberately positioned himself at the most vulnerable part of the defences, and used his expertise and undoubted charisma to help the Byzantine forces hold out for far longer than expected.

Alas for both Giustiniani and the Byzantines, this was a case of delaying the inevitable rather than giving any real hope of salvation. In late May Giustiniani was wounded (historians argue over whether it was through cannon fire or a crossbow bolt – in fact they argue about most of the details at this point) and was forced to seek treatment, leaving the battlements through the locked gate into the city itself. But when that gate was unlocked, some citizens panicked and attempted to flee. The confusion gave Mehmet II the opportunity for a renewed assault which resulted in the final capture of the great city. According to custom the Ottoman soldiers sacked the city for three full days. Thousands were killed, and great quantities of loot were carried off (including an estimated 30,000 civilians destined for the slave markets). A Venetian, Nicolo Barbaro, said the blood flowed "like rainwater in the gutters after a sudden storm". Dead bodies, he said, floated in the sea like "melons in a canal". Many of the Genoese defenders managed to escape, taking the wounded Giustiniani with them. He died soon afterwards and was buried on the island of Chios. Typically, Venetian sources blame his crucial disappearance from the battlements on cowardice rather than being wounded. Whatever happened around them, Venice and Genoa persisted with their mutual grudges.

The Ottoman predominance now put both merchant superpowers in the shade. After the disruption of the Silk Road trading links and the gradual loss of trading bases in the Levant and Holy Land, their access to the Black Sea was closed off. Attention was turning west, to the opportunities provided by Atlantic routes to the Orient, and that meant the Mediterranean was in danger of becoming a trading sideshow. Worse, Khizr's overtures to the Ottomans were bearing fruit. The alliance was allowing him to dominate North Africa's central and western coastlines, turning the Barbary Corsairs into a mortal threat for Christian ships carrying anything worth looting. If they were not worth looting for their cargoes, they were certainly worth looting for the humans on board, who ended their lives in slavery. Khizr was also starting to establish the Ottomans as a serious naval power. For the Genoese and Venetians, these changes were threatening everything they had achieved for centuries. The situation was desperate, and the Christian Mediterranean looked around for someone who could stand up against the looming threat from the East. Their man was Andrea Doria.

9

THE STEVE JOBS OF THE MEDITERRANEAN

*"An ambiguous character, a servant of many masters, an opportunist.
An entrepreneur of warfare, sometimes a pirate, sometimes a
Renaissance prince, pragmatic, but also
capable of conspiracies and sensational U-turns."* [1]
Pierangelo Campodonico

The two fleets could see each other approaching, and the crews watched nervously as the masts of the opposing galleys appeared between the waves heading slowly towards them. The oarsmen on both sides tried to save their strength as they worked their massive wooden oars through the Mediterranean water, the slaves among them adjusting the chains that secured them in the engine room of the great craft. Once the attack came, their survival would depend upon the sudden acceleration they could give the galleys, their firepower, and the audacity of their commanders.

Both the commanders were renowned and feared men. The Genoese were led by Andrea Doria, and the enemy by the pre-eminent Khizr Barbarossa. They had hunted each other for years, destroying bases, plundering ships, and wreaking havoc wherever they could. Now they faced each other on the open sea. The crew knew that no quarter would be given, and that the fate of the losers and many of the victors would be grim: they might be shot or hacked to pieces, or drowned, chained where they sat as their galleys plunged down into the depths, dragging their crew with them into oblivion. Any surviving losers would face execution or slavery, and even for the leaders that could mean years suffering in the chains of a galley slave.

The muscles were tense, and the eyes watchful, but no order came. Surely the two commanders had seen each other? The oars worked the water, the sails caught the breeze, and slowly, very slowly, the two fleets passed without exchanging so much as a shot. One astonished officer asked the now ageing Admiral Doria why the chance to confront Barbarossa had been passed up. "My old eyes see things your young eyes don't," he answered. Admiral Doria was a warrior and a fearsome opponent, but he was also very Genoese, and that meant he was a shrewd businessman. As Rome arguably discovered after the destruction of Carthage, sometimes it is better for business if the opponent stays out there, just beyond the horizon, concentrating minds and providing a purpose. Admiral Doria knew this, and as he was the man who breathed life and greatness back into Genoa, his men listened, and aimed their ships at the far horizon.

This telling little anecdote about Andrea Doria and Khizr was related to me by Pierangelo Campodonico, the head of Genoa's fabulous Galata Museo del Mare. The museum is on the edge of the harbour, on the spot where galleys had been built, fitted out and repaired since 1590. The name Galata comes from the Genoese district in Constantinople, just across the Golden Horn from the old city itself, topped by the Galata tower of 1348 that still stands today.[2] Campodonico's office lies down a corridor half hidden by a curtain. Small boys who have tired of the life-size replica of a galley or the "4D" experience of rounding Cape Horn in a rowing boat could find plenty in his office to amuse them, including several splendid models of grand ships and a submarine.

As well as having one of the coolest offices in Genoa, Pierangelo Campodonico is also chief cheerleader for the city's greatest son, Andrea Doria. When I asked about the admiral's personality, his first response was to chuckle and say, "*Un personaggio fantastico!*" He then ran through a list of his achievements and gave a careful comparison with another colossus of naval history, Admiral Nelson. Campodonico said that Andrea Doria was in many ways the opposite of Nelson: he followed his own interests, rather than any sense of loyalty or values; he was not the servant of the Spanish king, Charles V, but rather he was respected as an admiral who got the job done; he fought only when he was sure of victory, avoiding the type of risks that Nelson would take. This was not, as the Venetians inevitably alleged, because of any sense of cowardice, but because his fate was intimately bound up in that of his ships. Andrea Doria was also single-minded: once he stepped on board a ship at the beginning of one of his missions, he would not change his clothes until he had accomplished what he had set out to do, sleeping on the ship's deck and sharing hardships with his men.

Campodonico drew a portrait of a man who was also able to see beyond the confines of his age. At a simple level he was an innovator, seeing things with fresh eyes and constantly looking to improve. It hardly seems like an innovation to us now, but he stopped using free men to crew galleys, switching them for slaves and prisoners of war according to cold business and military logic.[3] He developed the use of cannon on galleys, and anti-personnel ammunition such as cannon balls that broke up in flight, spraying the decks of opposing ships with dozens of lethal chunks of metal. In one attack on a seemingly invulnerable Turkish fortress at Corone in the Peloponnese, Andrea Doria attached 40-metre ladders to the masts of his ships, which were then made more buoyant in the water to gain even more height. The ships approached the fortress's battlements with its soldiers taking cover below the decks, and then when they were close enough, the ladders were laid directly onto the tops of the walls and the soldiers spilled out along them into the fortress itself. During the same siege the admiral tied galleys together in pairs, facing in different directions. This allowed each pair to row within cannon-range of the fortress, let off a volley of cannonballs at the fortifications, and then rely on the backwards-facing partner galley to row them out of range of return fire while they reloaded. If you faced Andrea Doria in combat, you faced his brains as well as his courage and skill.

At a grander level, Andrea Doria was also able to recognise how the world was changing and adapt to it. He was a visionary. This, along with that intelligence and facility for innovation, explains Pierangelo Campodonico's answer when I asked what the great admiral would be like if born in our own day. "Probably a Steve Jobs," he said after a moment's thought. The answer also drew on Doria's undoubted ruthless streak – not just ruthless when it came to pursuing a goal or dealing with an enemy, but ruthlessness in business. Remember that anecdote about Admiral Doria passing Khizr – that was the action of a businessman rather than a simple politician or admiral, and arguably what you got if you employed a Genoese.

The main business of Admiral Doria was warfare. Andrea Doria made his name as a *condotierro*, and in many ways he never stopped being a mercenary, loyal above all to his business interests and the interests of his family. His affiliations are similar to those commonly associated with modern Italians, who trust first their family, then their wider relatives and close friends, then their locality, city, *commune*, region, and then finally Italy itself. Genoa was the type of place that encouraged adherence to such a strict hierarchy of trust.

As a *condotierro*, Andrea Doria owned the ships that he took to sea. Ultimately they were both his fortune and Genoa's fortune, but they were always his property. This was a fundamental difference between Genoa and Venice. When the Genoese left their rocky seashore to seek their fortunes on the waves, it was every man for himself; the Venetians were also forced to seek their fortunes out at sea, but the need for communal action to maintain their fragile existence on islands in the lagoon meant that they had a greater sense of the collective good. Genoa's capitalism was red in tooth and claw, and the city's constant factionalism and internal competition was both a consequence of their approach, and a driver of it. In Venice their system was red in the communal sense. As a consequence one can generalise by saying that the Venetian fleet was public, hired out to private merchants, while the Genoese fleet tended to be private, but could be hired out to the Republic. This system reached its apogee under Andrea Doria with the virtually privatised provision of Genoa's naval strength.

It was this naval strength, under Admiral Doria's leadership genius, that Charles V called upon when he commanded Doria to hunt down Khizr and wipe his threatening presence from the Mediterranean.

***

By 1533 the diplomatic skills of the younger Barbarossa, Khizr, had won a summons to Constantinople and an audience with Süleyman the Great. The sultan had become used to military success on land, but the Turkish navy was a comparative failure, and his summoning of Khizr was an attempt to rectify the situation by co-opting the Barbary Corsairs. For Khizr, this was the chance to secure official Ottoman backing that would allow him to achieve supremacy among the various statelets and petty dynasties of the Barbary Coast. According to the Bishop of Pamplona, Khizr set off for Constantinople in style with gifts including 200 Christian women for the Sultan's harem, each carrying a further gift of gold or silver in her hand. He was, unsurprisingly, well received, and spent a year in the capital building up the Ottoman navy.

By the following summer Khizr was ready to sail from Constantinople at the head of a mighty Ottoman fleet, and he put it to work in the way he knew best. He headed for the toe of Italy and sacked Reggio, then headed north and sacked the hapless coastal town of Sperlonga. The streets ran with blood, and the ships started to fill up with captive women, destined for the Eastern slave markets (although Khizr's main target, Giulia Gonzaga – reputedly the most beautiful woman of her day – managed to escape his clutches in her nightdress).

These raids, however, were just a warm-up for Khizr's new fleet, as he had more concrete ambitions back home on the Barbary Coast itself. The first of these was to sail south and claim Tunis from Khizr's rival, Moulay Hassan. This he did, but in doing so he galvanised the attention of Charles V of Spain, who found that this strategic base within easy reach of his Sicilian riches had swapped a relatively harmless ruler for a viper. His immediate response was therefore to assemble a fleet under Andrea Doria, with the aim of annihilating this menace.

The fleet was under Spanish patronage and Admiral Doria's control, but it was a coalition of both the willing and the desperate, from the Knights of St John in Malta to the Sicilians and Sardinians. By the time they had gathered near Sardinia in June 1535 the fleet may have had 600 ships in total. It was an enormous and intimidating force, and after a month of fighting the allies captured Tunis, in the process freeing another 12,000 Christians who were being held captive in the city. Barbarossa himself slipped out of Tunis at the last moment with some of his men, while the victorious Christians were indulging in the time-honoured practice of raping and pillaging their way through their prize (as with the capture of Constantinople, the conventions of war allowed them to do this for three days and three nights). Moulay Hassan was reinstalled in a puppet regime, and a garrison was established in what was now named Spanish territory.

Any whiff of victory, however, was short-lived. Although Andrea Doria was soon despatched along to Algiers, where it was thought

Barbarossa would seek refuge, the corsair showed his mettle by launching his own counter-raid north. He sailed into Mahon on the island of Minorca, where at first he was welcomed as part of the returning Christian fleet (the Corsairs even flew the imperial flag as part of the deceit). It was a mistake that some of the town's inhabitants would live to regret, as Barbarossa's squadron opened fire, capturing a Portuguese merchantman and sacking the city. The capture of Tunis suddenly seemed less of a victory than it had done.

Barbarossa's career, under the sponsorship of Süleyman, continued to flourish, and Venice in particular began to suffer from his predations, locked as it was into the Eastern Mediterranean. This led to complications when Charles V once again assembled a fleet to go on the counter-offensive, as ever under Andrea Doria: although Venice was by now a firm part of the efforts to destroy Barbarossa and the Ottoman fleet, antipathy between the two great maritime cities meant that the Venetians hated any thought that they were under Genoese command. Although the fleet that the Christians assembled was once again mighty, this and other rivalries among them meant that the total was rather less than the sum of its parts.

This latest grand fleet was not comprised solely of galleys. It also included heavily armed galleons, powered by sail and with room for far more cannon than on an oar-powered galley. This, however, meant that Admiral Doria faced problems in keeping his fleet together whenever the wind did not cooperate, and before long the various components of the Christian fleet were strung out and vulnerable to Ottoman attack. In fact it was the most heavily armed and cumbersome Christian vessel that fell prey to Barbarossa: a gigantic galleon commanded by a Venetian called Alessandro Condulmer found itself isolated. Condulmer's calculation was simple: could he keep the Ottoman galleys at bay long enough for Andrea Doria to arrive with his galleys? The answer was no, although Condulmer's cannon smashed Ottoman galley after Ottoman galley into splinters, and the galleon itself survived the encounter. The encounter was an opportunity to destroy Barbarossa which Admiral Doria missed, and historians are still debating whether he failed to appear due to simple malice towards the Venetians. Given the depth of antipathy between Genoa and Venice, their conflicting interests and Andrea Doria's ever-calculating mind, this seems possible, even reasonable. While the Venetians undoubtedly suffered the most from the entire episode, with their activities in the Eastern Mediterranean curtailed, Barbarossa was still on the rampage.

If his wrestle with the Barbary Corsairs was all that Andrea Doria was remembered for, he might be judged rather harshly. After all, Khizr survived the many attempts to stop him, whether as a pirate king or Ottoman admiral, and retired to Constantinople (where there is a statue of him, outside modern Istanbul's Naval Museum). Thanks to Khizr, the Ottomans did indeed end up with a navy that echoed, if not matched, the military prowess of their land army, with profound consequences for the Eastern Mediterranean and Black Sea. Khizr was undoubtedly a great man, and this book is not the place to do his long, fascinating and very complicated story justice. But although Andrea Doria is just one of a far wider cast of compelling characters that played roles in Khizr's story, he commands considerable regard in his own right. The Genoese admiral shared much with Khizr: he was a wily diplomat as well as a teak-hard warrior, and, like his Muslim opponent, his legacy went well beyond that of a simple military commander (and businessman). As well as battling the Muslims (and Venetians) on the waves, he also steered Genoa on a new course that was to revitalise a former superpower as the age of Mediterranean city states continued its relentless decline.[4]

Despite this, Genoa's greatest historical figure is not a particularly accessible hero. Andrea Doria has not attracted the adulation of other great figures with simpler and more clear-cut cases for inclusion in the pantheon. For much of his life he fought for the Spanish, but he was no Spaniard. He was Genoese, with all the complications this brings, and was never going to have statues built to honour his memory across either the Iberian or Italian peninsulas. There is, however, one monument to Andrea Doria that does him justice. There is a famous painting of him by Bronzino, depicting the admiral as Neptune. The painting is startlingly homoerotic, capturing the sheer physicality of the man and seeming to equate naval with sexual prowess. Andrea Doria is depicted with a naked, unabashedly powerful torso, and a piece of cloth barely covering his pubic hair. He holds a trident in one hand, and his flowing grey beard resembles seaweed. Andrea Doria was indeed a giant of his age: at a time when the average man was barely five foot tall, he was considerably over six foot. Life expectancy was somewhere between thirty and forty years (less if you ran into a storm or a galley full of pirates), yet Andrea Doria lived to the staggering age of 93, dying in

1560. That portrait is housed in Milan; but anybody on the trail of Andrea Doria can find plenty more memories in the port city that he called home.

***

The realm of the Doria family is concentrated around the perfect little church of San Matteo, a short stumble down striated paving stones from Piazza Ferrari and the throbbing civic heart of modern Genoa. The contrast could not be greater. There is the Piazza, with its fountain and the wall of the Palazzo Ducale, plastered with banners for the latest international exhibitions (and sometimes a small group with a timeless placard stating "No to war"); there is Garibaldi himself, astride his horse, guarding the entrance to the boxy Teatro Carlo Felice with an aspect bordering on listlessness; and there is Via Settembre XX (Via Venti to the locals) with its mosaics, neon and opportunities for buying handbags. Cross over, however, and wander down the steep slope of the Salita di San Matteo, and you cross the dividing line between the nineteenth century and the medieval.

Ahead is an arcade of heavy-set octagonal pillars in the familiar dark grey and white stripes that cover the entire building. If it is raining a Belarussian opera singer sometimes strums her guitar and sings *Katyusha* under cover of the arcade in the hope of a stray euro or two. Next to a well patronised *enoteca*, the Salita opens out into a small *piazza* with a terrace of red bricks laid out in a herringbone pattern. On the right is a church, looking handsome yet modest with its single-walled frontage, its large circular window, two flanking windows and a solid central door, all set into a striped marble and stone façade. Don Rapallo, San Matteo's abbot, may be standing on the steps of his church or on the terrace, greeting parishioners, imparting an air of quiet serenity, and pondering history. In the bottom right-hand corner there is usually a man sitting and enjoying a bottle of beer, taking things in and enjoying the view. In the corner just beyond the front of the church is a travel agency, and then an iron gate. That gate leads to a small cloister full of double-pillared arches and stony souvenirs of the centuries, and countless memories of the various Dorias that trod its stones, plotting and condemning, planning and imagining.[5]

Just to the left of that gate, above a busy and cheap canteen, is the house of one of them: Branca Doria. He was a bad sort, but very much a Genoese nobleman of his time. Branca murdered his father-in-law, Michele Zanche, in 1275, and has the honour of appearing in *Canto 33* of hell in Dante's *Divine Comedy*, with his body left on earth but his soul already in hell. It was not just Branca that Dante was targeting: in his view the Genoese as a whole were so corrupt and evil that their souls already inhabited hell while they still trod the earth. Unsurprisingly, given this uncomfortable situation, Branca's ghost is one of Genoa's most seen, walking from his house the short distance into the church with the blood of his victim still dripping from his hands.

The rest of the *piazza* is made up of perfectly handsome Genoese *palazzi*: elegant, not too showy, and full of superb detail visible to anybody who cares to look more closely. Above one doorway at the start of Via David Chiossone (habitually filled by a stout man with a quilted jacket and a cigarette) is an intricately carved lintel that shows St George running a dragon through with his lance. (When cash-strapped owners of *palazzi* had to rent out their ground floors to shops, they would often compensate by decorating their own main doors to make them stand out.) On the other side of Vico San Matteo, just to the left of the liquorice-striped arches of the arcade (and usually just behind a delivery van struggling to turn around), is my favourite building in Genoa, the Palazzo Doria.[6] It is not a fancy building, but it has those evocative dark grey and white marble stripes so favoured by the Genoese. The doorway is surrounded by carved marble, and the ground-floor windows are protected by more iron bars than the average jail. Three storeys up there is a corner balcony, supported by a small but solid marble pillar. Again, as with so many Genoese buildings, there is an incredible amount of detail hidden away here and there on the stone, as though the masons and designers were determined that a true effort had to be made to appreciate their work. There is nothing particularly remarkable about the Palazzo Doria, but it is deeply attractive in an unshowy and typically Genoese way: ornate yet modest, clever yet solid, and almost watching from the shadows to check if you have noticed it is there at all.

A Doria could feel safe in the Piazza San Matteo, if perhaps less so on the short walk to the harbour front and the open sea where so many of the family made their names. The church was founded in 1125 by Martino Doria, and, given the family's eminence in such a city of keen merchants, it is no surprise that it is dedicated to San Matteo, a tax collector. The interior you see now was renovated by Andrea Doria himself in the sixteenth century, no doubt taking a break from thinking about killing Muslim pirates and Venetians. Indeed, the vanquishing of Genoa's enemies is a theme of the church. A Roman sarcophagus that was captured when the Venetians were destroyed at the Battle of Curzola is embedded in the church's façade just under the right-hand window. The cloister next door was designed by a Venetian prisoner from the battle, Marco Veneto, and built between 1308 and 1310. There is also a Pisan banner from the similarly conclusive and bloody Battle of Meloria in 1284; links from Pisa's great harbour chain, destroyed by Oberto Doria, were only handed back to the original owner after Italy's unification. Inside the church, a hidden panel swings back to uncover Andrea Doria's sword, and in the crypt lie the coffins of both Andrea Doria himself and Lamba Doria, the victor at Curzola.

There are more clues about the great man in a grand *palazzo* that huddles behind the port and Principe Station, cut off from the waters by the intrusion of the *sopraelevata*. This is the Palazzo del Principe Doria Pamphili, and during the years when Andrea Doria dominated the Genoese Republic it was the political and military nerve centre of his rule. He planned campaigns, tested model galleys in the pond in the garden, and plotted a new course for Genoa. The Palazzo, which used to be positioned outside the city walls and directly on the water, is not a humble place.[7] It was built to impress, and during a visit from Charles V in 1533 his servants threw his silverware out of the window into the sea after each course in a display of ostentatious wealth. As a good Genoese, keenly aware of both the value and cost of everything, Doria had of course positioned a fishing boat just outside to reclaim the silver in their nets. One room is decorated by thrilling tapestries depicting the Battle of Lepanto. Lepanto was one of the greatest naval battles ever, when a Christian alliance took on the powerful Ottoman fleet established by Khizr. It was also a symbol of how times had changed, and even something of a side show. Whatever the successes of the wily Khizr, Admiral Andrea Doria's greatest achievement was in understanding these changes, and – as a visionary statesman rather than as a warrior – helping Genoa to reinvent itself to suit the new reality.

10

LEPANTO AND THE END OF THE MEDITERRANEAN ERA

"Silver is born in the Americas, passes through Spain,
and dies in Genoa."
popular saying

The drawing up of battle lines at sea was a slow and skilful business, not unlike the manoeuvring of yachts before an Olympic event, each craft trying to hit an exact point at speed at exactly the right time. On the Christian side the galleys and *galleases* bore names like the *Temperance* and the *Pyramid*, the *Padrona of Andrea Doria* and the *Bastard of Negrona.* The Ottoman ships tended to carry the names of the captains: *Uluj Rais, The Lord of Moria, Amdjazade Sinian* and *Amurat Dragut Rais.* They sported flags that caught the wind, gilded woodwork that caught the morning sun, and vastly expensive tapestries that spoke of the wealth of the ships' owners. The standard of the Christian commander, Don John of Spain, had a fabulously embroidered crucifixion scene on a red background on one side, and the Virgin Mary on the other. The ships bristled with cannons, especially the *galleases* at the front of the Christian lines, which were little more than floating tubs carrying as many guns as could be fitted on board. Armoured soldiers waited on the decks, clutching arquebuses, axes, primitive grenades and incendiary bombs, and halberds. The main, fixed cannon that was mounted on the front of a galley was called a *moiana* or the especially pleasing *sagro bastardo,* and was capable of hurling a 2.5 kilo iron ball a full 1,000 metres. Smaller cannons, mounted on swivel points, were called *smerigli petrieri.*

As the lines formed on 7 October 1571, the flagships of each fleet fired a single cannon shot to identify themselves. Then the lines closed at around 10.30 in the morning in the Gulf of Corinth, close to the town of Lepanto. The left flank of the Christians was the first to come under pressure, with the Ottomans aiming to loosen its hold on the shoreline and turn its flank. But Marco Quirini used his initiative to turn things to the Christian advantage by swinging his ships around behind the enemy.

In the centre the fighting was less refined: the great mass of warships crashed together like opposing charges of armoured knights, the flagships aiming directly for each other. Archers, crossbowmen and gunners fired from platforms onto the decks of opposing galleys, maiming oarsmen and killing the soldiers that gathered to storm onto enemy ships. Boats rammed each other in the dense smoke, like a seaborne Battle of Kursk fought with wooden ships rather than Soviet and Nazi tanks. It was carnage. The sea between vessels filled with splintered timber, drowning men and enough blood to stain the seawater red. The Turks began to run low on ammunition, and one account has Ottoman soldiers reduced to throwing fruit at the enemy. Some of the Christian slaves who had been chained to their oars in the Ottoman boats were able to free themselves and seek vengeance against their former captors. By 1.20 in the afternoon all the Turkish ships in the centre had been sunk or captured. Those who tried to swim to escape their fate were singled out by archers and gunners, one by one, and shot in the water. In El Greco's allegory of the battle (*Worship in the Name of Jesus*) the Almighty helps to destroy the Turks with fire and sea monsters.

On the southern edge of the battle the fighting resembled less a blood and thunder crashing together than a chess match. The commanders were the two most able seamen on either side: Gian Andrea Doria on the right wing for the Christians, and facing him the Barbary Corsair Uluch Ali.[1] They enjoyed the luxury of open sea in which to manoeuvre, and both were to face accusations of cowardice as a result. Uluch Ali was able to get the better of the limited exchanges between their wings, but it was too late to help Ali Pasha avoid defeat. At one point he had even succeeded in capturing one galley, the *Capitana of Malta,* killing all but six of its crew. But while towing the prize he was almost intercepted himself, and had to cut the tow rope, raise his sail and race for a gap in the closing Christian lines. He was one of the few Ottomans to escape the battle in one piece.

The victory over the Ottomans seemed decisive. Although a third of the Christians had been killed or wounded, 170 Turkish galleys had been captured, and many more lay shattered on the bottom of the Gulf of Corinth. Altogether 30,000 Turks were dead or wounded; 3,000 were taken prisoner (many were then killed); and 15,000 Christian galley slaves were freed. Ali Pasha himself had been killed in the melee at the centre; in one account a Spanish soldier cut off his head and offered it to the Christian commander, Don John, who waved it away asking what on earth he was going to do with it. One notable Christian casualty of the fighting was Miguel de Cervantes (the author of *Don Quixote*), who was wounded in the arm, and became known among contemporaries as the Cripple of Lepanto.

The Battle of Lepanto proved decisive in several ways. Some historians trace the centuries of Ottoman decline to those few bloody hours. It certainly ended Ottoman pretensions to dominate at sea as they often did on land. But the Ottomans themselves suspected that it was far from the end of their empire. The Grand Vizier Sokulla Mehmed Pasha said, "The Christians have singed my beard, but I have lopped off his arm [the Ottomans captured Cyprus in the run up to the battle]. My beard will grow back, but his arm will not." Less poetically, the noted historian Fernand Braudel called it a "victory that led nowhere". The Ottomans were soon to build another fleet, and the Christian alliance started to fall apart after the death of Pope Pius V in 1573.

But Lepanto was a remarkable moment in history beyond the simple weighing of the balance of power between the Ottomans and the Christians. It was the last cruel flourish of the great age of galley warfare that stretched back to Greek times, and indeed it was also the last flourish of the great age of the Mediterranean itself. As Lepanto played out, Genoa, a key part of the Christian victory on that day off the Greek coast, was facing another great challenge – adapting to a world where the Mediterranean was becoming a sideshow because of the political and economic shift to the Atlantic.

***

As we have seen, the growth of the interconnected late medieval economy had led to merchants looking beyond the confines of the Mediterranean littorals. The sea had become a conduit for the riches of Eurasia, the Middle East and the Orient, fuelling the rebirth of the Christian West. But as this trade was disrupted by events such as the Ottoman rise and the slow death of the Byzantine Empire, eyes started turning beyond the Pillars of Hercules and out to the Atlantic.

The woollen trade had led to Flanders and then England becoming important elements of the burgeoning European economy, and Genoese vessels were among those that had started venturing into oceanic waters, heading north but wondering what lay out in the far reaches beyond the horizon.[2] Maritime technology was shifting too, and even in the Mediterranean the traditional galley was gradually being replaced by the cog. These sturdier ships sailed in fleets two dozen strong, and gave seafarers the promise of being able to tackle those bigger oceanic waters in search of new opportunities.

Genoese sailors played a leading role in the opening up of the Atlantic, although they often had to work under the sponsorship of foreign powers such as Portugal, Spain and England, thanks to the constant conflict and feuding back home. Gradually, the Portuguese plotted a route around Africa that plugged into the trade centres of the Orient without having to go to the Levant or the Black Sea (this was a blow to the Venetians and their Egyptian trade with the Mamluks). The Spanish followed a similar logic to the Portuguese, but headed straight out into the Atlantic, in the hope of finding a new western route to the Orient. They of course came across the Americas, and vast supplies of gold and silver. This was to have a transformative effect back in Genoa, and provided an opportunity for a clever and visionary man like Andrea Doria.

Beyond his military and naval prowess, Andrea Doria's real genius was in recognising this great shift in gravity away from Genoa's familiar field of operations, and positioning the city to take advantage of it. By this time, despite its continuing influence, Genoa's glory days as an imperial power in its own right were well behind it. Bit by bit the merchant pirate pocket Hercules, with its diffuse empire of naval stations bonded together by intrepid and ruthless traders, had been overtaken by the emergence of grander and more complex powers. The city states of the Italian peninsula had been the product of collapsing central authority. But, partly thanks to the growth of the medieval economy that Genoese merchants had helped to create, urban manufacturing centres were becoming more potent and administration more efficient, and larger polities were once again starting to reassert control. On the Italian peninsula this led to conflict between factions in favour of either the Holy Roman Emperor or the Pope – the Ghibellines and the Guelphs. Some city states ended up firmly on one side or another; Genoa, predictably, contained supporters of both factions, adding to its perennial internal conflict.

These conflicts regularly paralysed the city. During one period of civil war between 1314 and 1331, for instance, Genoa was a place of sieges, massacres and food shortages. Trade withered, while other rising powers like the Catalans were able to step in and take advantage. The Genoese themselves came to recognise the value of periodic foreign control – from the Milanese to the French to the Habsburgs – as a safeguard against more potent threats and as a stabiliser in frequent times of chaos. Occasionally the city's people lost patience with the squabbles between leading families: a popular revolution in 1339 brought a man called Simone Boccanegra to the office of Doge with the remit of fixing Genoa's perilous financial situation, and ending the expensive and damaging conflicts that had riven the city and the Ligurian coast. The Spinolas and Dorias were duly exiled.

The Genoese may have been able to start a fight in an empty room, but they were innovative. Faced with gradual decline and occasional economic crises, they were forced to rethink the way they should configure their finances (as they had been doing anyway since those early methods of investing in overseas trade).[3] The Casa San Giorgio was established in 1407 as a group of creditors who could manage the Republic's debts. It became a quasi-public bank, and at one point even controlled the mint. In broad terms the Casa San Giorgio was like a Bank of England, three centuries earlier. It even issued the first ever cheque, and lasted until 1805 when it was closed down by Napoleon. The Casa had its problems, and ultimately reinforced the oligarchic rule of Genoa's main families who were the main shareholders, but it was also an effective innovation ahead of its time.

The Casa was based in the Palazzo San Giorgio, that self-standing musical box of a building that today is virtually desecrated by the crude concrete imposition of the *sopraelevata*. The oldest part of the *palazzo* is at the back, facing the chaos of Genoa's medieval centre. That part was built in 1260 with materials from Venetian buildings in Constantinople, demolished by the Genoese and shipped home. Like many Genoese buildings the Casa is almost gaudy with frescoes, dating back to 1606. They were revealed during renovations in the 1990s and have been restored. As with Genoa's many other frescoed buildings, the effect is mixed: they certainly add colour and a certain decorative frivolity, but for me they can make buildings look slightly cheap, as though builders were covering up plain façades as a way of dodging more substantial structural embellishment.

However the Casa was decorated, the Genoese talent for financial innovation gave them a strong hand in a burgeoning skill and industry that was increasing in importance in the Christian world. In particular, Genoese banks were gaining an important foothold in the Spanish port of Seville. By the time the fifteenth century drew to a close, Genoese banks were making substantial loans to the region's two great warring powers, Habsburg Spain and France. Their rivalry was focused on a battle for control over the Italian peninsula, and as ever this spilled over into friction within Genoa itself, with certain families allying themselves with each of the two powers.

At this time Andrea Doria was earning a good living as a notably effective *condottiero*, switching sides to whoever offered the best contract. In 1527 when French forces took Genoa from the Habsburgs, he was marching with the victorious French.[4] However, Admiral Doria could see the damage of constant turmoil, and began to consider the benefits of stability that would come with a longer-term allegiance to the Habsburgs. The first sign that he was working behind the scenes to prevent see-sawing between factions was when Cesare Fregoso, an expectant member of one of the main feuding families of the time, was not appointed as the new doge under French sponsorship.

Doria's next move came once he had finished honouring his contract with Francis I. He promptly took his services to the opposition, switching allegiance to Charles V of Spain. Once again he marched into Genoa at the head of an army, to remove the occupation that he had helped install not long before. Partly thanks to a recent outbreak of plague, and partly thanks to the unpopularity of French rule, he faced no opposition. He then resolved to put an end to Genoa's internal divisions, strengthen institutional order and bring stability to Genoa.

One of his first moves was to purge the Adorno and Fregoso clans, at the centre of much of the recent conflict.

The Habsburgs liked what they saw: Andrea Doria knew that this made him a more useful ally to the Spanish, who were keen to end Genoa's endemic volatility and keep control of this strategic Mediterranean port. He made sure that Charles V saw him as both the guarantor of Genoese loyalty and the provider of considerable naval power and financial know-how. This he achieved, and in return Genoa became a key Spanish ally, and a vital part of the machinery that processed the wealth of the Americas into military power in Europe.

This new role was critical for Genoa. Instead of being hamstrung by the wider relative decline of the Mediterranean, it was plugging itself directly into the new opportunities provided by global trade (and plunder) and the growth of international finance. Genoese expertise was also vital for Habsburg Spain. It had a vast but irregular income from American gold and silver, but in the days before modern bureaucracies and complex financial instruments it needed this transformed into a steady line of credit by the Genoese. Reliable cashflows were needed to operate its large and complicated empire, and wage the wars it was endlessly involved in. The Genoese again proved themselves to be innovators, using letters of exchange to move money across large distances, while German bankers for instance relied upon physical coins. The advantage that this credit facility provided was illustrated in 1568 when the English captured four Spanish ships laden with silver destined to pay Habsburg soldiers fighting in the Low Countries. Thanks to the foresight of Andrea Doria, Genoa had not just found some welcome stability, but was able to capitalise on its appreciation of money and its ability to innovate, just as the old world of galleys and Mediterranean trade was ending.

In the longer term, alas, Andrea Doria's successful repositioning as a Spanish ally can be seen as just a blip in Genoa's protracted decline. Being so tied in to Spanish fortunes was not necessarily a good thing once Spain ran into serious financial trouble. In 1575 Philip II was forced to suspend payments on Spanish crown debts (the costs of the fleet that had triumphed at Lepanto contributed to Spanish insolvency), and the relationship between Genoa and Spain became increasingly tense. A downsizing of the Spanish fleet also led to an upsurge in Mediterranean piracy, and slaving raids returned to the Ligurian coastline. By the early seventeenth century Genoa was trying to revive its maritime traditions, but with little success. Attempts were made to bring finance back into synchronicity with the demands of a maritime power. One was the creation of the Compagnia Genovese delle Indie Orientali, a conscious imitation of the Dutch Vereenigde Oost-Indische Compagnie (VOC or United East India Company). The capture of its two ships by the Dutch near Batavia exposed Genoese naivety: the new global trade was not simply a case of sending ships off to newly discovered territories, but in capturing, holding and defending these territories. Genoa, beyond the Mediterranean, was well out of its depth.

***

Before we leave the great age of the Mediterranean behind, it is worth a few more thoughts about that remarkable craft that dominated the sea for so long. The Galata Museo del Mare contains a splendid reproduction of a galley, complete with a forward-facing *sagro bastardo* flanked by two *smerigli petrieri*. With my mind full of the small but nimble sailing ships of Francis Drake and the larger, cannon-heavy Spanish ships that heaved across the waves to the New World, the galley does indeed seem like a relic of times past. But despite its problems it had held its own within an operating season outside the stormier months of the Mediterranean. Galleys were ideal for raids: the bow could ride up through the swell right onto beaches, and if the attackers had to turn tail and flee, the stern of a galley was similarly good for pushing off backwards for a watery escape. They were fast, and for many years were ideal for fighting in and around the islands and headlands of the Mediterranean. But the shift in opportunities from the Mediterranean to the Atlantic also made the galley seem like an anachronistic answer to a question no longer being asked.

For one thing galleys were not a robust form of transportation. Even in the Mediterranean they were confined to a specific operating season when their shallow drafts could avoid stormy seas. But there was no way they could deal with the higher, rougher seas of the Atlantic.

Technological advances also brought about their obsolescence. The growing availability of reliable bronze guns and then iron ones meant that the close-quarter oar-powered manoeuvrability of the galleys became far less important. Atlantic powers tried experimenting, starting off with cumbersome designs like the bulky sail-powered carracks, which were far more efficient for trading and had the advantage of being too tall for many galley crews to board. They converted small, agile caravels, and larger galleons, and then began to operate them in the galley's home territory, the Mediterranean. Sailing ships could make a broadside attack, unencumbered by oars, and had an all-round firepower that rendered them invulnerable to traditional galley attack unless utterly becalmed. Remember how Alessandro Condulmer's isolated galleon was able to hold off Khizr Barbarossa's galleys for so long, by simply sitting there and blasting the hapless attackers out of the water. Ship designers, responding to their increasing obsolescence but unwilling to give up on the undoubted advantages of galleys, looked for larger and larger craft on which to mount more guns. But like the *galleases* in the Christian lines, they often ended up being little more than clumsy hulks that did not enjoy all the advantages of true sail. Galleys were also resource-heavy craft that required great logistical support, and larger galleys meant larger logistical problems.

Recruiting enough men to row the galleys was a constant headache. Free men had the advantage of training, which could prove crucial when it came to those split seconds of synchronicity before the terrifying coming together of warships on the open sea. Free men could also bear arms, and leave their oars to join in the fighting, while slaves and prisoners of war sat chained to their benches. But who on earth would want the life of an oarsman on a galley? One way was to impose a levy, but another solution was particularly Genoese: as well as offering the oarsmen a share of the profits from a voyage, they were also allowed to carry a seachest (a *capsia*) on board, and use that for their own freelance trading. When a land was as rough and unpromising as Liguria, the promise of raising yourself above the level of abject poverty by heaving an oar on a Genoese galley was a sensible option. The effect of the Black Death, which destroyed the labour forces of port cities like Genoa, led to an even greater shortage of potential oarsmen, and – given that Liguria has never been able to support a large population on its barren slopes – this contributed to Andrea Doria's clear preference for chaining slaves and prisoners to the oars on his galleys.

Food and water was crucial, given the physical nature of the work, and whether free or captive labour, a good captain made certain that his crew was provisioned well enough to cope with the strain. In normal conditions crews rowed in shifts to allow breaks, and the captain would be well aware that simple matters like going to the toilet where you sat could lead to all sorts of health problems on longer voyages. Again, there were logistical implications: food and water for a large crew of oarsmen implied either taking up space that could be used for merchandise, or hopping from port to port, and never having much freedom or operational range.

With the life of the oarsmen being so tough, mutinies were not uncommon, and sometimes regulations were drawn up so that every party knew where they stood before things got out of hand. One, the *Tractatus Marinaroriem* in 1318, listed the conditions for Genoese seamen. It stipulated that if there were disagreements at sea, crewmen could disembark at certain listed ports where ships were heading back to Genoa. If it came to blows, the ship's captain had the right to strike the crewman first before any retaliation, but if the crewman struck an officer, they could claim sanctuary so long as they made it to the bow of the galley before being caught.

Sailors hardly had it easy after the galley was replaced by sail, but it is hard to think of any fate worse than that of a galley slave, chained to that great oar on unfriendly seas as enemy ships gathered speed for their frightful collisions. Yet despite the horror of galley warfare, there was something visceral and human about the galley that sailing ships would never have. The Battle of Lepanto may have been remorseless and bloody and grim, but with its banners flapping and the two lines quickening towards each other, full of wood and iron and human muscle, it was also a spectacle comparable to the clashing of gloriously armoured and robed knights. The age of the galley had lasted from the classical era exemplified by *Ben Hur*, and galleys would continue to be used for several centuries afterwards. But as the two great fleets clashed at Lepanto, the world had already moved on to wider oceanic horizons. Instead of Genoa passing into history during this great shift, Andrea Doria had helped it match the new challenges and find a new role for itself as the cashier of the Americas.

At a smaller, perhaps more heroic level, individual Genoese sailors found that this new age of oceanic adventure suited them too: the world was in need of their courage and their seamanship. Many perished, unknown and barely mourned, but the lucky few that succeeded would become rich and enjoy experiences their ancestors could never have dreamed of.

11

A CITY OF ADVENTURERS

"Oh young Italians, travel without waiting for the age when
you will be forced to be prudent, when you will be
aching and full of regret! Travel!"
Captain Enrico D'Albertis

In Genoa the public transport system is just as likely to take you up and
down as from side to side. Buses rev noisily around the hairpins between
blue-collar apartment blocks with blue-chip views of the Mediterranean,
climbing the suburbs high above the port. Passenger lifts are just as
important as the orange buses, if not quite as crowded. ("Ah, these are
worse than Quito," gasped an Ecuadorian woman on one recent trip.)
Just as the cobbles hit a sharp gradient and climb out of sight, in
between a *palazzo* with a frescoed foyer and a glass shopfront displaying
the crispy golden suns of their *farinata*, a ticket machine will guard the
entrance to an *ascensore*. These lifts offer a short cut to the next tier of
Genoa's amphitheatre, whether a concrete-reinforced street corner or a
tree-shaded *piazza* with a schoolgirl leant against a wall, texting her
friends. If it is sunny, pensioners will line up on benches, talking and
taking in the view.

Perhaps the best view of all is near the top of the *funiculare* that sets
off from Zecca, curving up through its rocky tunnel, pausing at its five
stops, before arriving in the shadow of the old city fortifications, high

up in Righi. On a clear autumn day I validated my ticket in the machine down below and climbed on board. The scattering of other passengers were wearing hats and padded jackets, despite the sunny warmth. It was, after all, November, whatever the thermometer said. And don't forget the extra altitude, the passengers might have added, as though they were ascending Mont Blanc.

Outside, the flywheels roared and the steel cables took the weight. Inside the carriages, local opinions were being exchanged. "How disgusting," one middle-aged woman said to another as we neared the Maddonetta stop. "I saw one politician take the bus just before the elections, but she lives in a four-bedroom villa in Albaro. If I see her on a bus I'll ask her to get off, the hypocritical cow."

The other woman nodded sadly in agreement. "Yes, disgusting."

"I'm sorry for the young ones, who'll have no jobs and no pensions. I wish the mayor was so poor and hungry he'd have to lick walls to eat." The curls in the woman's elegantly coiffured hair bounced in unison as the carriage ground to a halt, between imposing metal gates and lemon trees that evoked the medieval trade with the Levant. "They're all corrupt. They should simply hang a few of them as an example."

"Yes, disgusting," said the other woman, getting up and issuing a carriage-wide farewell before heading out onto the stepped platform. The cables that hoisted the cars up and down ran off on their concrete track beneath us, and, far below, a view of La Lanterna and the ferry port was framed by coloured apartment blocks topped with well-kept terraces. The first woman turned to another of the passengers.

"Have you seen her? The little girl?" she asked, suddenly all smiles at the thought of a neighbour's infant daughter. The doors slammed shut and the cables once again took the weight of the carriages (and the winter coats of the passengers). There is something intimate about travelling on interesting bits of machinery – a bus is a bus, but when public transport involves a carriage and a mountainside it is remarkable how people start talking to each other.

The *funiculare* may reach higher up the city's slopes, but Genoa's most remarkable piece of public transport engineering is one that foregoes diagonals – this one combines the up-and-down with side-to-side, all in one ingenious contraption. Just off the street edge at Balbi, not far from Stazione Principe, you can step into a small, red, box-shaped capsule – the type of thing you might find on a tunnel of love ride at a 1950s US funfair. First the capsule trundles a couple of hundred metres into the rock face in a gentle S shape, before pausing, transforming itself into a lift with several clunks and a whirring of cables, and being hoisted 70 metres upwards. It is an unnerving experience, not unlike being inside a €0.90c version of Willy Wonka's Great Glass Elevator. I always feel like telling fellow passengers that it is all powered by "sky hooks", but I do not think many Italians are familiar with Roald Dahl.

There are two of these red capsules, and where they pass each other at ground level, at the point where horizontal becomes vertical, you can see that each is really little more than a steel and glass fairground box with none of the usual attachments that a lift might use to hoist itself up and down. As it travels upwards, the windows offer a neat view of the other shaft, along with the reminder that you are not being pulled upwards with ropes attached above. Don't normal lifts have steel cables attached to the roof? Maybe, and maybe not: I rarely think to look. But then again, few lifts pretend they are carriages on a miniature underground railway before climbing 70 metres up an open shaft.

Do these magical craft ever break down? "Oh yes," the attendant loitering next to the ticket machine had said. "Especially when moisture builds up where the motors change direction. That's quite complicated. But," he added, "that's what I'm here for." With that, he smiled and wandered off to light a cigarette.

This marvellous sideways-and-up contraption is a fitting way to arrive at one of the most extraordinary places in the whole of Genoa: a neo-Gothic turreted fantasy, perched on an outcrop in the amphitheatre above the port, and a monument to the centuries-old Genoese reputation for adventure and discovery.

***

Captain Enrico D'Albertis was an eccentric and a true traveller, and sported a beard that could have been home to an entire colony of weaver birds. Just one of his eyebrows would have made most other men's moustaches wilt with envy. He was born in 1846, in an era when there was just enough danger in travel to make a journey to the tropics an event, with the likelihood but not the stone-cold certainty that one would catch malaria, be punctured by a dart from a blow-pipe, or lose a limb to some virulent fungal infection.

It was also an age when crossing the sea was virtually the only way to travel any significant distance, and this suited an intrepid sailor who had grown up with the whiff of the salty Mediterranean in his nostrils. By the age of sixteen he was in the *Marina Militare*, heading off to Egypt, to the Canary Islands, and around the North Sea. After naval service he went into the *Marina Mercantile*, and was master of the *Emilia*, the first Italian ship to thread its way south through the Suez Canal and into the Indian Ocean. On his final return trip from Calcutta to Genoa he brought a Bengal tiger cub home as a pet, although it soon ended up behind bars in a zoo.

Captain D'Albertis, however, was no company man, and by 1875 he had built his first yacht, called the *Violante*, and equipped it with a cannon to deal with the pirates who still infested the dark parts of the Mediterranean with the spirit of the Barbarossa brothers. Once, while heading towards Gibraltar, he was intercepted and boarded by the Spanish navy, who had interpreted his armament as a sign that he was a pirate himself. The *Violante* was replaced a few years later by the *Corsaro*, which allowed D'Albertis to celebrate the 400th anniversary of Christopher Columbus's voyage of discovery by crossing the Atlantic using only home-made copies of fifteenth-century navigational instruments.

In total D'Albertis circumnavigated the globe three times, but he also found time to explore other forms of transport. He managed to ride from Genoa to Turin (which is mostly uphill: remember that the former is a sea port and the latter recently hosted the Winter Olympics) on a crude and heavy velocipede that boasted iron wheels, Heath Robinson brakes and no gears. Later in life he fell in love with seaplanes, and remembered his first flight as the happiest day of his life.

He also tended to fall in love with married women, including Margaret Brooke, the *Ranee* of Sarawak in Borneo. Another of his enduring loves was Amalia Micone Salvago: when she was widowed he jumped in and promptly married her, before instantly regretting it. Married life obviously suited him less well from the inside than the outside, and the couple separated later on their wedding day. By way of apology for his abrupt change of mind, Enrico gave her his house along the coast in Varazze, built a small hut nearby in Noli, and they then resumed the relationship as an affair. He was evidently a man who did not like to be tied down.

Towards the end of a life where he both acted and looked like a character from a Tintin book, Captain D'Albertis built his castle above Genoa. After his death it became the splendid museum that you can visit now, a window on the world featuring oddities like a stuffed duckbilled platypus, intricately inlaid Muslim muskets and a totem pole. The building itself is an even greater treat than the exhibits. At the centre of the castle is a fabulously ornate gothic staircase, made from different coloured marbles and decorated with an iron chandelier of winged dragons. His fearsome wood and iron velocipede sits at the foot of the stairs, mocking the modern Italian cyclist's obsession with lurid lycra and space-age titanium. Displays of weapons from Sudan and China hang from the walls, along with a crossbow, the weapon of choice of so many Genoese mercenaries through the ages. The Salotta Turco echoes the nineteenth-century fashion for all things Oriental, whether original or synthetic, with its mishmash of scimitars, opium pipes and sail curtains suspended in billows from the ceiling, all suffused by the heady smell of dark wood. His *Cabina del Capitano*, a room no bigger than a suburban bathroom, recreates D'Albertis' poky wood-panelled ship's cabin, complete with twine-sprung bunk bed. It is the ultimate nautical escape cave for a retiring adventurer with a bottle of whisky and a desire for some peace.

The ghost of Christopher Columbus, the inspiration for that back-to-navigational-basics jaunt across the Atlantic, haunts the castle. A wistful marble figure of the explorer as a supple young man, with tousled hair and elfin features, perches on a colonnaded castle terrace, staring out beyond the rooftops and container cranes to the sea beyond. A mural of the *Niña*, *Pinta* and *Santa Maria* setting out on their history-shaping voyage to the New World decorates a wall inside the castle itself. D'Albertis, like Columbus, could only have come from Genoa, or perhaps Venice. Indeed, panoramas of the two great medieval rivals feature either side of the monumental fireplace in the castle's Sundials Hall, where D'Albertis indulged his other hobby, designing a grand total of 103 sundials. On the chimney his family's coat of arms is accompanied by the motto "*tenacitor catenis*", stronger than chains. The room is also home to half a dozen timber and hide chairs, decorated with leather fringes suggesting Davy Crocket's Wild Frontier jacket.

Like a flamboyant Wilfred Thessiger, D'Albertis was a man who could not wean himself off adventure. He never looked anything less than intrepid, with luxuriant facial hair even as a young man. His theatrical style translated well into photographs, whether posing in a leather flying cap or pith helmet, or perched precariously on top of a ladder in the rarefied air above Genoa's rooftops, pointing off into the heavens. But when it came to exploration, rather than adventure, D'Albertis' cousin Luigi was the real star of the family.

Luigi D'Albertis, like his relative, was lucky in that earning a living was never a fundamental preoccupation of his life. In the early twenty-first century trustafarians become documentary-makers and bloggers; in the mid-nineteenth century they grew enormous beards and challenged the world to kill them while working out what lay in blank parts of the world atlas. Luigi kicked things off at the age of eighteen by joining up with Garibaldi, but by the time he turned thirty he had swapped the life of a revolutionary for that of a naturalist.

In 1872 Luigi journeyed to the Arfak Mountains in New Guinea, which European eyes had never before seen. He was frequently ill, and was given to using his gun to ensure the natives were "brought to their senses". In the meantime he gathered samples and specimens for scientific study.

After his health had recovered Luigi attempted a second expedition, involving the copious use of dynamite to scare the natives and collect yet more specimens: "I fished with dynamite and captured some large fish – too large to preserve and too interesting to eat." Despite his fondness for using explosive gathering techniques, Luigi D'Albertis was to give his name to a whole host of animals, including a python, several beetles, and a number of birds (the *Drepanormis Albertisii* is a type of bird of paradise). On that second expedition Luigi achieved another first: travelling the full 580 miles navigable length of the Fly River, in a 16-metre steam launch carrying ten people, a dog and a sheep. He dealt with hostile natives with a combination of fireworks, dynamite tied to rockets, and shotguns. "An explosive cartridge was thrown in the water with a long train of powder," he wrote, "so that it should go off exactly when the canoes came up to it. Happily the rising tide favoured our project, and the dynamite exploded just in front of the first two or three canoes". A marble bust of him in the Castello D'Albertis during his New Guinea phase (there were five expeditions in the 1870s) shows Luigi with his beard styled into two lengthy and diabolical forks – quite fitting given the whiff of cordite that doubtless hung around him.

Luigi was a close friend of another Genoese gentleman naturalist (and entomologist) of the time, Giacomo Doria, who founded the city's Museo Civico di Storia Naturale di Genova. Giacomo Doria was also able to spread his already famous name yet further: by the time he died it had been given to a tree kangaroo, a bird of prey and a slug. The exclusive circles in which these men travelled can be gauged by the following passage, in which Luigi describes being stranded in a jungle at the edge of the known world and then bumping into friends and relatives as though at a bus stop: "This afternoon I was sitting in front of a small hut when the mail steamer arrived from Singapore... How shall I tell how I felt when I found that the passengers the boat carried were two of my best friends, Dr Beccari and my cousin, Capt. Enrico D'Albertis?"

The keeper of the family flame is a smartly dressed woman called Anna D'Albertis. She is often to be seen at the Castello, and works there helping to piece together fragments of her impressive ancestors' lives. She remembers the building from visits as a young child, after Enrico had died (leaving it under the watchful eye of a uniformed caretaker). There was a large and dusty table, covered in a confusion of things like bottles of champagne and First World War gasmasks. There was a white peacock in the garden, but during a visit by her brother's school class it happened to be hit by a stone and sadly died.

The views from the Castello D'Albertis are among the best in this city of stunning vistas, and Anna was keen to show us the most stunning of all, up the vertiginous, inadequate steps that run around the inside of the Castello's boxy main tower. Outside, the whole of Genoa is spread out, with ferries and container ships loading and unloading; suburban buildings scattered round the amphitheatre of hills as though waiting for a performance by the sea; and the slow, ugly crawl of car lights on the *sopraelevata* cutting a path from one side to the other. My eyes watered from the wind as I watched a Hainan container ship edge its way out of the port like a multi-coloured floating tower block. Off beyond La Lanterna the sun managed to find its way through a fleeting gap in the November clouds, lighting up a patch of rough sea. It was not a day to be out on the Mediterranean on the type of craft that Enrico D'Albertis favoured. (In keeping with Genoa's maritime heritage they still carry stormy weather warnings – *Mare molto agitato* – on the electric signs at bus stops, as though it was still a city where the women looked out for their husband finishing their shift on a Doria war galley in time for tea.) A plaque on the tower commemorates Giuseppe Verdi's climb up those same steep, narrow steps on 24 March 1894. Back inside, one wall was covered with the etched names of others who had stood up there and taken in the view that had inspired generations of Genoese to head out into the unknown, satisfy their curiosity and make their fortunes. Back then, said Anna, "even if you stayed at home you could get measles and die. So why not die in a shipwreck?"

***

Enrico D'Alberis was one of many famous explorers to come from Genoa and the Ligurian littoral. The harshness of the coast and the uncompromising Genoese approach to seeking a fortune bred a long line of firm-jawed mariners who wondered whether their big break was just over the horizon. Some did it for the glory of Genoa, and some for the glory of another foreign power, but each was careful to profit from their discoveries personally. Nicoloso da Recco claimed the Azores for Portugal; Lancelotto Malocello reached the Canaries in 1456 and gave his name to the island of Lanzarote; Antoniotto Usodimare discovered the Cape Verde islands, and explored great chunks of the West African coast; and Leon Pancaldo circumnavigated the globe as Ferdinand Magellan's pilot in 1519-20.

Two of the region's sons had very similar experiences of exploration. Giovanni Caboto, who became better known as John Cabot, reached the Americas thinking that he had actually visited Asia.[1] Instead of the Japanese islands (Cipango) he had in fact bumped into North America, possibly Newfoundland. As he was living in England he sailed under the patronage of King Henry VII, in a tiny caravel called the *Matthew* with a crew of eighteen. These were brave men. The following year, in 1498, Cabot disappeared without trace while leading a new expedition of exploration.

Preceding Cabot was another explorer who aimed for Asia and ended up in the Americas. Christopher Columbus, as the English-speaking world tends to know him, was the eldest son of Dominico Colombo and Suzanna Fontanarossa. His father was comfortable, if not rich, and was able to send the young man to the University of Pavia to study subjects that included geography, navigation and astronomy. The eldest son of a wool weaver who had made a success of his life might have been expected to follow his father's profession in other parts of Italy, but Genoese men were made of more adventurous stuff, and at the age of fourteen Columbus left university and headed out to sea.

Although little is known of this period of his life, Columbus certainly travelled widely. "I passed twenty-three years on the sea," he later wrote. "I have seen the Levant, all the western coasts, and the North. I have seen England; I have often made the voyage from Lisbon to the Guinea coast." Given his Genoese heritage it is no surprise to find that he fought Venetians in galleys off the coast of Cyprus. He even made it as far as Iceland in 1477 ("the sea was not frozen, but the tides there are so strong that they rise and fall twenty-six cubits").

At around this time he began to settle down, getting married in Lisbon to a woman called Philippa (of Italian descent), and devoting much of his time to illustrating books, and drawing maps and charts. It was an age of enthusiasm for exploring the Atlantic and deep curiosity about what lay on its farthest shore. Genoese merchants, like others across Italy, had begun to suffer from the fall-off in trade as it shifted around the Cape route to the Orient, while the Ottoman Turks stifled business in the eastern half of the Mediterranean. The Spanish, and others, were starting to wonder whether the next opportunity lay directly to the west.

On Friday 3 August 1492 Columbus set sail with his three ships on probably the most famous voyage ever. "Set sail from the bar of Saltes at 8 o'clock, and proceeded with a strong breeze till sunset sixty miles, or fifteen leagues south, afterward southwest and south by west, which is in the direction of the Canaries." By mid-October, they saw land: the *Pinta* "makes signals, already agreed upon, that she has discovered land. A sailor named Rodrigo de Triana was the first to see this land." This sighting changed the world.

The voyage did not take place under a Genoese flag, as Columbus had left the city way back in the 1470s. So how much pride can the Genoese take in the famous sailor? David Epstein, in his book *Genoa and the Genoese*, makes a strong case for Columbus still being extremely Genoese in outlook.[2] Firstly, he was shaped by a deep awareness of the Muslim threat. After visiting Genoa's last imperial outpost on the island of Chios, he saw a desperate need to rekindle trade by finding another route to the Orient. He also spoke of a desire for a new crusade to recapture Jerusalem. Secondly, he had an utterly ruthless approach to slavery. As soon as he arrived in Hispaniola he sized up the commercial potential of the human stock. In fact his Spanish patrons were taken aback by his suggestions for establishing a slave trade, but as a Genoese, slavery had been a key part of life, trade and economics for centuries. Lastly, just before he set sail on his final transatlantic voyage in 1502 he wrote to the protectors of the Casa San Giorgio that his heart remained in Genoa wherever he travelled. He then promised a tenth of his income from the New World (so long as taxes were reduced on food on wine), although to Genoa's misfortune this promise never found its way into his will of 1506. It is also worth throwing in a description of Columbus from Bishop Las Casas, which makes him sound like exactly the type of uncompromising and obdurate seaman that Genoa had been producing for centuries: Columbus was "a robust man, quite tall, of florid complexion, with a long face" but also "rude in bearing, and careless as to his language. He was, however, gracious when he chose to be, but he was angry when he was annoyed." Forget which flag he sailed under, Columbus was Genoese from the toe of his boot to the tip of his nose.

Despite the lack of obvious tourist sites that theme park Italy is so good at, Genoa certainly treats Columbus as one of its own. The shame is that the main thing they have to show for it (and a staple for cruise-ship passengers to take photos of) is a curious little half-house, just down a cobbled path from the mighty Porta Soprana. The building is known as the "Columbus House", and (in a city blessed with the Castello D'Albertis and the superb Galata maritime museum) it is one of the most underwhelming museums I have ever visited. In truth, the building only dates back to the eighteenth century, and was chosen to represent Columbus's house in the 1890s to mark the 400th anniversary of the great man's epic-making voyage. I feel that Columbus, as well as Cabot, the D'Albertis cousins, da Recco, Malocello, Usodimare, Pancaldo and a string of others, through Andrea Doria and beyond, deserve more.

A 'bewildering phantasmagoria' – Genoa's *centro storico*. The shamelessly concrete *sopraelevata* is just visible on the right, cutting through the port.

La Lanterna – a glimpse of Genoa's iconic landmark through the precipitous streets and *vicoli* that surround its port.

The crude concrete imposition of the *sopraelevata* slicing its way through Genoa's port, almost taking off the nose of the Palazzo San Giorgio.

The church of San Matteo, final resting place of various Dorias who spent their lives hunting and killing Venetians, Pisans, Muslims and Mediterranean pirates.

A *fruttivendolo* or *bezagnin* on the Piazza delle Fontane Marose.

Emanuele Brignole, the charitable pioneer behind the innovative Albergo dei Poveri.

Welcome to the ancient principality of Seborga, former home of *Sua Tremendita* Giorgio Carbone, whose ambitions went beyond selling flowers.

Vernazza, a jewel of the Cinque Terre that cannot escape the harsh geography that makes it so beautiful.

Portofino, a stunning hangout for celebrities who wish to be photographed by paparazzi while having a secluded holiday away from the cameras.

A young Columbus looking out to sea from the Castello D'Albertis – Genoese from the toe of his boot to the tip of his nose

The counter at Viganotti, and Genoa's version of Willy Wonka, Alessandro Boccardo.

Arte Culinaria – Second Lieutenant Giuseppe Chioni dreams about pesto and other food after defeat at Caporetto.

Genoa CFC at the Derby della Lanterna – Italy's oldest club calls on history to taunt their rivals.

Sampdoria fans at the Derby della Lanterna – Genoa CFC's stylish rivals respond with colour and noise.

12

THE GRAND TOURISTS

"Genoa is the crookedest and most incoherent of cities; tossed about
on the sides and crests of a dozen hills."
Henry James

The walls were a kind of duck-egg blue and the ceiling was a riot of
colour thanks to many hours of intricate brushwork from a gang of
skilled Renaissance painters. The panels showed helmeted men doing
deals and storming walls, while the few women on display wore blouses
that all seemed to have become loose enough to expose their breasts. The
long red curtains were a mistake, apparently, and the 5-metre-high
marble fireplace was quite unlike anything I had ever seen before:
festooned with gruff naked men with curly beards, flags, axes, shields
and a cannon. The flag of Saint George hung outside the double-height
windows, and men in green smocks kept themselves busy, running
orders and serving espressos. Occasionally a door would open and a pair
of eyes would pop out to see if everything was in order, then the door
would shut discreetly.

"The Palazzi dei Rolli are a photograph of a historical moment, a
precise picture," explained Gregorio Gavarone. If you poke your head
out of the window and look up and down Via Garibaldi, he explained,
it will look just as it did 500 years ago. Gavarone suited the backdrop of
the Palazzo Doria. He wore a suit and green silk tie with an ease and

comfort that I will never achieve, and spoke in melodious, rhythmic Italian, every so often breaking off to answer a question in English. Gavarone was the president of Genoa's foremost gentleman's club, the Circolo Artistico Tunnel (CAT), occupying a rather opulent complex of rooms in the Palazzo Doria at Via Garibaldi 6.

The CAT recently moved to its present location after several dozen years across the road in another exuberant *palazzo* that is now occupied by Deutsche Bank. It required rather a lot of work to get it into its present state, after the previous public-sector occupants left it with fluorescent striplighting and lino flooring. Despite the apparent mistake with the red curtains, the makeover seems to have been a stunning success. The CAT's current premises, as the name suggests, used to be part of the Doria empire, and one of their number – Clemente Doria – both owns the *palazzo* and maintains an apartment at the top of the building. Just as Via Garibaldi is largely unchanged since the building of its Palazzi dei Rolli, so are the owners and residents: the old, wealthy and powerful families that have been the heart of Genoa for centuries.

The silver and gold that the Spanish brought back from the Americas came to Genoa, and while it was recycled to fund the Habsburgs' countless wars across Europe, much of it stuck in these steep streets above the Mediterranean. The glories of the Palazzi dei Rolli provide a rough idea just how sticky those Genoese streets were. As well as being magnificent *palazzi* in their own right, the Rolli were, in effect, upscale guesthouses, with gradings provided by the municipality. Each grade of Rolli was suitable for guests of a particular status, and when such a guest arrived the lucky host from the relevant properties was chosen by ballot. At the very top of the tree that meant hosting a pope or an emperor. Lower down it might mean having a duke or a minor royal for a couple of weeks. It was a system that encouraged ostentation, and the result was the creation of one of the grandest collections of buildings in Europe.

Long before the Strada Nuova itself was completed in 1716, Genoa's fortunes started to turn. The problem was that in tying itself quite literally to Spanish fortunes, misfortune for Spain inevitably led to misfortune for Genoa. In the first decades of the seventeenth century Spain was getting itself deeper and deeper into debt, thanks to the ruinous sums it was spending on war, and this led to it defaulting on its debts. In Genoa, the boom that had begun with Andrea Doria's visionary retooling of the city was at an end. Once again the city faced a long decline. But like Rome after the Empire and Florence after the Renaissance, Genoa now had a mighty physical inheritance that would continue to attract visitors for centuries.

***

Forget the modern cruise ships towering over its old port: Genoa had its golden age of tourism well before the era of Thomas Cook and mass travel. The city was an integral part of the Grand Tour for northern Europeans. Part of this was simple geography, with the port lying in a convenient spot on the way from the South of France to the established glories of Ancient Rome and Renaissance Italy. But part was the Rolli effect – the gradual accumulation of treasures and marvels by the city's rich, who housed them in *palazzi* worthy of any rank of guest.

Genoa's geography was the first obstacle for visitors, who tended to reach the city from Nice by boat, thanks to the execrable state of Liguria's roads. The Aurelia, that Roman route from the ancient capital to Gaul and Spain, had fallen into disrepair on the rocks of the Riviera (it was rebuilt under Napoleon's rule). So, seemingly, had many of the seafaring skills of the past.

"No mariners in the world are as cowardly as the Italians in general, but especially the Genoese," wrote a distinctly unimpressed John Molesworth, the British envoy to Turin in 1723. "Upon the least appearance of a rough sea, they run into the first creek when their feluccas are sometimes wind-bound for a month." A traveller called Andrew Mitchell wrote a similar passage in 1734, blaming the laziness of the sailors as well as the conditions. They were scared to use the sails and stuck to their oars, staying close to the coast. The sailors themselves, Mitchell said, were poor quality.

The weather in the Mediterranean in the winter took many by surprise. One tourist in 1754 hired a felucca to take his entire retinue along the coast from Nice. "In the winter it is so bad a way of going that I would not advise anyone to go in one of those boats," he warned. "Not that there is any danger at any time in them from the sea; the Genoese being so great cowards: but there is danger of being put on shore and being obliged to continue several days where you can neither get house to cover you, bed to lie on, or bread to eat. Then again they are in continual apprehensions from the Barbary Corsairs..." Whatever the seas and the state of the land routes, the pirate problem remained.

Once they arrived, many tourists were dismayed at the swarming, chaotic city that greeted them. "There lies all Genoa, in beautiful confusion," wrote Charles Dickens, who started off being distinctly unimpressed by the city. But who can blame him when he described the medieval centre as "a maze of the vilest squalor, steaming with unwholesome stenches, and swarming with half-naked children and whole worlds of dirty people". The fragrance of the smaller streets was "like the smell of very bad cheese, kept in very hot blankets". An earlier visitor in 1778 worried about crime: "The police is ill regulated at Genoa and murderers are frequently left to escape with impunity." It was a common and generally justified concern.

Dickens was visiting Italy (and France) in 1844 as a break from writing. Luckily for Genoa, he chose to give the city time, rather than stomp through like many Grand Tourists, with a nod to the Palazzi dei Rolli and their treasures while holding scented handkerchieves to their noses. The novelist's keen interest in people's lives, however base, and his willingness to get out and walk around paid dividends in Genoa – then as now not the obvious tourist city. Ignoring that smell of bad cheese kept in hot blankets, he walked through streets "as narrow as any thoroughfare can be" that forced the rich to abandon their carriages for the sedan chairs that can be seen as exhibits on the ground floor of several of the Palazzi dei Rolli today. He noted the "long strings of patient and much-abused mules, that go jingling their little bells through these confined streets all day long", and the houses that were "immensely high, painted in all sorts of colours, and are in every stage and state of damage, dirt, and lack of repair". Some of this will be familiar to those who take time to tramp the *vicoli* with open eyes today (sadly, not the mules). Indeed there is a surprising echo in modern Genoa of much of what Dickens saw.

The apothecaries seem to have played as large a role in nineteenth-century life as the pharmacies do among the health-sensitive residents of the city today (and all of Italy). Inside, Dickens noticed that they were full of "grave men with sticks", who sat in the shadows discussing what was in the newspapers. These men were actually doctors, hanging around in the hope of snagging some passing trade off any customer feeling particularly grim. Peasant women seemed to be constantly washing clothes, laying them out on flat stones and bashing them with wooden mallets. Dickens wondered how they would ever get them clean given the all-pervasive dirt. Babies were heavily wrapped to prevent any movement, and Dickens saw some hung up on hooks and left dangling, to avoid inconveniencing anybody (a very different attitude to children exists today in Italy). He also remarked that theatre audiences were cruel and ready to pounce on any mistakes.

Around a fifth of the people he saw in the streets were priests and monks. Although he noted that the "splendour and variety of the Genoese churches, can hardly be exaggerated", he was less kind about the men of the cloth. Dickens found them rather unprepossessing, from their "repulsive countenances" to their "sloth, deceit, and intellectual torpor". When he wandered down to the port, he saw two portentous officials (again an echo of the modern day) wearing cocked hats and searching people for contraband. They barred the way to both monks and ladies, as "sanctity as well as beauty" were apparently vulnerable to the temptation to smuggle items hidden in both habits and dresses. The merchants of Genoa's golden age would surely approve of such thoroughness.

Dickens even passed his keen gaze over the process of death. Just as in the days of the plague, the dead were not treated with particular kindness. Once a day they were gathered up and dumped in common pits ("this promiscuous and indecent splashing down of dead people in so many wells"). The Genoese were astonished that Swiss soldiers stationed in the city were provided with the posthumous luxury of coffins if they died. Funerals were conducted by a group called a *confratérnita*, on a rota as a form of penance, each wearing a loose cloak and hood with holes for breathing and seeing.

But even as Dickens wandered the streets, noticing the babies dangling from hooks and the washerwomen, he also took note of the *palazzi*. He, too, was a fan. "When shall I forget the Streets of Palaces: the *Strada Nuova* and the *Strada Balbi*!" He wrote about their heavy stone balconies, walls alive with Old Masters, massively barred lower windows, and "dreary, dreaming, echoing vaulted chambers". He also left a good description of how the more modest *palazzi*, like the redoubtable Palazzo Grimaldi where I am writing this, were used in normal life. One of Dickens' friends was an English banker who had his offices in a building on the Strada Nuova. The *palazzo* had an elaborately painted hall (as dirty as a London police station); a couple selling walking sticks (the man with a "hook-nosed Saracen's Head with an immense quantity of black hair"); three blind beggars and a legless man on a cart; a hatter's shop; and a yard that seemed not to have been visited in a hundred years. A similar jumble can be found in a modern-day *palazzo*: architects and gallery owners are especially keen on such locations, but you might also come across the offices of accountants and lawyers, artists' studios, and flats owned by pensioners and university lecturers. Paint peels, ceilings dazzle with frescoes, and worn black marble staircases still echo with an endless tip-tapping of footsteps going up and down, up and down. Residents sue each other, argue, invite each other around for dinner, argue about leaving doors open or shut, and of course complain about politicians.

The Grand Tourists certainly relished the special beauty of the architecture: the *Description of Italy* by Richard Lassell asserted that the "*strada nova* for a spirit surpasseth in beauty and buildings all the streets in Europe that ever I saw any where; and if it did but hold out some rate a little longer it might be called the Queen Street of the world. Ordinary houses are out of countenance and dare not appear in this street, where every house is a palace and every palace as beautiful as marble pillars and paintings can make it."

The artist Peter Paul Rubens was so impressed that he published a book devoted to the *Palazzi di Genova* in 1622, giving detailed descriptions and illustrations of the city's most notable buildings. It was not just that he admired them; he actively wanted them to inspire people back home in the Spanish Netherlands, and have ready-made plans, sections and elevations to copy. His own Rubenshuis in Antwerp, his home and studio, was his personal homage to Genoa's grand designs. Others did not have such a practised eye. Lord John Pelham Clinton wrote that the *palazzi* infinitely exceeded his expectations, but he was also modest about his own abilities: "I have just taste enough to admire a good picture, when it is pointed out to me, but not judgement enough to find it out by myself."

But while the Palazzi dei Rolli were the main ostensible draw for Grand Tourists, when they set foot in Genoa they knew that the seedy port was famous for another reason: sex. From descriptions many gave of the quality of Genoa's women, this might seem unlikely. Charles Dickens was especially cruel, and wrote that the withered, intensely ugly old women reminded him of witches, but then suggested they would never been seen with broomsticks as they are an instrument of cleanliness. The English chaplain down the coast at the Tuscan port of Livorno, the Reverend John Swinton, called Genoese women "the proudest creatures in the universe, and most intolerably and insufferably insolent, especially to their husbands". Hester Thrale, close friend of Samuel Johnson, warned that "the generality of the women here are the most ugly hags in the universe. Their heads are of a monstrous size, their complexion swarthy and olive-coloured, their features large and their mouths exceedingly wide... what sort of beauty is suited to the Italian taste I know not, but I'm certain an Englishman would be shocked at the sight of them." The modern Italian woman (or man) would not be particularly impressed by such an assessment, but at least it cannot be counted as entirely accurate: a Genoese woman called Simonetta Cattaneo was the model for Botticelli's *Venus*. (As the husband of a Genoese wife I also feel duty-bound to protest.)

Genoese women must have had certain allures, however. In 1729 a tourist disapproved of how married Genoese women took escorts and lovers (*cicisbei*), which he thought set a bad example to visiting British females.

Meanwhile homosexuality, commonly seen as a vice by most northern Europeans, was often associated with the Mediterranean in general and the Italians in particular. Some of the Grand Tourists who turned up in Genoa found that it was a vice they were quite keen on experiencing. In 1716 a British envoy called Davenant informed his counterpart in Paris: "I met with a very dirty piece of business upon my arrival here. The 4th instant Mr Cresswell was arrested by an order of a Deputation of the Senate, which has the inspection in cases of sodomy, they call them here *il Magistrato dei Virtuosi*. He was immediately carried to the prison of the palace, with a young Genoese boy he had lately dressed up, and nobody is admitted to see him. He has been so public in his discourse and actions that they can fix on him the fact above 38 times, in his own house, the streets, in porches of churches and palaces..." As Rosella the transsexual prostitute would agree, the grit of base human desire fits neatly alongside the grandeur in Genoa.

But Liguria is not just about this old port city, and many of the Grand Tourists travelled east and west along the coastline to the undoubted beauty of the Riviera. One place that used to lie east of Genoa's *centro storico* but would now be considered the poshest suburb of the city itself is Albaro, full of glorious old villas rolling down to the Corso d'Italia footpath and the Mediterranean. Like Nervi and Voltri on both outlying wings of the city, Albaro used to be considered a destination in its own right, and at one point was the place that Lord Byron called home.

Charles Dickens stayed in Albaro during his visit, in the Villa Bagnerello ("or the Pink Jail, a far more expressive name for the mansion") which was owned by a butcher. On the one hand "the mosquitoes would tempt you to commit suicide", but on the other, it was "one of the most splendid situations imaginable. The noble bay of Genoa, with the deep blue Mediterranean, lies stretched out near at hand; monstrous old desolate houses and palaces are dotted all about; lofty hills, with their tops often hidden in the clouds, and with strong forts perched high up on their craggy sides."[1]

The lanes around Albaro were almost as narrow as in the *vicoli* of Genoa, if just wide enough to allow travel by carriage rather than sedan chair. In one lane locals had to measure the narrowest point so that they could match it up with the wheels of a carriage they were trying to squeeze through. Not long before, an old lady had wedged her carriage so firmly between the walls that the walls were jammed fast and she was stuck. "She was obliged to submit to the indignity of being hauled through one of the little front windows, like a harlequin," wrote Dickens.

The writer thought that the surrounding countryside was beautiful, and recommended climbing one of the neighbouring mountains. There was then, as now, an air of genteel decay, with overgrown courtyards and piebald statues, rusty gates, dull, empty fountains, and stacks of firewood in halls "where costly treasures might be heaped up".

The hill forts that ringed the city like a gigantic upturned "V" also impressed visitors, when they were not being used by one army or another as a vantage point to bombard Genoa. "The height and distances of these forts, their outlying loneliness... seem to make Genoa rather the capital and fortified camp of Satan," wrote Herman Melville in 1857. Those hill forts still stand, laced together by their nine miles of walls. They are still in very good condition, but (like much in Genoa) without enough real thought about how the people of the city, or visitors, could make best use of them.

Following the coast to the east you come to the Promontorio Portofino, which helped inspire Friedrich Nietzsche in the 1880s. He said the Promontorio was somewhere to "anchor and never leave". He wrote part of *Thus spoke Zarathustra* during those nights when the sound of the waves prevented him getting to sleep. The village of Portofino continued to inspire fine literature, until in 2008 *OK!* magazine paid a reported £2.5 million for exclusive coverage of Wayne Rooney's wedding there.

Next along the coast is the Milanese-friendly resort of Santa Magherita (where Clark Gable spent a holiday), after which it cuts back in to Rapallo. This serial diplomatic venue has a long list of eminent foreign visitors.[2] Ernest Hemingway and W. B. Yeats both dropped in, and Ezra Pound lived in an attic on the sea front for twenty years up to the end of the Second World War. He wrote *The Cantos* in Rapallo, and broadcast in favour of Mussolini, before having to move to Genoa as the unwilling guest of the US Counter-Intelligence Corps.

Passing the renowned Cinque Terre, which Lord Byron called "paradise on earth", you get to the Gulf of Spezia, at the far eastern end of Liguria. This is where Byron swam five miles across the bay, from Porto Venere and Lerici. Mary and Percy Bysshe Shelley also lived near here, although Mary was never happy about it, noting that "the very jargon of these Genoese is disgusting". In 1822, after Mary's near-fatal miscarriage, Shelley set off for Livorno by boat despite bad weather forecasts. Unhappily, the boat never reached its destination, and Shelley's body was washed up a while later having already provided supper for numerous fish. When what remained was cremated on the beach, his skull split open from the heat and his brain reportedly made a fizzing noise on the bonfire.

D. H. Lawrence also lived near Lerici, in a house called the Casa Rosa, while in a scandalous relationship with Frieda von Richthofen (whom he later married). They then moved to the Riviera Ponente, on the other side of Genoa, to the Villa Bernada in Sportorno. When the villa was demolished in 2002 to make way for holiday homes, the inspiration for one of the most infamous characters in English literature was lost. The villa had been owned by a war hero called Angelo Ravagli, who took English lessons from Lawrence and helped him to fix a smoking chimney. When D. H. Lawrence returned from a trip to Sicily he discovered his wife and Mr Ravagli having an affair (their relationship apparently lasted for four years). It is believed that Ravagli was the model for Mellors, the gamekeeper in *Lady Chatterley's Lover*. As well as securing a form of literary immortality, Ravagli did rather well out of the whole affair. When Lawrence died in 1930 Ravagli left his wife and three children and moved with Frieda to New Mexico, where they lived off her late husband's royalties. After she died he inherited those royalties with the rest of her estate, and returned to Liguria where he and his pots of money were welcomed back into his original family.

The most important holiday spot on the Riviera Ponente is Sanremo, within sniffing distance of the French frontier. The town owes its fame to a publicity campaign that kicked off with a piece in *The Times* by a Dr Panizzi, explaining the health benefits of the mild winter climate. Dr Panizzi also wrote a pamphlet explaining his argument, and brought his PR machine to London with a full-scale publicity tour that was aimed specifically at convalescents.

The hills around Sanremo are also the centre of Liguria's flower-growing industry, and as you come off the *autostrada* every possible area of flat, terraced land seems to be covered in greenhouses, like enormous silver-grey concrete blocks discarded by a careless giant on a beach holiday. In my experience you will have plenty of time to ponder these and enjoy the view of Sanremo from above, as the whole area seems perpetually clogged with awful traffic jams.

Although I have little positive to say about this present-day Ligurian Monaco-lite, with its glitzy casino and smartly dressed lady shoppers, there are plenty who have appreciated its previous charms. Edward Lear lived (and died) in the town, and Pyotr Ilyich Tchaikovsky was part of a vibrant Russian community. The palms that now line the Lungomare Imperatrice were first donated to the town by Tsarina Maria Alexandrovna, and in 1920 it also gained onion domes thanks to the building of a Russian Orthodox church. Fans on the trail of international treaties after visiting Rapallo will be pleased to know that the Mandates of the League of Nations, including the British Mandate in Palestine, were agreed in Sanremo.

Another resident of Sanremo with a very direct impact on Liguria (and far beyond) was Alfred Nobel. His dynamite was crucial in blasting holes in the rocks of the entire coastline, allowing the whole of Liguria to be laced together by rail and road. Nobel died in Sanremo in 1896, and his laboratory is open for any visitor able to escape the traffic jams of the town centre. Flowers from Sanremo are still used to decorate the Nobel Prize Award Ceremony in Stockholm each year.

If its traffic jams were not ghastly enough, Sanremo is notable for one further infamous contribution to the wider world: the annual Sanremo Music Festival, which gave the world the model for the Eurovision Song Contest (the Italian entry for the Europe-wide contest is still chosen at the Sanremo Festival). Thankfully, some of Liguria's other contributions to the world have been slightly more benign; but in the infamy stakes, foisting the Eurovision Song Contest on the world surely ranks up there with Genoa's role in the Mediterranean slave trade and its brutal treatment of the populations of Sardinia and Corsica.

13

NAPOLEON AND THE FRENCH INFLUENCE

"They thought themselves amply rewarded, in having an opportunity to contribute to the happiness of their native country, by rescuing it from the Genoese darkness, which was worse than that of the Goths..."
James Boswell

Two bowls were placed in front of us: one contained smooth, white sugared almonds that resembled pebbles from a bowl outside a spa in London's West End; the other was a jumble of colours and textures, some bringing to mind rainbow crystals of hoar frost forming around twigs in a ferocious cold snap.

"We are small and ugly, yet do grand things," said Pietro Romanengo, Genoa's sugar king. He wore a green silk tie that was patterned with rows of alert hares, tucked into a blue V-neck jumper. His hair was silver and neatly combed, and a walking stick was propped up against the chair. A worn but functional grey plastic mobile phone sat on the desk next to the two bowls of sugary delights, and on his crowded bookshelves were 1001 recipes for things to pleasure the tongue and rot the teeth.

Romanengo is the name of a Genoese sweet dynasty that began doing business in the eighteenth century but also draws inspiration from the city's millennium-old trade with the Levant and the Eastern Mediterranean. The company specialises in candied fruit and nuts, and its existence is testimony to how Genoa's merchants helped to change Europe's economy a thousand years ago. During the time of the Crusades, Europe discovered the preservative qualities of cane sugar. The Genoese adapted the technique for predictably practical ends, preserving lemons in sugar to help keep sailors healthy at sea. Sugar was traded through the city and Genoese merchants started smelling the possibilities and the money. By the fifteenth century *paste di Genova* were well known by those who could afford them.

In the basement beneath Pietro Romanengo's office, pistachios were swirling around in what looked like a sugar-dusted cement-mixer. Leaves of greaseproof paper hid chunks of candied pineapple and chestnuts, resting on wire grids held taut by wooden frames. There were trays of seemingly dainty but disarmingly dense multi-coloured cakes, capable of super-gluing fingers and teeth together. Tiny pink sweets the size and shape of pumpkin seeds were designed to explode in the mouth leaving nothing but sugar crystals and rose essence. In one room coffee fondants were stacked, drying ahead of the Christmas rush, while violet crème rhombuses waited for a chocolate coating and the final flourish of a crystallised violet petal. Jars of sweet tree resin, *conserva di manna*, sat on shelves, and an 1850-vintage dessicator of flower petals was being used as a storage cupboard.

Romanengo still uses the same techniques that were handed down from those early years when sugar was a preserving marvel from the East: boiling quartered oranges and entire tangerines, pears and pineapples in sugar syrup. They are then left for ten days to steep in large yellow baths. The resulting sticky, oozing delights can keep for years if stored in jars, and, if glazed in sugar, they can last for three months in the open air. The clients included Giuseppe Verdi and royal households across Europe, and in the Genoa of today the business does very well on the Italian predilection for giving beautifully wrapped high-status sweet things whenever visiting friends. It is a niche that Romanengo occupies well, many centuries after Genoa's traders first brought back the products and technologies that he still uses today.

As well as the sugary link to Genoa's medieval trading past, the company has its roots in a second key period of Genoese history. The birth of Romanengo itself and the magnificent presentation that it still glories in, spinning sugar in imitation of nature, owes much to the French, and to an era that stretched from when the Palazzi dei Rolli were being built through to the unification of the Italian peninsula (with a great deal of Ligurian help). The family's shop in the *centro storico* opened in 1814, not long after Napoleon had controlled the city, and as Pietro Romanengo readily admits, the French influence helped shape the company. Not only was the shop styled to look French, but all the machinery that they used in their confections were French too (they still are).

France has a long history of involvement in Genoa and Liguria. Remember that before throwing in his lot with Charles V of Spain, Andrea Doria worked for Charles's rivals in France. When Spain went into its inexorable decline in the seventeenth century, France was once again on the rise. And just as northern Italy had been the battleground between the French and the Spanish Habsburgs back in the great Admiral's day, it was soon to be the great battleground between France and the Austrian Habsburgs. In fact Genoa was often a front-line city in the War of the Austrian Succession (the latest in a series of fabulously complicated dynastic wars that Genoa seemed to get caught up in throughout its history). The French were able to take the city after a bombardment by the forces of Louis XIV, but in 1746 it was the Austrians' turn to capture it. Their occupation was brief, and gave the stage to one of the least likely heroes in Genoese (and Italian) history – a small boy called Giovan Battista Perasso.

On 7 December Austrian occupying troops were helping a team of oxen heave an artillery piece through the thick mud of a Genoese street, but got stuck. They started conscripting locals to help, beating them for good measure. Giovan Battista Perasso – who has gone down in history under the more manageable nickname Balilla – shouted "*Che l'inse?*" ("Shall I start?"), and started throwing stones at them. Others joined in, the Austrians retreated hastily, and a legend was born. Nobody really knows how old he was, but the nickname *Balilla* suggests he was young lad. "*I bimbi d'Italia / si chiaman Balilla,*" according to the Italian national anthem ("The children of Italy are all called Balilla").[1] There is an all-action statue of the young chap in mid-hurl in the Quartiere Portoria where the incident took place, and the phrase *Che l'inse?* has since entered into broad use among Italians, particularly the ones throwing missiles at authority figures.[2]

The type of ostentatious grandeur represented by the Palazzi dei Rolli, however, meant that the man or woman (or stone-throwing youth) on the Genoese street was almost as likely to take exception to inequality in the city as to occupying Austrian troops. The French Revolution of 1789 struck a chord with many Genoese, who took to the streets wreaking havoc and destroying symbols of the grand families that had dominated the city for centuries. (Arguably, those families still do. It remains remarkable quite how much wealth in Genoa lies in the hands of people who carry the same names as the wealthy from almost a millennium ago.)

Fighting between the army of Revolutionary France and the opposing coalition (prominent among them the Austrians and Piedmontese, with support from the British Royal Navy) soon spilled over into Italy. The French made progress but the Allies counter-attacked at Savona, before the French secured their supply lines to Genoa. As the focus of fighting shifted north of the Alps, the French gave control of the relatively poorly resourced Army of Italy to a young Corsican artillery officer called Napoleon Bonaparte. His brilliance led to a run of crushing defeats for the Allies, and took the French to within a hop and a skip of the Austrian capital, Vienna. A new military genius had arrived on the European stage.

The irony of Napoleon's rise to his exalted position in history is that he was almost not born French at all. He came into the world on the island of Corsica in 1769, which had been part of the Republic of Genoa for centuries.[3] From 1755 onwards Corsica had achieved a great measure of *de facto* independence, and when French forces occupied the island in 1768 Genoa agreed to sell it to Paris.[4]

This was a pragmatic decision on the part of Genoa – it was a long time since it had been a superpower, and it was hardly in a position to hold on to the last fraying fragments of its Mediterranean empire. This was probably a good thing, as Genoese rule was brutal and harsh. In 1765, after taking his Grand Tour around Europe, James Boswell visited Corsica, and was caught up in what he described as "a constant struggle against the oppression of the Republic of Genoa", and published his first book, *An account of Corsica*.[5] The book listed infamy after infamy committed by the Genoese, for instance explaining how the Corsicans were forced to sell their merchandise to Genoa for little money, and how this amounted to a sort of legal plunder in scarce years that resulted in famine. Frequent revolts by the peasantry were put down with the type of violence and bloodshed that betrayed the occupier's weakness rather than strength. It was a shabby end to a once great but long gone empire.

For Genoa, the late eighteenth and early nineteenth centuries marked more than just the end of its imperial status. The ailing Genoese

Republic, which had been in existence since 1005, was finally put out of its misery in 1797 by Napoleon. The Ligurian Republic flickered briefly in the pages of history before it too was extinguished, chopped into three sections of coast and incorporated into the French Empire. This was not an entirely bad thing, although the 25,000 Italians who ended up taking part in Napoleon's doomed invasion of Russia might beg to differ.

With the coastline around Genoa such a focus of Napoleon's campaigns against the Austrians, it is no surprise that the region provided him with the launch pad for one of his most important victories. Republican France had consolidated its territorial gains from the first war against the coalition, including Genoa and Liguria, but Imperial Austria (and others) remained twitchy about French expansionism. The British Navy won an important victory at the Battle of the Nile, and a reinvigorated Second Coalition made solid progress in northern Italy in 1799. By 1800 the Austrians were besieging Genoa while the Royal Navy sat just off shore, its cannon firing at will on French positions. The French troops were eventually forced from the ring of fortifications above the city, but succeeded in holding out for sixty days within the city itself. It was not easy for them, and it was certainly not easy for the Genoese. Food stocks ran out, cannon fire landed in built-up areas of the city, and plague once again thrived in the squalor.

For the French, however, the siege was a useful diversion. Napoleon, fresh from seizing power in a *coup d'état* in Paris and declaring himself First Consul of France, marched into Italy over the Great St Bernard Pass. He was looking for the moment when he could take on the Austrians and force a decisive battle. Thanks to the siege of Genoa he got it in the village of Marengo in Piedmont, just across the border from Liguria, against a weakened Austrian army. The French won, and Napoleon had the victory that allowed him to secure his position as First Consul. Ahead of him lay the rest of Europe and his destiny in history. Even though he would ultimately fail, Genoa's brush with Republican ideas would help inspire a couple of revolutionaries who would play leading roles in the unification of Italy, with unforeseen consequences for the countries on the other side of the Atlantic.

14

UNIFICATION AND EMIGRATION

"Without a country you are the bastards of humanity."
Giuseppe Mazzini

Klemens von Metternich called him "thin, pale, poor, and as eloquent as a hurricane, as able as a thief, as indefatigable as a lover". It was a remarkable tribute to a hollow-cheeked, sad-eyed visionary who was born in Genoa in 1805. "I have united armies which fought bravely though made up of different races; I have reconciled kings and emperors and sultans," Metternich continued. "But nothing and no one has created greater difficulties for me than a devil of an Italian." For Giuseppe Mazzini, the unification of Italy was a semi-religious mission that was intended to push the new Italy into a leading role in some future United States of Europe. At a time of great political ideas, it was an intoxicating message for bored, middle-class young men with a romantic streak, and paved the way for the unification of the Italian peninsula.

Whereas his fellow Ligurian Giuseppe Garibaldi was a natural hero, all proud nose, testosterone and galvanising speeches from balconies, Mazzini was the opposite. He dressed in black and his eyes always seemed on the verge of tears. A photograph of him just before his death in Pisa in 1872 shows him looking cerebral and distinguished but also disapproving, and even somewhat disappointed. This is understandable, as the great philosopher of the *Risorgimento* was an idealist and a dreamer, fated to be let down by the harsh realities of political life. Genoa had a proud tradition of producing fearless, pragmatic adventurers, but this man, one of the four key figures in Italian unification, was something different.

Mazzini founded La Giovine Italia (Young Italy) in 1831 while in exile in Marseilles.[1] It was a dreamy conspiracy as much as a movement, aiming at fomenting unrest and insurrection with the eventual aim of creating a democratic, unified Italian peninsula. The two main enemies were the Austrian Habsburgs, who dominated large swathes of the north (Metternich was responsible for dismissing Italy as nothing more than "a geographical expression"), and the deeply reactionary forces that centred around the Papal States (the papacy even saw street lamps, vaccinations and railways as the work of the devil).

Mazzini's ideas inspired a series of plots and attempted coups, each one ending in failure. Mazzini himself fled Genoa, only to be expelled first from France, and then Switzerland. He finally ended up in England, where he was known for seeming to exist largely on coffee.[2] Critics charged him with being a dreamer who worked safely in exile, sending idealistic young men to their deaths in crazy schemes. Although he was active enough to pick up a couple of death sentences during his life, the charge is not without foundation. In one instance, two brothers deserted their posts in the Austrian navy and decided to take part in a planned insurrection in Calabria. Despite their mother tracking them down in Corfu, and bluntly telling the pair that they were idiots, they persisted with their plans. When they landed in Calabria they were dismayed to find a complete lack of the type of revolutionary fervour that Mazzini had promised, and were soon arrested in an inn. The brothers, plus seven others, were promptly executed. (One exhibit in the fabulous Museo Nazionale del Risorgimento Italiano up in Turin captures the archetypal bored young romantic who was particularly susceptible to Mazzini's ideas. In a later age such young men might have driven a double-decker bus from London to Kathmandu, or ended up running a yoga studio on an island in Thailand. Back in the nineteenth century they invariably wrote poetry and died fighting for people who did not share their fervour.)

The closest Mazzini came to achieving his aims was when revolution swept the continent in 1848. Faced with widespread revolt, the Pope fled in February of the following year, and a constituent assembly was formed in Rome. It proclaimed a republic and invited Mazzini (by then in exile for seventeen years) to return as its effective leader. For three months he exercised power with care and tolerance, for instance abolishing clerical censorship without attacking religion itself, but the "Rome Republic" was doomed, along with his broader plans for a tolerant and liberal new Italy. As well as facing counter-revolutionary forces, Mazzini was also seen as the enemy by another powerful force hoping to evict the Austrians from Italian territory: the Piedmontese.

While Mazzini and Garibaldi (more of whom soon) were Ligurian, the other half of the quartet who would be feted as the driving force behind Italian unification were from deeply conservative Piedmont, centred on Turin (as we saw earlier, thanks to the post-Napoleonic settlement, Genoa was firmly under Piedmontese control within the Kingdom of Sardinia). The leading Piedmontese politician, Camillo Benso – better known as Cavour, and the third of our quartet – saw revolutionaries like Garibaldi and Mazzini as enemies. His aim was to further the interests of Piedmont, and the type of democratic idealistic nonsense that they spouted was seen as dangerous. Cavour was a chubby, calculating character, a high-achiever who was more used to making enemies than friends. A rather cruel terracotta figure dating from 1854 caricatures him as dominated by an enormous rounded belly that entered any room long before the rest of him appeared. Cavour was the devoted servant of the fourth figure in our quartet: King Victor Emmanuel II. The king appears on horseback in statues across Italy to this day. In contrast to Garibaldi's heroic countenance, Victor Emmanuel's appearance is slightly ridiculous, from facial hair that did not know when to start or stop, to his braided Gilbert and Sullivan uniforms. Poor old Mazzini is rarely afforded such commemoration: even in Genoa he only gets a shopping gallery named after him.[3]

The other statue that is to be found all over Italy is that of Garibaldi, a simple man with a complicated personality. Garibaldi was democratic to a fault in his belief in human dignity, but still believed that a benign dictatorship was the way to get things done ("Sometimes you have to force liberty on people for their own good"). He possessed military cunning and campaigning ability in abundance, but lacked genuine political nous (Dennis Mack Smith wryly notes that he was "Unskilled in public speaking – except from balconies..."[4]) and clever politicians like Cavour were able to exploit him for their own – and Piedmont's – ends.

Garibaldi was born in 1807 in Nice, to a Ligurian family that worked the coast along towards Genoa, and set about a heroic life that reads like that of an improbable central character in a novel. He was a cabin boy on a Russian ship sailing to Odessa at the age of fifteen, and earned a master's certificate as a sea captain a decade later. He sailed in the Piedmont navy, but could not resist taking part in a Mazzini-inspired insurrection that led to him escaping a treason charge by fleeing to the colonies of Ligurian emigrants in Brazil. He traded brandy, sugar and flour along the coast, but unlike most Genoese he was no businessman: Garibaldi was a natural revolutionary, and soon found his place in the navy of the rebellious Rio Grande Do Sud. He operated a boat called the *Mazzini* in a piratical manner familiar to so many other generations of Ligurians in times gone by, although unlike them he made a point of freeing any (African) slaves he encountered.

After fourteen years of swashbuckling in the names of various freedoms, Garibaldi returned to Italy during the revolutionary years of 1848 and 1849 to lend military assistance to Mazzini, who was making the most of his moment of success with the "Republic of Rome". Their improvised army managed to hold off the Papal forces until the French arrived and chased the revolutionaries away, killing 5,000 of their number (including one of the slaves whom Garibaldi had freed in Brazil).

So began Garibaldi's second transatlantic exile, this time (at first) in the US. He worked for nine months in poverty as a particularly unlikely candle-maker on Staten Island, before his need for adventure once again got the better of him. He sailed a cargo ship along the Peruvian coast for three years, and another (the *Commonwealth*) off the US. Then the news came through that Cavour was allowing him to return to Piedmont provided he abstained from politics. He crossed the Atlantic once again.

Predictably Garibaldi's regular service did not last, and after a handful of years he resigned his commission in the Piedmont army, fired by the desire to bring revolution to the *Mezzogiorno*. He called for a "million rifles and men", but settled for around a thousand. In lieu of uniforms his volunteers wore red shirts, and they set sail from Quarto, a suburb of Genoa, to attack the south via Sicily. An impressive monument now marks the rough spot where in 1860 the fabled *Thousand* clambered into rowing boats and set off to board two steamers – the *Piemonte* and the *Lombardo* –which were anchored just off shore. Now, almost every pizza parlour and beach hut for several hundred metres in either direction has a name commemorating the event.

Giuseppe Abba was a typical volunteer. He had spent time in the Aosta cavalry but without ever tasting the thrill of action, and he sped to Genoa when he heard about the latest venture: "Garibaldi is going and I am to be one of the fortunate few who will go with him." Abba describes Garibaldi as a majestic figure with a common touch, a man who could spend time explaining to a sentry how to tell the time through the stars like a shepherd king. For his part Garibaldi was well aware that his volunteers were mainly, as he put it, "almost all the sons of cultivated families from the country's urban centres". But he explained the lack of popular peasant involvement in his campaign because they were under the influence of the Church, "the reverend ministers of lies". Despite the fine words of those involved, the men who set out to unite the peninsula and free Italians of every sort from oppression and reaction were desperately few in number and very middle-class in background.

From Quarto the two steamers headed east along the Ligurian coast, trying to track down a couple of smugglers' boats that were carrying "ammunition, percussion caps, and small firearms". But despite searching between "Monte Portofino and the lighthouse in Genoa" they gave up, called in at Comogli for oil and sawdust, and set off to liberate Italy.

What followed has gone down in the history books in a blaze of red shirts and a volley of musket shots. The truth, of course, is more complicated, and those complications help to explain the unseen upheaval the *Risorgimento* caused later on. Mazzini might have provided the inspiration and Garibaldi the audacity, but it was the wily Cavour and the ambitious Victor Emmanuel II who added Piedmontese muscle to the whole affair (along with some timely French assistance against the Austrians in the north). Even at the time it was obvious that this was not the type of grassroots uprising in the name of Italy that Mazzini or Garibaldi might have expected or wished for, and perceptive observers might have remarked that the *Risorgimento* was in fact carried out in favour of a Greater Piedmont. Rather than be celebrated as the philosophical father of unification, Cavour made sure that Mazzini was portrayed as a terrorist and revolutionary, and later tried to write him out of the story altogether. Mazzini died in 1872, still on the run and staying in Pisa under an assumed name. He was buried in Genoa a week later, and his funeral saw 100,000 people take to the streets, in defiance of the Mazzini-less version of history that Cavour had been peddling. Police records show that Garibaldi, who had fallen out with the romantic revolutionary some time before, was one of that 100,000.

Giuseppe Mazzini was buried in Genoa's fabulously ornate necropolis at Staglieno. The cemetery is one of the most remarkable sights in the city, full of impressive, dusty arcades and bombastic family tombs that hint at the riches that the city has produced. Yet Mazzini's grave still manages to stand out, carved like a grotto into the hillside and fronted by two massive pillars and a heavy door. The great man's name is spelled out on the stone above the pillars, and ornamental wreaths and inscriptions decorate the walls like adhesive notes around a computer screen. Mazzini's grave gives off the impression of a secluded office, a place where the ageing visionary could retire to continue his work undisturbed, now that the tiresome and disappointing business of mortal life was over with.

From the country of Italy to the football shirts worn by the Italian national team (blue is the colour of Victor Emmanuel's House of Savoy), the legacy of that curious quartet of visionary, revolutionary, king and schemer persists to this day. But the *Risorgimento* would also have an unforeseen impact that reduced the Italian population by half and had its own significant bearing on world history. It would trigger off a wave of mass emigration that would funnel the populations of whole villages through Italy's ports, Genoa chief among them, and change the character of the countries on the other side of the Atlantic for ever.

***

Italy as a country has only ever enjoyed moderate support from its citizens, and even those who devoted their life to its birth could see its flaws. Despite Garibaldi's spectacular successes in uniting the peninsula behind his red shirt, and thereby entrancing the world with his exploits, he was nevertheless haunted by the failures of that most striking and glorious achievement. At its core, the *Risorgimento* contained a tragic flaw, which was condemning the *Mezzogiorno* to something approaching the status of a Piedmontese colony. For example, Cavour's position and ultimate influence over the newly united Italy led to tax laws being drawn up that benefited the more modern economy of the north: in one case, cows (likely to be the property of landowners) were not taxed, while mules (the agricultural muscle of the peasantry) were. The taxes were needed for the new roads and railways that benefited northern cities like Turin and Milan, rather than the subsistence agriculture of the south. Rebellions broke out in the south just weeks after unification had been won, forcing the creation of a modern 100,000-strong army to quash the dissent. But conscription for the army was itself resented by the peasants, as it siphoned off vital agricultural manpower for a cause they did not quite understand. In turn the rebellions in the south caused resentment in the north, exasperated by the lack of gratitude: a former prime minister of Piedmont, Massimo D'Azeglio, perceptively suggested that "unification was a process of making Italians dislike one another... like going to bed with someone with smallpox". Even during Mazzini's plotting or Garibaldi's campaigning there had been a lack of understanding about the brutal power dynamics in the south, or the restricted horizons of the common people (one story suggests that some southerners thought they were fighting to free "Italia", the daughter of a northern king). In many ways, Cavour's ruthless promotion of his favoured Piedmontese interests under the banner of a unified Italy was the canniest course.

Meanwhile, conditions in the *Mezzogiorno* remained appalling for many. Ignazio Silone from the Abruzzo remembered a village of one hundred hovels, hemmed in by the mountains and by time. "In the interiors, which seldom possess a floor, the men, women and children, and their goats, chickens, pigs and donkeys live, sleep, eat and reproduce, sometimes in the same corner."[5] Illness was a fact of life, and by the early twentieth century malaria was killing many thousands of Italians a year.

But just as life was as bad as before, if not worse, a new option was opening up, with steamship fares from Genoa to the New World falling as low as $10. Thanks to the new railway lines that were being laid, even getting to Genoa and other ports was easier. The modern world was presenting poor Italians with a radical means of escape from misery.

Emigration across the Atlantic was not new. Between 1783 (the founding of the American Republic) and 1871 (the birth of the Italian nation) around 12,000 made the journey. The numbers of Italians were far lower than for other nationalities: up to 1860 1.5 million Germans and 2 million Irishmen moved to the US. As a traditionally adventurous bunch from Italy's main port, the Genoese were heavily represented in amongst the artisans, traders and political refugees who left the peninsula to build new lives in the Lower Mississippi and the booming cities of the north-east. True to their roots, the Ligurians tended to be driven by adventure, opportunity and the uncertain political situation. Some, like Garibaldi himself, looked to South America for sanctuary or a new beginning, although the death of 9,000 Italians in a Brazilian smallpox epidemic made many prefer to head further north.

One place that still bears the imprint of those early migrants is Buenos Aires. Boca, the famous working-class district in the port area, was a gathering point for Ligurian immigrants. The iconic coloured houses owe much to a wave of migrants from Varazze, including fishermen and carpenters. The name of the district (and one of the world's best- known football teams, Boca Juniors) comes from the tiny multi-coloured fishing village of Bocadasse, now within the city limits of Genoa itself. The Genoese tongue, which was influenced by an array of languages from Arabic to English, survived for many years in the households of emigrants.

The wave of emigration that was unleashed in the years following the *Risorgimento*, however, was different: 80 per cent were from the south, driven by grinding poverty and hunger. Many of the millions who left had their last experience of Italy when they stepped onto a steamer in the port of Genoa, the country's gateway to the world.

***

There was nothing particularly unusual about the voyage of the *Galileo* from Genoa to Montevideo and Buenos Aires, other than that among the passengers was a journalist called Edmondo De Amicis (1846-1908). He wrote a vivid bestselling account of the trip, called *On Blue Water*, from when the *Galileo* was at anchor in Genoa, "filling up with misery", through to its final docking in another continent and another hemisphere. The account was successful because it was based upon something so typical in the late nineteenth century, when so many men, women and children from the length and breadth of the peninsula decided that they had had enough. For them it was time to do what

Columbus had done – head across the wide Atlantic towards the horizon in search of something new.

For De Amicis the story began in Genoa, although for the "interminable procession of people" that he saw boarding, the journey began when they summoned up the courage to leave whichever hardscrabble village their families had called home for centuries. They came from across Italy and the frosty, muddy villages of Central and Eastern Europe, huddling up on the cobblestones of Genoa's *vicoli* while they waited for their ships to sail off to barely understood new opportunities. "The greater part, having passed a night or two in the open air, lying about like dogs in the streets of Genoa, were tired and drowsy. Workmen, peasants, women with children at the breast, little fellows with the tin medal of the Infant Asylum still hanging around their necks."

Many held their tickets in their mouths, as their arms were full of trunks, bags, mattresses and folding chairs. "Poor mothers that had a child for each hand carried their bundles with their teeth. Old peasant women in wooden shoes, holding up their skirts so as not to stumble over the cleats of the gangplank, showed bare legs that were like sticks." Droves of cattle and flocks of sheep were urged on board, and passengers from the upper decks carried small dogs and bundles of books. Donkey engines hoisted cargo on board. The great ship, wrote De Amicis, "like some grim sea monster that had fixed its fangs into the shore, still went on sucking Italian blood".

One photo from the first years of the twentieth century is a chiaroscuro image of rich women picked out in shining white, helping the black-clad, sun-wizened women about to embark. The rich ones sport gloves and bright hats bedecked in ribbons, while the poor ones have their hair pulled tightly back on their bare heads, and carry babies so thoroughly swaddled that they look almost rigid.

In Genoa, the crowding of emigrants into the port area was a real problem. They came in their thousands, without the money to provide for themselves or rarely even the ability to communicate with the dialect-speaking locals. To ensure they did not miss their passage they arrived early, and filled the *vicoli* of Genoa's port with their sleeping bodies and their luggage. One enterprising businessman decided that there was a profitable way to solve the problem, and opened the Regia Casa degli' emigrante near the corner of the Salita della Provvidenza and

Piazza S Ugo. A brochure for the Casa advertises it as vital preparation for that journey to a new life. It shows a handsome *albergo*, several storeys high, offering services such as accommodation, vaccinations, training on how to get past the Ellis Island immigration officials, and haircuts. It was still going strong after Mussolini put an end to mass Italian emigration, but it had switched to catering for emigrants from elsewhere in Europe. Unfortunately, in early June 1930 the entire building collapsed. A front-page report in the *Biblioteca Gallino* says the incident happened just after 9 p.m., leaving two Poles dead, sixteen injured, and eight others missing. The article noted that 350 guests had been staying at the *albergo*, including Armenians, Arabs and Hungarians. Further casualties, it said, were to be expected.

Emigrants had other worries beyond crumbling medieval buildings. Genoa was known as the worst of the Italian ports for the sharks who preyed on gullible, vulnerable and unworldly emigrants. These ranged from dodgy travel agents and providers of fraudulent services to thieves who vanished after offering to help carry heavy suitcases and trunks. Laws were passed in 1901 to help protect the emigrants, for instance by providing official health examinations, or simply by giving them better information about their trips and disabusing them of common misconceptions about life in the US. There were other hurdles, and some carried certificates from the Municipia di Genova saying they had the means to support themselves in the US and would take responsibility for their own future.

On the *Galileo* Edmondo De Amicis was below decks when they set sail from the port, hearing "Genoese, French, Italian, Spanish", and comparing his new surroundings with being in prison for the first time "In those low, narrow corridors, tainted with the reek of bilge-water, the smell of oil lamps, the fragrance of sheep-skins, and with wafts of perfume from the ladies". His account of sailing across the Atlantic ranges from sexual encounters on board between passengers to seasickness, and the third-class quarters where 1,600 people "lay huddled together, some thrown across the benches like the dead or dying... amid a tangle of ragged wraps".

The voyage was often an ordeal, but in some cases it was a never-forgotten highlight of the emigrant's life. In 1925 one steamship company, the Navigazione Genovese Italiana, published the diary of one passenger who had enjoyed it so much that he did not want to leave the ship once they arrived at their final destination. The passenger had sold all his sheep to fund his emigration to Illinois, where a cousin lived. Despite his enjoyment of the voyage, the diary reveals one area of concern: like a true Genovese he had spent some of the passage worrying about being presented with a large bill at the end for all the ice cream he had eaten.

Angelo Calosso, who left Genoa for Argentina in 1926, kept a detailed log of his journey. At times the waves were like "moving small hills... the corridors looked like a mad-house..." On the tenth day, at around 7 a.m., the ship crossed the equator. A beauty queen was selected, the men raced and the women took part in a tug-of-war contest. They may have still been thinking of the moment when their ship had pulled out of the port of Genoa, with its swarming medieval centre and the hills that sat high above the docks like an amphitheatre, but they were off to begin again in a New World.

***

When the *Galileo* sighted the coast of Uruguay, twenty-two days after leaving Genoa, Edmondo De Amicis noted a group on board who talked of Garibaldi's exploits in that country. One woman started weeping as the thought that she would never see her homeland again swept over her. When the passengers filed onto the dock at Montevideo, some were dressed well, others far dirtier than when they had embarked. Toes poked out of worn-out shoes, buttonless jackets were held shut to conceal bare chests underneath, and some, De Amicis notes, were "even hatless". He watched the *Galileo* disappear off towards the horizon on the River Plate, its flag catching "the early rays of the American sun. It was as if Italy, with a last salute, commended her wandering children to their newly adopted mother."

The Genoese, like most of the early emigrants, maintained strong links to their families back home. In L'Archivio storico della Provincia di Genova there is a series of cards from a family that left Chiavari for Peru in the nineteenth century. The first was posted on 12 September 1882 from Lima by Francisco Raggio (he wanted it to arrive for Christmas), and was written half in Spanish and half in Genoese dialect. The next is from Francisco's son, Vittorio, who sent his card to his mother in 1921 (by then she was back in Chiavari). The photo shows him resplendent in suit and spats, alongside Eva Luy Rojas, who is introduced as his fiancé (she writes, "To my future mama..."). There is a third, from 1925: the couple are happily married, and are showing off their two children to their grandmother, who is safely back in Liguria, on the edge of the Mediterranean.

The migrants heading to the United States joined an increasingly large and diverse community. Every immigrant stepping warily off the Staten Island ferry was met by an average of five Italian Americans. The earliest immigrants often resented the rough newcomers from the *Mezzogiorno*: they undercut wages, and with their uncouth manners and peculiar dialects they represented an Italy that was unfamiliar and even embarrassing to them. As the Genoese in the US tended to be in the earlier waves before the years of genuine mass migration, they were generally well established and considered themselves "settlers" rather than "immigrants". They were at the core of San Francisco's northern Italian community, one of the few not outnumbered by southerners. The Genoese lived on the lower reaches of Telegraph Hill, and helped build both San Francisco's fishing community and their wine-making industry. The Genoese who joined the Californian Gold Rush in their traditional hard-wearing working trousers also left a lasting contribution to Western social history: those trousers were adapted by Levi-Strauss and became known, through a corruption of the French for Genoa, as "jeans". One folding postcard of San Francisco ("The Queen city of the West") was sent back to Genoa by a man called Mario with a brief note to one Ernesto and his family, saying "in the postcard it looks much better than in reality".

The Genoese were among the teachers and organ grinders of south Philadelphia, and brought marble to the docks in Baltimore (part of a triangular trade that took grain to England, then coal down to Genoa, where the marble was hoisted on board). They were merchants in food, olive oil and wine in Boston, and among the wealthy Italian Americans of Chicago, who looked down upon the later, rougher arrivals. Some struck out on their own, and established communities like Genoa, Wisconsin. This was set up by immigrants from Liguria and Piedmont in 1854 (with the original rather heavy metal name of Bad Axe City) on the east bank of the upper Mississippi, and depended on the river for transport. A strong Ligurian merchant community in New York's Greenwich Village disappeared once the influx from the *Mezzogiorno* began in earnest.

One particularly well integrated member of the Genoese immigrant community, with a particularly Genoese name, was Francis B. Spinola. He was born on Long Island in 1821, and by turns became a New York state legislator, the commissioner of New York harbour, a Civil War general, and a congressman. There were other noted successes: Marco Fontana from Genoa set up the Del Monte fruit company, and Amadeo P. Giannini drew on the city's long financial heritage to set up the Bank of America. The Bank started off as a way to get finance to Ligurian settlers in California, who found credit hard to come by. When the San Francisco earthquake of 1906 struck, Giannini was able to rescue his deposits before they were consumed by fire, and began to lend again from an impromptu open-air office with a desk built of planks and barrels. Remarkably, all of those post-earthquake loans were repaid, and what was to become the Bank of America was on its way to greatness.

Migration helped to spread local food specialities around the world. The emigrants often carried a few basics with them, but once they were established some of the more enterprising among them set up supply chains to bring over the familiar favourites from their previous home. One note, written by Agostino Lanata from Chiavari, accounts for the 30 barrels of wine (each holding 65 litres), 106 kg of mushrooms, and 96 kg of cheese that he shipped to his brother in Argentina in November 1896 on the *Duca di Genova*.

The end of the great exodus came in the mid-1920s, by which time around 4.5 million Italians had entered the United States, and many more had headed off to new opportunities in Argentina, Brazil, Australia and beyond. The end came partly thanks to the fascists putting a stop to mass emigration, and partly thanks to the discriminatory 1924 US laws that targeted would-be immigrants from the south and east of Europe. On Staten Island, where Garibaldi spent his unlikely and unheroic few months making candles, the Italian community had grown to such an extent that a third of all the whites that lived there by 1935 were from Italy. The impact elsewhere was similarly dramatic, not least back in Italy, where rural communities, especially in the *Mezzogiorno*, were gutted by emigration. Garibaldi himself was aware of the link between the establishment of a new state called Italy, and the impetus its failings gave to those who saw better lives far, far away. He called emigration a "significant evil" that was directly related to the failures of "this miserable, poverty-stricken, humiliated Italy we see now, governed by the dregs of the nation". Garibaldi and fellow Ligurian Mazzini had been instrumental in bringing Italy about in the first place, and the last sight so many of those emigrants saw of that new country they had despaired of was those mountains and rocky cliffs that once meant home.

The Galata museum in Genoa displays a superb reconstruction of the conditions on board the emigrant ships, one that De Amicis would recognise. It goes one step further, and suggests that Italy is now host to the emigrants who come to its shores in search of a better life. It is not a message that is always well articulated in Italy, but in this port city the Equadorians, Senegalese, Colombians and others seem to fit in far better than they do in more judgemental cities. This is to the credit of the Genoese.

15

THE GREEN FIST OF PESTO

"Pesto speaks Ligurian. Only take a smell, and your ears will pick up
the vernacular: it is both harsh and tender at the same time, built
from drawled noises, whispered syllables, grim vowels."
Paolo Monera

One obvious consequence of the spread of Ligurians around the globe
is that the world has been introduced to the magical sauce called pesto.
This green alchemy is a direct answer to the harsh geography of Genoa's
hinterland, where there is barely any flat ground to grow anything. The
history of Genoa kicked off with that search for grain and other products
that they simply did not have access to. But the herbs that are the vital
element in Liguria's signature dish could be grown even on its steep and
rugged slopes, and thanks to pesto this unlikely region has a seat at the
hallowed top table when it comes to Italian food.

To Ligurians pesto is like crack cocaine. At a gathering of two
extended families on a hillside olive grove above Varazze, I saw universal
gasps of delight and even amazement when a multitude-sized bowl of
pesto was brought out as a meal's *primo piatto*. In Genoa it is eaten at
lunch by oily blue-collar workers and bored state employees, bustling
housewives and striking bus drivers, wealthy footballers and still
wealthier shipping tycoons. Across the world, supermarkets aisles are
stuffed with it (although often very flimsy versions), and weary mums

cook it up at dinnertime knowing that it is one of the things even the most finicky of children will take an almost Genoese delight in. My own recommendation is to eat the pasta and pesto from a white bowl (or plate if you are a barbarian like me). When you are finished, the remaining green oily puddle is so vivid that it gives the pleasing impression of having just devoured a Martian.

***

One of the first mentions of a recipe for pesto was in 1863, in *La Cuciniera Genovese* by Giovanni Battista Ratto. In this land without much in the way of agriculture it relied upon traditional ingredients such as olive oil, cheese and pine nuts, and a herb base that could be cultivated intensively on small patches of land. It could be added to soups or used as a sauce for pasta, and was a fantastic way to give returning sailors a shot of green vitamins after months out at sea.

Even the basic essence of pesto as a basil sauce has been open to question. In his superb study of Italian food, *Delizia*, John Dickie notes a reference to pesto in an 1844 dictionary that suggests the basil could be swapped with either parsley or marjoram. On the whole, however, it is the supplementary ingredients that have been argued over. In 1909 *The new cuisine of regional specialities* notes the use of "Dutch cheese", and under the heading "*taggioen co-o pesto*" a 1910 dictionary of Genoese dialect describes how the sauce can be used with pasta.

One of the most remarkable documents in Italian culinary history also mentions pesto. It was written by Second Lieutenant Giuseppe Chioni from Genoa. He was taken prisoner along with around 300,000 of his compatriots at the disastrous Battle of Caporetto in the First World War, and sent to an officers-only prison camp near Hanover in Germany. The Italian government had no policy of providing for POWs, and was frankly embarrassed by the debacle of Caporetto and the impact that mass surrenders might have on the home front. Chioni had to rely upon the Red Cross and meagre rations distributed by the Habsburg authorities. One in six of the POWs died, often from diseases related to malnourishment. One soldier, Giovanna Procacci, wrote in his memoir that "hunger became a kind of delirium: we talked of nothing but eating, and waited only for the moment when the miserable bowl of slops was distributed".[1]

Chioni and his comrades passed the time and fought off the hunger by talking about the foods that defined each region of the still-young country of Italy. He himself recalled that "Long periods of fasting force us to stay curled up so that the cramps of hunger feel less strong... each of us has remembered the exquisite meals and appetising sauces prepared by the delicate and caring hands of a far-distant mother or wife."[2] In 1919 Chioni returned to his native Genoa, got married and enjoyed a honeymoon in Tuscany. A photo from the time shows him still looking remarkably fresh-faced and young, despite his experiences on the battlefield and prison camp. He then returned to his pre-war job as a deputy stationmaster, and set about writing down the recipes they had discussed in the prison camp in Germany.

The result was called *Arte culinaria*, and I was lucky enough to see the desiccated and blotched original, wrapped in paper, stored in the L'Archivio storico della Provincia di Genova. Along with recipes for delicacies such as roast hedgehog (the trick is to include *pecorino* rind in the stuffing), Chioni of course includes a recipe for pesto. Some of it is familiar, such as the use of a pestle and mortar, and the addition of raw olive oil to lubricate the mixture. Other ingredients reflect a more unorthodox approach: parsley, spices and onion. He also misses out pine nuts.

The recipe would raise eyebrows now: there are orthodoxies and heresies in the pesto world. In an echo of the type of secret society beloved by *Da Vinci Code* readers, a Pesto Confraternity was formed on the 500th anniversary of Columbus bumping into the Americas. There is a Grand Master, and an Order of Paladins and Knights. The tricky concept of a definitive recipe is avoided, but there are seven core ingredients: basil, *Parmigiano-Reggiano* cheese, Sardinian *pecorino* cheese, pine nuts, garlic, salt and Ligurian extra-virgin olive oil, all mashed together carefully with a wooden pestle in a marble mortar. If you really want to get it right, the basil should come from one of a handful of little farms grown in a most unlikely suburb of Genoa.

***

Alberto Sacco lifted a small posy of leaves to my nostrils and invited me to sniff. It was like being punched in the nose by a large, green fist. Since 1831 his family has been growing basil in Prà. It is, so they all say, the best basil in the world. And given that the Genoese were clever enough to come up with something as simple yet intoxicating as pesto, the world ought to believe them.

The recipe for pesto is as simple and yet as complicated as any classic. Smash up those seven core ingredients in just the right quantities, and there you have it. But then there are variations that might involve walnuts, *Fiore Sardo* cheese, and the absence of garlic. But at its core, pesto's green alchemy is based upon basil leaves, and quite simply the better they are, the better the pesto.

Prà itself is an improbable spot. I drove there from the centre of Genoa, dropping off the *sopraelevata* near La Lanterna, then out through Sampierdarena and the often derelict shipbuilding yards of the western suburbs. If you go by train from Genoa you will trundle through those shabby suburbs, perhaps passing a Roma family camped out under a motorway flyover, and then get off next to the container port.

On the day of my visit the November wind was unusually bitter and there was a sifting of snow on the mountains ahead that lead up to the Beigua. Alberto was waiting at the gate of his basil farm, looking like a battle-scarred *Serie A* centre-half enjoying his busy retirement. He had a cigarette in one hand and was busy exchanging banter with a friend passing on the other side of the street. Then he turned to shake hands, and pointed into his office.

It was not really an office so much as a large room containing a row of enormous stainless steel fridges and somewhere to sit while doing the accounts. Despite being the fifth-generation Sacco to grow basil in Prà, there was a photograph of Torino players on the wall, and Alberto was quick to say that he also liked Manchester City (although less so since they had become successful – supporting Juventus' city rivals probably makes him feel comfortable in underdog shoes). In one fridge there was a wheel of cheese big enough to do service under a bus. In another there were slabs of frozen *semi lavorato* – basil mixed with oil and a bit of salt, and then frozen.

It is an operation that bears little resemblance to a traditional farm, but that is what it is. There are nine greenhouses, and they occupy a smallish, steeply sloping chunk of land that is sliced in two by a motorway. From the office you walk through a motorway underpass and up to the greenhouses above you, one to each terrace, with a car-wide track zigzagging up the middle. A small patch of land is used as a kitchen garden, and at the bottom of the slope is a large pile of cow manure – being organic is one of the ways Alberto can try to compete with the big boys. A rusted contraption at the door to one greenhouse had been employed to drive a winch that Alberto's father used to transport heavy items up and down the slope. Now they used a nifty blue tractor-like thing that cost the best part of €50,000.

From the top of the hill I could understand a bit more of Prà's geography. The greenhouses lay below, down the slope, on a series of giant steps, and beyond them the cars whizzed by on that section of *autostrada*, sheathed in grey metal cladding. Behind that sat a motley collection of rather featureless apartment blocks, two or three streets deep, before a road, then a railway track, and then the water. That water was only a temporary distraction before the multi-coloured container port was built on an artificial island like a toy building kit. Beyond that can be seen the open Mediterranean. Building the port changed the climate, said Alberto. Before then the basil had more sea air, and the mild sea air also stopped it ever getting too cold. When he was a boy he used to swim down there, and the whole area was farmland.

Each of the greenhouses was around 40 metres long, and filled by a hypnotic, intense smell of basil, tinged with a trace of diesel from the heating systems. In his father's time that trace was coal. Each greenhouse contained yet more terraces, each a carpet of verdant green. Sprinkler pipes ran overhead, and a billowing snake of polythene full of warm air fed along one wall.

The picking was done by hand, inch by inch, from a low wooden bench that brushed the highest leaves. Alberto and his brother sat side by side, one using the left hand and the other the right. Alberto could pick sixty bunches in an hour. "It's a gift. My brother can only do thirty." He grinned and moved his hand like a robot's grip. "*Machino mane.*" It looked like very hard work but he reassured me that he would rather be there than in an office, although nine hours of picking sometimes gave him backache. It takes two days to clear a greenhouse, with the smaller plants left in place to continue growing. The picking often takes place at night, after the plants have been watered to make them perky. In summer it gets too hot to work inside anyway. The stems of each sprig are wrapped in a piece of brown paper, and secured with a rubber band from an old metal tin labelled "Butter Cookies. Product of Denmark".

Despite what Alberto said, basil growing really is a tough business. He works twelve months a year, and only has Sunday afternoons off. His last proper holiday was seven years ago, and when he takes his wife and children skiing, he drops them off and drives back home to his greenhouses (he says he hates the feeling of snow beneath his feet). Growers also have a fungal illness to deal with. It affects basil and vines, but with vines you have a long growing season and plenty of time to deal with it; with basil you can see the leaves turn yellow and then lose the lot in 72 hours.

There are no big companies growing basil in Prà. There are just five or six families, each running their own semi-vertical farms. So why Prà? Alberto said that every region has a typical food, and that food tastes as it does because of where it is grown. In Parma the ham tastes different, and so Parma ham is famous. In Prà the basil has always had the perfect mix of sun and sea air, and is distinctive as a result. It was a disarmingly simple explanation, but experts say that the basil from Prà is distinctive because it has no minty tinge to it.

Competition is tough, but the Prà label is well respected in a region that devours pesto in gargantuan quantities. (Do you eat pesto often? Oh no, said Alberto dismissively. Only two or three times a week.) The big producers in Liguria can ship in *semi lavorato* basil from places like Vietnam, or they can grow their own crop once every 48 hours with pesticides and lots of machines. It is not the same. Alberto's plants need two weeks before they can be picked in the summer, and as long as 35 or 40 days in the winter (that is why they preserve some as *semi lavorato* blocks, to keep production of pesto up during the darkest months).

Is it worth the undoubted effort? Well, through many lunchtimes of testing I can swear that there is a world of difference between the astonishingly zingy real thing and the disappointing imposter that hangs around in murky jars in the pasta aisle of supermarkets the world over. And yes, Prà pesto is a step above even that zingy real stuff. Like wine, or good quality steak, there is a difference, and once you have tasted it, it is obvious.

***

It was one of Italy's best-known chefs that suggested a trip to Alberto's greenhouses at Prà. Luciano Belloni was a well-shaven, jocular and animated man, who suited his beautifully pressed gold-buttoned chef's smock, its blue collar carrying a circle of gold stars and Italian tricolour piping. He had the stubby and harassed fingernails of a hard worker, set in immaculately washed hands, and despite his 70 plus years he bounced off the fittings of his restaurant with energy and bonhomie. In Genoa he was better known under the name of his restaurant, Zeffirino's, and he was a global evangelist for good pesto.

Zeffirino has been the proud supplier of pesto to the Vatican for forty years. On the wall of his restaurant there was a richly illuminated certificate (although the word does not seem right when it is signed by the Pope himself) from John Paul II, giving a very specific special blessing to every member of the family, from (the original) Zeffirino Belloni downwards. No sooner had Obama settled into the White House than he was sent a packet of Zeffirino pesto. Zeffirino's clientele has included Barry White, an astronaut, Mikhail Gorbachev, Roger Moore, Gina Lollobrigida, Fidel Castro and Cassius Clay, and one of his posters carries the legend *Ambasciatore della Cucina Italiana nel Mondo*. Most of the Italian cooking that he promotes across the globe is Ligurian.

The first course that he served was, of course, pesto. On one side of the plate there was a predictably spectacular pesto with homemade pasta, and on the other something richer but slightly less intensely green: *Paffuttelli alla Frank*, a type of pasta stuffed with fruit that he invented for Frank Sinatra himself.

Zeffirino met Sinatra ringside at a boxing match at Madison Square Garden forty years ago. He has always loved sport, and represented Italy at wrestling (useful for when customers refuse to pay, he said). He even hosted exhibition boxing matches at the restaurant. On this occasion he was in New York to present a trophy, and, as is his way, began talking to Sinatra. After that meeting, the singer started demanding Zeffirino's food as part of his backstage rider, and the friendship led to Zeffirino setting up a restaurant in Las Vegas with a 12-metre-high bar. (The Genoese of times past, not least Andrea Doria, might have found it hard to stomach that this new venture was situated in "The Venetian" casino. Guests are invited to "indulge in Grand Venetian style", and there is a "Grand Canal Menu" for lunch.) Sinatra used to sign his letters to Zeffirino "Cousin Frank".

The second course was the most succulent bream that I have ever eaten, cooked with traditional Ligurian ingredients, including wine, pine nuts and aromatic *taggiasca* olives. As a motto on the ceiling said, "A fish has to swim three times: first in water; second in oil; third in wine." Before serving my wife he offered me the fish's head – women already have enough brains, he suggested. It was no surprise that like most of the world's best restaurateurs and chefs, he was a showman as well as an extremely skilful cook.

He also had a keen business sense, something that a good number of Italians have been blessed with over the years. Zeffirino catered for the Costa cruise company, although obviously not at the all-you-can-eat-breakfast-buffet end of the scale. His restaurant was open from noon until midnight, which handily caught the new Russian tourists that came through Genoa, either from cruise ships or on their way to spend their bundles of roubles on Riviera properties (the website, tellingly, is in Italian and Russian). The Russians, for some reason, seemed to like eating and drinking in the middle of the afternoon. He had restaurants in Brazil, Germany, Hong Kong, Las Vegas and near Portofino, all staffed by family members. (What if a son or daughter chose a different path? "I'm like Mussolini: you're either with me or against me," he answered with a chuckle.) "Fake" Zeffirino restaurants apparently exist in several countries.

Zeffirino's approach was all about attention to detail rather than short-termism. He had harsh words for those Italians, like Roman taxi drivers, who take advantage of tourists without thinking about tomorrow. He was also keenly aware of the importance of building a brand, telling a story. He has files full of old receipts for shipments of pesto to popes and presidents, and whole archives full of press cuttings. Celebrities were as much part of the Zeffirino brand as the Vatican and basil sauce, and we spent the gap between courses listening happily to him telling us some of his more memorable anecdotes (it was a quiet service).

One involved Zeffirino becoming good friends with Luciano Pavarotti, who had a flat above the restaurant, halfway up the mosaic arcades of Via XX Settembre. Thirty or so years ago, Zeffirino was called in to arrange the catering for a month-long Pavarotti tour of China. Pavarotti himself required three entire containers full of food to last the month, but his girlfriend was outraged and told Zeffirino that three containers would kill him; they settled on one, containing a tonne or so of food, including gallons and gallons of pesto and 1,600 bottles of Lambrusco. In China they turned part of Pavarotti's suite into a version of the Genoese restaurant, complete with pictures hanging on the wall. At noon every day the singer settled down for lunch with his father, Zeffirino, and the chef's brother. At dinner they did the same but were joined by TV crews and journalists. One night Pavarotti reacted to constant requests for him to sing by saying he would, but only if they could find a Chinese who could join in. Somebody dug out a member of the hotel's kitchen staff who could sing opera, and between them they kept going for two hours. The party went on that night until 5 a.m., after which the hotel staff cooked a private Chinese banquet that included everything from noodles to jellyfish.

Like Alberto Sacco with his allegiance to Torino, Luciano Zeffirino also looked beyond Liguria for his roots. In his case it is to Emilia-Romagna, from which he came to Genoa at the age of nine; he immediately became fluent in Genoese dialect, which (unlike his Italian) he speaks without a "foreign" accent. His home is now indisputably Liguria, the region that gave the world a sauce he loves so much that he built a culinary empire around it.

***

As Alberto Sacco's grumbles about Vietnamese basil suggest, the world of pesto is not without controversy. In 2002 the head of Liguria's regional government, Sandro Biasotti, announced that he was boycotting Nestlé products, accusing the multinational of "copyrighting" two types of basil (to be named "pesto" and "San Remo"). The conflict was resolved peacefully, but there remains tension over the importation of foreign (i.e. non-Ligurian) basil, and an organisation called Prà Basil Park was set up in 2006 to defend the interests of producers. (Two months later gigantic hailstorms smashed many of the Prà greenhouses, and destroyed 80 per cent of the crop.)

To Ligurians these things matter, because pesto is accepted as one of the mortal world's unarguable good things. Any restaurant will sell bowlfuls of the stuff, spiked with the odd green bean and lump of potato, even though diners eat it several times a week at home. Despite the best efforts of the Grand Master of the Pesto Confraternity, recipes continue to differ, even at the highest level of pestology. Luciano

Zeffirino uses walnuts in his version, and Alberto Sacco is not alone in producing a garlic-free pesto over in Prà. During the infamous G8 meeting in Genoa in 2001, the sixteen Michelin-starred Ligurian chefs who cooked for the assembled world leaders were instructed to produce a garlic-free "basil sauce" rather than pesto, apparently in deference to the garlic-averse Silvio Berlusconi and the Japanese delegation.[3] For some this reflected the sanitisation of an unapologetically earthy city during the summit. In response, Genoese anti-globalisation protesters threw garlic bulbs at Berlusconi. The Genoa G8 summit is now remembered for its violent confrontations, the killing of a young protester, Carlo Guiliani, by a *carabiniere*, and a brutal *carabinieri* raid on a school used by campaigners and journalists. Alluding to the beatings, Beppe Grillo, Genoa's agitator-in-chief, noted that "After the G8, Genoa isn't the same any more. *Pesto alla Genovese* means something different now."[4]

The last word on pesto, before I head off to the kitchen to cook some with the pasta twists known as *trofie*, goes to John Dickie, who gave the best single-line description of eating it that I have ever read. If this is not your experience, then you are probably not eating the proper stuff: "To eat *pesto* is to have the olfactory sense so pervaded by fragrance that solid food is exalted to a point fleetingly within reach of the spiritual realm."[5] It is not the type of sentence that could have been written about many foodstuffs. Pesto is special.

16

THE ENGLISH GIFT OF FOOTBALL

"Football is a public game of two groups of young men, on foot and unarmed, who pleasingly compete to move a medium-sized inflated ball from one end of the piazza to the other, for the sake of honour."
Giovanni Maria de'Bardi

It was at around four in the afternoon that the other boat appeared and started to follow them. They were out of sight of land, but knew they were not far from the coast of Somalia. It had been thirty-one days since they had pushed off from a beach in Sri Lanka, all sixty of them, Singhalese and Tamil alike, crammed into an open fishing boat 22 metres long. The boat was so small and unsteady in heavy seas that they had to crowd to one end to counterbalance the engine.

There were five men in the other boat – more teenagers than men, really. They were armed, and their smaller, quicker boat soon caught up with the Sri Lankans. Niranga remembers that they were feral and very dirty, and looked like animals. They threatened to shoot everybody on board, and took everything of value: gold, money, navigational equipment. They also took the food: curry, lentils and tinned salmon. It was not a sophisticated pirate attack, but it left the sixty Sri Lankans adrift in the Indian Ocean, somewhere near Somalia and the Horn of Africa, facing death. Modern Somali piracy is sometimes treated as a harmless solution to hard times, an ingenious business model worthy of dissection in the *Harvard Business Review*.[1] In reality it involves kidnapping, murder, torture and mutilation. The pirates abandoned those sixty Sri Lankans with every expectation that they would all suffer a desperate and painful death.

For eight days the boat sailed north, the skipper navigating by the stars and sun. For food they caught octopus and fish, eating them raw. They ran into storms, with waves so big they would sail slowly up their crests before crashing down on the other side. Those on board started to fall ill, and many just sat crying. Niranga clutched a photo of his wife and four-month-old son, and thought he would never see either of them again.

Somehow, the skipper's skill got them to Egypt. But by this time nobody had any papers, so they could not disembark. They anchored near a lighthouse at the entrance to the Suez Canal. A street trader took pity on them, and they used his mobile phone to contact the agent that had organised their fated voyage. Through him, they were able to get hold of enough money to buy water and potatoes. They also bought a GPS device, because although the only option for them now was to turn back, they knew that they had to avoid going close to the Somali coast.

The potatoes ran out after just four days, but the metabolisms of those on board had slowed down so much that food was not their main concern. Water was another matter, and when it ran out after fourteen days they were reduced to catching the rain in nylon sheets. Many fell horribly ill. Niranga remembers the skipper lying next to those suffering the most, trying to comfort them.

Eighty-five days after pushing off from a Sri Lankan beach they arrived back home, at midnight. Niranga's muscles and sense of balance had eroded so severely during weeks on the open sea in a small boat that when he stepped ashore onto the sand he could neither stand nor walk. He had a massive beard and his fingernails had grown long, like claws. When he made it to his house his father-in-law thought he was a ghost and would not let him in. His family had given up hope that he was alive, and had given alms in recognition of his presumed death.

Over a decade on, and Niranga's life is beyond anything that he might have imagined when he stepped, unsteadily, back onto Sri Lankan soil. He wears a sharp suit, with his black, tousled hair as immaculate as any Italian's. He has a good job, and his family lives with him in Genoa. Above his chair hang a couple of sporting medals, the blue and red pennant of the Genoa CFC football team, and a cricket bat. That cricket bat is not merely a reminder of his South Asian roots: Niranga is the captain of one of Genoa's most venerable sporting institutions, and the bat is a reminder of the debt that Italy owes to Genoa for introducing its favourite sport, football.

***

For the Genoese who knew their history, the opening of the Suez Canal in 1869 was an important moment. Ever since the Ottomans had captured Constantinople and Khizr Barbarossa had commanded the Eastern Mediterranean at the head of an Ottoman fleet, the sea that had had given Genoa life had struggled to breathe. Now, once again, it was a route to the Orient. Britain was especially keen to use Suez to reach India and beyond, and Genoa became an important coal station on the way. This linked in with the development of the Italian railways, and in particular the track that led up through the pass from Genoa to Turin, which opened in 1854. These developments buttressed Genoa's traditional role as a trading conduit for northern Italy, and soon it was developing its own manufacturing industries on its western fringes in places like the former fishing village of Sampierdarena. With the British ships came services such as maritime insurance and finance. And with these services came an influx of Brits, setting up two places of worship in the city, a cemetery, and an enthusiasm for organised sport.

Cricket itself had first appeared in Italy in 1793, in Naples, thanks to a visit by part of Nelson's fleet. But it was in Genoa that the game gained its first true foothold. On 7 September 1893 the Genoa Cricket and Athletics Club was founded, with a Mr G. D. Fawcus as the first cricket captain. A scribbled piece of paper from the time lists the club's officers, and notes that the patron of the new venture was HBM's Consul, C. A. Payton.

In 1896 an English doctor named James Richardson Spensley joined the club, and within a year became captain of their new "Foot-ball" team. This new venture obviously took off, and the organisation's name duly changed to Genoa Cricket and Foot-ball Club. The club remains Italy's oldest, affiliated to the new Federazione Italiano del Football since 1898.[2]

From Genoa the game spread within the "industrial triangle", up to Turin and Milan. Several aspects of the modern game were visible quite quickly. Rules on payments to players in this nominally amateur era were routinely flouted, and there was a lot of misbehaviour by supporters: a Genoa CFC–Juventus game in 1905 had to be replayed after fans climbed onto the pitch; in 1912 stones were thrown at the referee during an Andrea Doria–Inter game; and in 1920 a Genoa CFC supporter attacked one of Pro Vercelli's mid-fielders during a match. Fans also started travelling with their teams on Italy's railways. A photo from 1923 shows a group of Genoa CFC supporters on their way to an away match, next to a railway carriage. They are waving banners and graffiti have been scrawled on the train ("Fan Carriage" and the especially pleasing "Foot-ball, acute mania"). A couple of years later a total of five matches were needed between Bologna and Genoa CFC to decide a highly controversial championship. There were violent clashes between fans, even involving gunfire, and Bologna's final triumph in a game played in an empty stadium left Genoa CFC stranded on nine championships won (denying them the right to sew a star onto their shirts like Italy's other most successful clubs – that tenth title has remained firmly out of reach ever since).

James Richardson Spensley's name is still well recognised among those Genoese who know their history. The city's multimedia Museo della storia del Genoa (note the English spelling), tucked away behind the Palazzo San Giorgio and virtually under the *sopraelevata*, has a treasure-trove of Spensley memorabilia. There is even an official copy of his birth certificate: he came into the world in Oak Villas, Lordship Lane, Stoke Newington (in north-east London) on 17 May 1867. Photos show him with his beard cut into different designs: from a smart, clipped style suitable for any Victorian gentleman; to something far more woolly and expansive, resembling that of Edward Lear; he also appears clean-shaven; and in a photo taken on the outbreak of the First World War Spensley poses with grand moustachios, wearing a smart uniform and leaning on an officer's cane.

The museum documents the key role that Genoa CFC played in making *calcio* the national sport of Italy. Its creditable approach to energy efficiency means that at quieter times the lights switch on and off every five seconds, thanks to a proliferation of badly calibrated motion-sensing switches. It is also studiously dismissive of the existence of a second team in the city, other than in an array of video screens showing Genoa CFC triumphing over Sampdoria in various *Derby della Lanternas* from years gone by. My father-in-law would not be pleased (but then again, he would not visit).

Genoa CFC was also responsible for introducing the English word "mister" into Italian football: even today it is widely used as the word for the team manager. This dates back to 1912 when the former Blackburn Rovers player William Garbutt (or Guglielmo Garbutt, as he was known in Genoa) became Italy's first professional coach, introducing hot showers and systematic training sessions. He could often be found wearing a bowler hat, or stalking between his exercising players, looking very much like a man whom nobody would cross.

Garbutt's career also took him to Naples (while managing Napoli he adopted a local orphan, Concettina Ciletti) and Bilbao. But like Spensley, his name will always be associated with Genoa, the city and the football club. He was on another stretch in charge of Genoa CFC in 1940 when Italy entered the Second World War. He lingered longer than he should have done before fleeing, because the team had just reached the cup final. Garbutt and his Irish wife, Anna, eventually fled to the mountains the day before the match (which they lost anyway). After being captured, they were thrown into prison. But Genoa was a city with a great deal of sympathy for the man and his reputation, so the couple were released and sent into exile down south to a small village near Salerno. When Mussolini fell in 1943 they were allowed to leave. Tragically Anna was killed while taking shelter from an Allied air raid in a church near Imola.

Even after the war there was no separating Garbutt from Genoa. His return for yet another spell as manager brought large crowds onto the streets, and when this last stint in charge ended in 1948, he stayed on for a few more years as a scout. Guglielmo Garbutt, the original "mister", had been in charge of Genoa CFC for a grand total of sixteen seasons. He died in 1964 after a retirement in Leamington Spa (where his adopted daughter Concettina cared for him). Few noticed his passing in England, but in Italy every major newspaper carried an obituary.

Other key figures from the club's history are venerated in the museum, including the Genoa CFC and Italy goalkeeper during the 1920s, Giovanni De Prá, who was apparently noted for his *plasticità* (plasticity). On the way out there is a fan's banner featuring a badly-printed Andy

Capp (the cartoon character who hails from where I grew up in north-east England), along with the inscription *"..Perche' un tifo cosi' tu non l'avevi mai visto! Fossa Grifoni."*

***

Although the reference to cricket never left the Genoa CFC badge (except during the fascist interlude when it was briefly *Genova 1893 Circolo del Calcio*) the actual sport disappeared entirely, other than in the gin-soaked imaginings of the odd Englishman who washed up in the port. In 2007, however, that changed, when Genoese cricket spluttered back into life like an accidental phoenix.

Mark Ebury is an English teacher at the Deledda International School in Genoa. Back in 2007 he was searching for a physical activity for his pupils that did not involve the inevitable *calcio*, when a Scottish/Pakistani friend left him two cricket bats before disappearing back on the plane to Britain. Mark started teaching the pupils the basics of whacking a ball about, when a secretary at the school spotted the bats and made the connection to that fabled but largely forgotten sport associated with the early days of Genoa CFC.

The secretary's unexpected interest in this link back to Genoese history led first to a series of phone calls, and then to a meeting between Mark and a group of enthusiastic but rather cricket-ignorant Italians. They were keen to breathe life back into the whole idea of "Genoa cricket", but with little idea of what on earth cricket involved. Mark told them (no doubt leaving out the bit about games lasting for five days), and suggested some kind of English-themed family charity cricket match, complete with slices of cake and teapots. They countered with more ambition, contacted the local newspapers and set up an exhibition match in a fully-fledged stadium.

The match itself was a remarkable success. Mark trained two teams of Italian school kids, and doctored the rules heavily to make sure they did not get bored. A whole gaggle of players from the subcontinent also turned up, along with India's local diplomatic representative. They batted and bowled on a strip of fake grass that Mark had bought from a local shop, at stumps that his father had knocked up to order from a few bits and pieces of wood.

The next dizzying step was to enter the national championships: fifty or so wannabes turned up to trials, and a selection was made including Indians, Sri Lankans, Pakistanis, Bangladeshis and Englishmen (an Italian made the team in the second season). At the first two-day tournament in Bologna at *Serie C* level, the team finished seventh out of sixteen teams. Now, under the captaincy of Niranga, they are in *Serie A* and aiming for the national title.

I met Niranga and the rest of the team at a book launch in the Museo della storia del Genoa. The book being launched was all about Italian cricket, which struck me as rather a niche interest despite the story of Genoa CFC. The room, however, was full. Genoa's team stood in their club tracksuits in front of display cases full of football memorabilia, and several rows of seats were filled with some of Mark's more eager pupils and their intrigued parents. The panel talked with straight faces to this Italian audience about the qualities that cricket taught its players, like patience and fair play, and everybody applauded gamely. Certain aspects of cricket are actually rather suitable for the Italian temperament – such as sensitivity to changes in the weather and the wearing of natty white outfits (not unlike the ever-dapper Italian navy). Niranga and his mainly Asian team smiled and felt part of one of Italy's most important sporting institutions. The fact that the current incumbent of the position first held by G. D. Fawcus had also fallen prey to the age-old Genoese institution of piracy on the high seas, albeit in a modern Somali incarnation, was a neat little twist of history.

17

SHIPBUILDING IN MODERN ITALY

"Great naval architects designed her, great seamen of the old Genoese
lineage man her."
Introduction to an advertising pamphlet accompanying the launch of
the *Andrea Doria*

When the collision happened, some people had gone off to bed, to their
tourist class bunks and their wood-panelled first class suites. But many
were still up, enjoying a last night on board, before a scheduled arrival
in New York at 9 a.m. It was, after all, only just past 11 p.m. on 25 July
1956. Nineteen-year-old Melania Ansuini, who was migrating to
California, was dancing to the sounds of an impromptu band made up
from other emigrants, in the social hall for tourist class passengers. The
first class lounge was also still busy, full of passengers drinking cocktails
and champagne, smoking and talking. The Italian Line had
commissioned artists to decorate the lounge, and the walls were hung
with paintings and tapestries and a mural by Salvatore Fiume that paid
tribute to the great Italian masters. Dominating the room was a massive
bronze that purported to be the great Genoese admiral Andrea Doria
himself, in full armour and with his sword slung by his side (looking
rather like Robocop). Above him hung a silver-coloured Doria coat of
arms. For centuries the crest had been kept in one of the various Palazzo
Dorias dotted around Genoa, and had been donated by the Marquis

Giambattista Doria. If anybody was listening carefully they might have heard the ship's fog whistle give its shrill blast every hundred seconds.

The *Andrea Doria* was nearing the end of its 101st transatlantic crossing, from Genoa to New York. Although it was dark and they were surrounded by thick fog, the crew of the *Andrea Doria* had spotted the other ship as a green blip on its radar at 17 miles. It was heading in the opposite direction, directly towards them, 20 miles north of where eastbound ships were supposed to sail. At first this was troubling but not necessarily a problem: although ships were meant to pass port-side to port-side, their bearings suggested that they would comfortably pass starboard to starboard, perhaps a mile from each other. When the distance between them had narrowed to three and a half miles, the captain ordered a nudge to port, to widen the gap. When the crew were finally able to make out the lights of the approaching ship through the thick fog they realised it was turning slowly towards them. The other ship seemed to be making a doomed attempt to pass the *Andrea Doria* port-side to port-side. That cautious, abstract monitoring of green blips had become an all-too-real emergency. In most cases, ships about to collide would both turn towards each other, as glancing blows from streamlined prows do far less damage than a head-on collision directly into the side of a ship. But Captain Piero Calamai, a Genoese sailor from a sailing family, also made a final attempt to outrun contact, and ordered the *Andrea Doria* to steer hard left. The wheel spun around, but nothing was instant on such large ships. The ship continued straight for several long seconds before its rudders began biting into the seawater, and it started its slow turn to the left.

Then the other ship hit. From the bridge the crew of the *Andrea Doria* knew it was coming well before contact was made. The painted metal prow of the *Stockholm* smashed right into the starboard side of the larger ship, ripping through its skin and demolishing several cabins. The shock waves shuddered through the ship, and the waves thudded the *Stockholm's* prow again and again into the hole it had made, fully 10 metres inside the *Andrea Doria's* hull. Some passengers were killed immediately, including Maria Sergio, a doughty-looking mother from Calabria, and her four young children. One passenger, Linda Morgan, was asleep in her cabin wearing her yellow pyjamas. She woke up to find that her whole bed had somehow ended up inside the prow of the *Stockholm* (her only serious injury was a broken arm). The lights spluttered all over the Italian ship and went out in some rooms. It was a while before the full nature of the collision became apparent, and the *Andrea Doria* started to list heavily to one side as sea water poured into her ruptured hull. A few lifeboats were lowered into the chilly water, but most of the passengers, told to wait at their muster stations, were still oblivious of any need to abandon ship. One passenger, Frank Clifton, found himself and just three other passengers in a lifeboat with forty crewmen and many empty seats. When they reached the safety of the *Stockholm* the other ship's crew treated the escaping crewmen with justifiable scorn.

The *Andrea Doria* began to lurch further onto its side, and it soon became clear that the ship had to be abandoned. Some of it was orderly, but for others there was a frantic, chaotic rush to safety. Passengers dangled above the waves of the Atlantic on cargo nets and rope ladders, while lifeboats fought the swell to get underneath them. Children were thrown into blankets held as emergency safety nets, while adults took their chances and let themselves drop, sometimes into the sea and sometimes into the smaller craft, injuring themselves in the hope of escape. Thanks to the heavy list of the ship the eight gravity-launch lifeboats along one entire side of the *Andrea Doria* could not be lowered into the water and dangled uselessly high above the water near where many of the passengers had gathered. Crucially for the rescue effort, another liner, the *Île de France* (under the improbable-sounding monocle-wearing stand-in master Baron Raoul de Beaudéan), was also not too far from the Nantucket lightship; it turned around and headed to the scene to help, saving many lives.

Two men, Thure Peterson and a waiter, Giovanni Rovelli, worked for hours deep down in the stricken ship, trying to free passengers trapped inside their cabins at the point of impact. They knew that at any moment they might be outflanked by rising waters, or that the *Andrea Doria* would simply lose all buoyancy and slip forever into the dark waters. Peterson's wife, Martha, was among those who were stuck, surrounded by the twisted steel and splintered wood that used to be cabin 56. The two men managed to reach her using car jacks to prop open walls, but she finally died from the injuries that she had sustained in the collision five hours earlier.

With the *Andrea Doria* sinking lower in the water, whirlpools formed around it as water poured in through gashes into its belly, and lifeboat crews had to pull with all their might to escape the suction. The ship's captain, Piero Calamai, told Junior Second Officer Guido Badano, "If you go back to Genoa and see my family, you will be my witness. You can say I am at peace with myself. I did what I had to do." His clear intention was to go down with his ship, but at 5.30 a.m. on 26 July he joined one of the last three lifeboats and escaped.

Unknown to the brave crewmen leaving in those last lifeboats, one passenger remained on board. Robert Hudson was also a seaman, and had recently injured his back on a freighter. He had been heavily drugged to deal with the pain, and only woke at 5.10 a.m. to find the emergency lighting on and the ship about to sink. He climbed along half-submerged dark passageways, through wrecked door frames and up mangled stairwells, and finally found a way out. He then had to convince a lifeboat to come and rescue him, despite the risk of being sucked under with the sinking hulk of the 29,000 tonne ship. Thankfully the lifeboat crew did turn around and pick him up, and he happily landed up on the tanker *Robert E Hopkins* with a change of dry clothes and a large glass of bourbon.

At just past 10 a.m., the *Andrea Doria*, a ship with Genoa in its DNA, sank beneath the waters of the North Atlantic. The final photo is of the last patch of stern on its port side, sinking under boiling water with one screw in the air, and the word "Andrea" visible above smaller lettering spelling out "Genov..." It sank into almost 70 metres of water, leaving a whirlpool that span around for fifteen minutes afterwards. Altogether 1,660 people had been taken off. The final death toll was 51, of which 46 were passengers on the *Andrea Doria* and the others were from the *Stockholm's* crew.

Some of the survivors went on to live remarkable lives. One, a priest called Tom Kelly, had led a band of men to gather life jackets from the perilous lower decks. He eventually left the priesthood and married a former nun. Another passenger, Mike Stoller, was a song writer, travelling thanks to the royalties from a song called "Black denim trousers and motorcycle boots". When he cleared customs in New York after the accident, his writing partner Jerry Leiber told him that Elvis Presley had just recorded their song "Hound dog". He would go on to write twenty other songs for Elvis, including "Jailhouse rock". The father of Linda Morgan, the young girl who woke up to find herself and her bed jammed into the wrecked prow of the *Stockholm*, was the ABC radio newscaster Edward P. Morgan. Despite believing at the time that he had lost his daughter in the accident, he continued to broadcast about the sinking of the *Andrea Doria*. Later, when he found out that his daughter had survived, he went back on air:

"Within the space of 24 hours this reporter has been pushed down the elevator shaft to the sub-basement of despair and raised again to the heights of incredible joy, washed, one suspects, with slightly extravagant rivulets of some heavenly champagne."

The relieved father signed off his broadcast with "This is Edward Morgan, saying goodnight from New York."

Captain Piero Calamai never recovered from the accident. At the time of that last voyage he was 58, tall and with a muscular frame. His face was weathered by many years at sea and he had a bulbous nose. He had been at sea since graduating from Genoa's Nautical Institute at the age of eighteen, and was earning a handsome $625 a month doing a job that most Genoese could only dream of. Years later, one of the *Andrea Doria* passengers on the night it sank, George P. Kerr (the head of Procter and Gamble in Europe), spotted the hunched captain walking the streets of Genoa like a zombie. For the last fifteen years of his life Captain Calamai did not talk about the *Andrea Doria*, but on his deathbed in 1972 he cried out to his daughter Marina, "Is it alright? Are the passengers saved?" Most of the rest of his crew had more peaceful retirements, in Genoa, Camogli and other small coastal towns and villages of Liguria.

***

The *Andrea Doria* was a proud part of the golden age of Italian transatlantic shipping. It had been launched from Genoa's Ansaldo yard on 16 June 1951, after nine million man hours of work, and was equipped with the most modern equipment, from radar screens to an automatic pilot. It was also beautiful, even by the standards of the age, with all its vertical lines raked slightly backwards, so that even when it was sitting in dock it suggested elegant speed. It was the first transatlantic liner to have separate swimming pools for each passenger class, along with separate dining rooms, movie theatres, gymnasia and promenades. Only the chapel and hospital were communal. It was the thirteenth largest passenger vessel in the world.

The ship made its first Atlantic crossing in 1953, running into a storm that left twenty passengers injured. On the fateful voyage, its 101st, it left Genoa for Cannes, Naples, Gibraltar and then across past the Azores towards New York. It was carrying 1,134 passengers. The 190 in first class included two movie stars, two ballet stars, the mayor of Philadelphia, and several prominent journalists and businessmen. The 267 in second class were mainly middle-class people on holiday. The 677 passengers in tourist class, including Maria Sergio and her four children, were largely Italian emigrants from poor villages, looking to start a new life on the other side of the Atlantic. On B deck there were nine cars, including one experimental model that had been built by Ghia of Turin for Chrysler. For those rich enough to enjoy the first class facilities, it was the Concorde of its age, despite its rather more stately speed and more expansive opportunities for a stroll at sundown. For the other passengers it was everything from the streamlined means to a new life of opportunity, to a once-in-a-lifetime chance to explore another continent.

The *Andrea Doria* was the heir to a generation of remarkable ships that marked the country's coming of age. Perhaps chief among them was the *Rex*. A vision in Art Deco, the *Rex* was higher than the Colosseum, longer than a football stadium, and achieved immortal glory by capturing the Blue Riband (*Nastro Azzuro*) for the quickest transatlantic crossing. She had handsome, unbroken and pure lines, carrying the promise of streamlined power from her bow to her stern. Other ships, like Germany's *Bremen*, looked utilitarian by comparison. Federico Fellini used the *Rex* as the symbol of a hard-working, internationalised Italy, and posters of her still adorn shops in Genoa's *centro storico*. She was pre-war Italy's chance to show that it could rub shoulders with the French, British, Germans and Americans as a modern industrial nation.

Genoa was one of the centres of that modern Italian industry, and the city's shipyards were where those streamlined ocean-going behemoths were born. Contemporary photos show the Genoa shipyards to the west of the old port, crammed in against the mountains and with their dry docks virtually on the beaches of Sampierdarena. The prows of vast ships under construction surge up under the noses of housewives pegging their clean laundry to lines strung between the top floors of apartment blocks. Daredevil workers clambered up endless rickety ladders, propped against half-finished hulls that reached most of the way to the sky, balancing tools in one hand and gripping the rungs with the other.

The completion of a new ship was always an event, and when the *Rex* was launched by King Victor Emmanuel III and Queen Elena (the ship's "Godmother"), 100,000 people watched it slip between the cranes into the Mediterranean. That was on 1 August 1931; it then took a further year for the interiors to be finished. Passengers were able to spend their time dancing, swimming, smoking, boxing, fencing, playing tennis, exercising, drinking, eating, or watching shows. There was even a tanning salon, and a special balcony in the chapel so that first class passengers could pray without mixing with the common people. First class passengers could also drive their cars (or have them driven for them) directly into the hold through doors on the sides, and once there they found lifts that took them directly to their cabins. It had four classes: first, special, tourist and third, and enough jobs and demanding passengers to keep 876 crewmen busy.

Despite the fanfare (not least from the fascist authorities), the *Rex* had an inauspicious start. On its maiden voyage, stuffed with celebrities and aiming for a record-breaking run across the Atlantic, it broke down before reaching Gibraltar and had to be towed. Several disgruntled passengers jumped ship and took the *Europa* from Germany instead, only to find the *Rex* at anchor in New York when they arrived.

In May 1933 the *Rex's* sister ship, the *Conte di Savoia*, almost captured the Blue Riband, which at the time was something like a combination of the land-speed record, launching a successful Mars probe, and being voted the world's best airline. For Italy, a young country that felt keenly its recent poverty and relative backwardness, capturing the transatlantic record sat next to imperial ambitions as a sign that they had arrived on the world stage. Mussolini was watching closely.

When the *Rex* made its Blue Riband run, its rival the *Europa* held the transatlantic record for Germany. The Italian Line was goaded by an article in the *New York Times* that suggested that the Italians were simply not up to the task. The voyage started well on 10 August 1933, but the effort was almost derailed in the mid-Atlantic when (like the ill-fated *Andrea Doria* two decades later) it ran into an area of thick fog, with visibility down to just 30 metres. A decision had to be made by Captain Francesco Tarabotto, a La Spezia native with an oval face and a neatly clipped goatee beard: should he make a run for it and risk everything, or should he play it safe? The captain decided to go for glory, and without the benefit of radar he radioed ahead to make any boats that might be in the area aware that the *Rex* was coming through. His foolhardy bravery succeeded, and they arrived in New York in record-breaking time. The transatlantic stretch had taken a couple of minutes less than four days and 14 hours, at an average speed of 28.92 knots. Fascist Italy had its *Nastro Azzuro*.

A cable arrived in New York on 8.07 a.m. on 18 August, congratulating the captain "*per il record magnifico del* Rex", signed simply =Mussolini=. Notices were put up in Rome saying "At the order of the Duce all goals are reached!" *Il Duce* was also credited for his decision to build a modern, world-class fleet in the shipyards of Genoa.

The glory did not last too long. The *Rex* lost the Blue Riband, and in 1936 Italy's image abroad suffered from that other prestige project of Mussolini's, the invasion of Ethiopia. In response the owners of the *Rex* tried to attract more American passengers by merging second and tourist class. At the same time there was an increase in numbers of Jewish passengers, fleeing persecution in Germany, and new features on board the *Rex* were a kosher menu and a rabbi (Max Green from the United States).

During the Second World War the ship was moved to Trieste, and photos from the time show the *Rex* looking decidedly shabby compared to its glamorous heyday. On 8 September 1944 she ran aground near the Slovenian coast, and was attacked by British and South African Beaufighters. They raked her with cannon fire and rockets, leaving her on fire and sinking onto her port side. The final end came slowly, and in 1947 the Yugoslavs began to rip the *Rex* apart in the shallow waters to salvage its steel. It was an ignominious end to a craft that had encapsulated the thrusting ambitions of an entire nation, in sweeping lines that proved that machines could be as beautiful as anything produced by nature.

***

After the demise of the *Rex* had echoed the collapse of fascism, in post-war years the Genoese shipyards grew from strength to strength. The *Andrea Doria* was one of hundreds of ships that were launched from the Ligurian coast as the Italian economy recovered from war and the *Duce*.

SHIPBUILDING IN MODERN ITALY

Even today, Genoa has its share of maritime engineering, and for a different market has developed a niche centre of excellence for refurbishing and converting yachts for oligarchs. It is a proud tradition for a city that reached its heyday in the years when the Mediterranean was dominated by the galley. In keeping with those days, this continued vitality also hints at victory in the continuing rivalry with Venice.

The Museo Navale in Venice is a fantastic place to visit, although much more old school than the splendid Galata Museo in Genoa. It is stuffed full of schoolboy treasures, most of them scale model ships of varying sizes, from galleys to container ships, and everything in between. (We also owe them a debt of thanks for letting me squeeze in a lightning visit ten minutes before it shut, while the kindly staff helped my wife change my son's nappy in the ticket office. I came back to find two of them entertaining him while my wife disposed of the mess. In surprising areas Italians are truly world leaders.) Especially pleasing for the Genoese visitor, however, is the magnificent display of models from the golden age of transatlantic shipping. Again and again the ships catch the eye with their elegance and that special aesthetic only generated by mechanical and industrial ingenuity. The *Conte di Savoia* is there, as is the *Cristoforo Colombo* – the sister ships of the *Rex* and the *Andrea Doria* respectively. Other names are just as evocative, like the *Virgilio* and the *Michelangelo*. It was an era when Italy began to take on the industrialised giants of the Western world, and do it in style. But again and again, the ships displayed in the museum in that great Adriatic city carry the name of its Tyrrhenian rival across their sterns: *GENOVA*.

18

SURVIVING MUSSOLINI

"A child who, even while not refusing to obey, asks "Why?"
is like a bayonet made of milk."
Fascist slogan for boys in the *Balilla* movement

The curve of Genoa's harbour ends with a lump of rock that rises above
the *mole vecchio* and the medieval centre. That rock is the Quartiere
Portoria, a network of swanky streets and toy dogs that are reminiscent
of Recoleta in Buenos Aires. The *sopraelevata* skirts this rock on the
coastal side, next to small shipyards dedicated to sprucing up the
personal yachts of the financially well-lubricated. On the land side
Genoa reaches out past Piazza de Ferrari and down the splendidly
galleried Via Settembre XX, with its mosaic floors and the odd
unfortunate on their knees holding up a placard saying *Ho Fame* ("I am
hungry"). Beyond the viaduct of the Corso Andrea Podestà and the
Mercato Orientale, the bottom of this main shopping street reaches an
open area, one of Genoa's two reminders of those little-discussed years
of Italian fascism. This is the monumental Piazza della Vittoria,
complete with its own triumphal arch and a slope decorated with
flowering displays showing Columbus's ships heading off on their voyage
of discovery. In truth it is not a particularly monumental *piazza*, and
feels more like a useful area of overspill parking than a focus for the
glorification of a fascist rebirth. (The weed-tufted arch is quite nice, with

galleys built into its four corners, although I am not sure it feels particularly *triumphal*.) Not far away is the Torre Piacentini, Italy's first "skyscraper". Like the Piazza della Vittoria it was built by Mussolini's favourite architect, Marcello Piacentini, in 1940, and is also distinctly underwhelming: despite having been the tallest high-rise building in Europe until 1952, by Manhattan standards it doesn't even get to tickle the sky, let alone scrape it.

There are little footnotes from Mussolini's years throughout Genoa and Liguria, but in keeping with the Piazza della Vittoria and the Torre Piacentini there is nothing of any particular substance. Both of Genoa's football teams were touched by fascism: Genoa Cricket and Football Club had to change its name to the rather more Italian "Genova 1893 Circolo del Calcio"; and the two teams that eventually became Sampdoria (Sampierdarenese and Andrea Doria) were merged temporarily in 1927 under the fine name of "La Dominante". The fascists were keen on renaming things in grandiose ways: on the western arm of Liguria, Porto Maurizio and Oneglia (the birthplace of Andrea Doria) were merged under the bombastic new name "Imperia". At the other end of Liguria, La Spezia gained a few pieces of typical fascist architecture, including a post office that is heavy on the right-angles. Back in Genoa, the Stazione Marittima was built as the terminus for great passenger liners like the *Rex* and the *Conte di Savoia* (the wonderful bust of Christopher Columbus is worth seeing – it looks like Klaus Kinski in one of his manic phases). As we saw in the last chapter the building of great ocean-going liners owed something to the impetus given by Mussolini, and just behind La Lanterna the wharfs were named after Italy's colonial exploits: Ponte Etiopia; Ponte Somalia; Ponte Eritrea.

The strongest link between the city of Genoa and the fascists, however, was the adoption of a great Genoese hero as the role model for the fascist youth movement. Balilla, that brave and foolhardy young boy who threw his stones at occupying Austrian troops back in 1746, turned out to be just the type of role model that the fascist authorities were looking for.

Under fascism boys could expect to join the Balilla, the Italian version of the Hitler Youth, at the age of eight (they left for the Avanguardista at fourteen). As well as enjoying spanking new uniforms and marching, they faced compulsory reading that included stirring examples of self-sacrifice for the state: "How can we ever forget that fascist boy who, when near to death, asked that he might put on his uniform and that his savings should go to the party?" It was a sad debasement of a genuinely heroic (if reckless) character.

Balilla has given his name to an array of shops and cafes across the city, especially in Portoria, as he has done for a couple of submarines and a fistful of Fiat cars. Thanks to an infamous winemaker from up near the Austrian border, Balilla has also lent his name to a bottle of gratuitously labelled wine. In 1995 Alessandro Lunardelli from Friulli launched its historical series, and hit the headlines with "labels that remind us of the life lives [*sic*] of celebrated personages of Italian and world political history such as Che Guevara, Churcill [*sic*], Gramsci, Hitler, Marx, Mussolini, Napoleon and Sissi". The bottles now account for half of their sales. An €8 bottle (from *cabernet franc* to a more refreshing *pinot grigio*) carries a picture of a 1930s youth standing to attention in ill-fitting shorts, above the label "*Il Balilla*"; this can also be purchased with an even smaller chap in uniform giving the fascist salute above the label "*Figlio della lupa*". It is the same price for those coveting labels sporting Mussolini ("*Credere Obbedire Combattere*"), Hitler ("*Ein Volk, ein Reich, ein Führer!*") or Stalin ("*Il Compagno*"). A more limited range of similarly tasteless Friullian grappas comes in at €12. Italy's relationship with twentieth-century dictatorship certainly remains much more nuanced than Germany's.

***

Genoa's experience of the war years was based on two facts: firstly, tucked up in northern Italy it was well out of the way of any actual land fighting; and secondly, it was an important port and armaments hub, and therefore an Allied target. The port itself was attacked from both land and sea. A photo from October 1942, taken from the heights above the city, shows a terrifying blaze of incendiary bombs being dropped on the port in a night raid by Allied aircraft, each one leaving a fiery trail as it falls on the city. Other strategic parts of the coast that were heavily bombed include Recco and La Spezia. The bombardment of Genoa by warships standing offshore suggested a certain historical familiarity. Visitors to Genoa's *Cattedrale di San Lorenzo* can find a hefty British naval shell, the size of a large child but doubtless much heavier, that hit the cathedral without exploding. Newspaper reports from the war years condemn the "wild" British bombardment, after shells also apparently landed on a school, a convent and a hospital wing housing female patients.

The most infamous wartime episode was a ghastly incident during an air raid on 23 October 1942. A woman named Ginetta was caught up in the raid.[1] After an unpaid apprenticeship she had become a waistcoat maker (her waistcoats always had five buttons; she remembers that the pockets were the hardest part), and on that October day she was living with her family on the Vico della Fata (the vico of the fairies). When Ginetta heard the air-raid siren she went with her parents to the underground Galeria delle Grazie, not far from the Torre Piacentini. It was a recognised air-raid shelter, but on that occasion more and more people crowded in, and Ginetta remembers that people started pushing, and some could not breathe. Her father could tell that something was not quite right, so he took his family and pushed through the crowds towards the exit. It was a wise decision: while Ginetta's family braved the bombs outside, more than 300 people were eventually crushed to death inside the Galeria.[2] She remembers that the corpses of the dead were laid out near the Bank of Italy building, and their relatives had begun to search among them for her family. Genoa never suffered as much as cities like Rotterdam, Warsaw and Berlin, but air raids were a frequent reminder of the city's strategic importance. Ginetta remembers one occasion when she was caught in the open during a raid, as she returned from a doctor's appointment. The earth shook as the bombs rained down on the Brignole area, and even the solid steel girders of the railway bridge were moving with every explosion; Ginetta survived despite having nothing more than a doorway to shelter in. During one naval bombardment in February 1942 her mother went missing wearing only slippers and a light top; the family eventually found her trying to find safety (and warmth) under the fruit and vegetable baskets of a *fruttivendolo*.

After the fall of Mussolini in 1943 the Nazis moved in. There was significant partisan activity in the Ligurian mountains, and the Germans were swift and brutal in their reprisals. The SS Commander in Genoa in 1944 and 1945 was a man called Friedrich Engel, who earned the nickname the "Butcher of Genoa". In 1999 a court in Turin convicted him in connection with several reprisal massacres in which 246 Italians were killed. Engel admitted being present at the shooting of 59 prisoners of war in Turchino, in a pass through the mountains north of Genoa, and in 2002 a court in Hamburg convicted him of 59 counts of murder. This was then overruled as his direct responsibility could not be proven, and he died in 2006 at the age of 97.

The partisans were especially successful at the end of the war, jumping in to capture the city before the fleeing Germans could destroy chunks of infrastructure. *The Milwaukee Journal* of 30 April 1945 carries an *AP* report about a "dramatic two day uprising" that left tram cars, water utilities and phone lines in place. One Major Robert Sharkey was even able to telephone the head of the city's resistance from just along the coast at Rapallo, and when the Allies entered the city they found that it was "doing business as usual". A total of 14,000 Nazi and Fascist troops were forced to surrender before they could flee.

The gorgeous fishing village of Portofino, nestling in its picture-perfect little harbour to the east of Genoa, also had a lucky escape. As the Germans were withdrawing, some ghastly halfwit of a Nazi commander ordered one of his officers to blow the place up before leaving. Luckily the officer was able to be talked out of this act of mindless vandalism, and Portofino swiftly became what is today: a stunning hangout for celebrities who wish to be photographed by paparazzi having a secluded holiday away from the cameras. The dinky little harbour is walled in by a question mark of multi-coloured houses, and the boat crane at the far end can also be used for lifting piles of roubles to be spent in Portofino's boutiques.

Genoa's port did not escape the war unscathed. Jetties and quays were destroyed, along with over 80 per cent of the warehouses, cranes and port infrastructure. A total of 139 mines had been placed in the water by the Germans, including 73 in the port itself, and ships had been scuttled to block entrances and exits. There is a memorial under La Lanterna to the fifteen British servicemen who were killed in de-mining operations. (During reconnaissance of the port a wealth of old wrecks were discovered: 338 ships and 600 other vessels were found on the sea bed, including 140 Italian naval ships, 134 Italian merchant ships, 63 French and one British ship.) The Palazzo di San Giorgio, on the edge of the harbour, was also a mess. The roof of its famed *Sala Compere* was destroyed, and the arches that held the weight of the building were heavily reinforced with wooden scaffolding to prevent their complete collapse. In comparison to other cities in Europe, however, Genoa had escaped lightly. But shortly after the war ended, Genoa and La Spezia both found themselves at the centre of the intrigues that followed the collapse of the Third Reich.

***

The Villa Bombrini in the posh suburb of Albaro is now best known for being the Conservatorio Nicolò Paganini, a beautiful tree-shrouded building stuffed to the gills with grand pianos, violins and musical talent. But at the end of the Second World War, while Europe picked up the pieces after the devastation and horrors of Nazism, it had a different function. It was the location for the offices of the Delagaciòn Argentina de Inmigraciòn en Europa (DAIE), run by Carlos Fuldner, an Argentine-born German and former SS captain. The DAIE played a vital role in plotting the escape routes for some of the most prominent Nazis, fleeing Europe on the rat run to South America.

Between 1947 and 1951 Genoa hosted some of the most wanted men in Europe. Joseph Mengele stayed in a private house at Via Vincenzo Ricci 3 in May 1949, before leaving on the *North King* under the name Helmut Gregor. From late spring 1950 until June, Adolf Eichmann stayed in a hotel at Via Balbi 9, and then travelled as Ricardo Klement to Buenos Aires on the *Giovanna C.* Klaus Barbie stayed at another Genoese hotel in March 1951, in Via Nazionale Lomellini 6, before his passage on the *Argentina Corrientes* as Klauss Altmann. Erich Priebke and hundreds of other Nazis were funnelled off to South America via Genoa, along with other wanted men like Ante Pavelić, the head of Croatia's grotesque Ustaše regime.

The fugitives took advantage of the chaos surrounding the end of the war, with millions of displaced and desperate refugees trying to rebuild their lives from the rubble. Red Cross passports were issued to many of those who had lost papers during the war. The DAIE helped escapees obtain these documents, along with new identities and Argentine visas, and then secured their passage to new lives in Argentina, Paraguay and Bolivia. Some of those bearing most responsibility for the atrocious suffering and bloodshed of the war years were able to start new lives from the moment their ships cast off from the dock in Genoa, away from the clutches of the Allied intelligence services who were combing Hitler's defeated forces for war criminals.

There was some involvement from churchmen too. Barbie was met in Genoa by the Croatian priest Krunoslav Draganović, and researchers have linked other local priests to the rat run too. Attempts have also been made to associate the deeply conservative Archbishop of Genoa himself, Giuseppe Siri, but the evidence tends to point towards him turning a blind eye to the situation during chaotic times, rather than active involvement. In September 2013 Genoa's local newspaper, *Il Secolo XIX*, reported that it had still received no details of an internal Church investigation into these matters, despite promises a decade earlier.[3] Suspicion lingers on.

***

While prominent Nazis slithered out of Genoa towards South America, many of Europe's surviving Jews looked for their own escape from the blood-stained continent through the Mediterranean ports. Flare-ups of anti-Semitism in Poland and elsewhere hurried them on their way, and many also sought to avoid internment in the squalid processing camps set up by the Allies.

Getting away, however, was not easy: because of sensitivity about Jewish–Arab relations in Palestine, the British in particular tried to regulate the numbers of Jews heading for their Promised Land, imposing strict quotas. Italy was seen as a relatively easy jumping-off point for the Jewish refugees, and became a centre for *Aliya Bet* (illegal immigration) to Palestine. They came in their thousands, some by themselves or in small groups, and others in the more organised *Bricha* (flight) from northern Europe. In response Jewish groups already in Palestine sent people to help the refugees, including Mossad agents.

In 1946 the head of the Mossad in Italy, Yehuda Arazi, decided that for the sake of efficiency it would be best to concentrate all the Jewish refugees in one place, rather than spread them out all over the coast. He chose La Spezia, the port at the eastern end of the Ligurian moustache, which sits facing towards Tuscany in front of a mountainous and perfect semi-circular bay. Convoys of trucks were arranged to bring the refugees to La Spezia in April, and despite almost being intercepted by both Italian and British security forces, they boarded two ships called *La Fede* and *Fenice,* and prepared to sail.

The British, though, had other ideas, and demanded that they disembark. They were determined to stop the 1,014 refugees on board from adding to an already unstable situation in Palestine. But 1946 was not a year for Jews to back down on their demands to leave Europe behind in exchange for the Promised Land. The refugees' leaders said they would blow up the ships if any British soldier touched one of their people, and a stand-off developed. Journalists arrived to report on what was happening, and the frustrated refugees raised the stakes by declaring a hunger strike. What was becoming known as the La Spezia Affair was creating a lot of international sympathy for the Jews, and very bad press for the British.

It was a battle that the British knew they could not win, faced with two ships containing over a thousand determined refugees, including a hundred pregnant women, many concentration camp survivors and 200 partisan veterans. After a month the authorities backed down and announced that the ships could leave. Celebrations went on well into the night. The *La Fede* and *Fenice* were renamed the *Eliahu Golomb* and *Dov Hos*, and for the last 60 miles of their voyage to Haifa they were escorted by a British destroyer, the *Charity*. From the end of the war until 1948, 35 ships made their illegal passage from Italy to Palestine, more than from any other European country, and the La Spezia Affair was the moment when the exodus gained its momentum.

***

There is one other peculiar reminder of the war years in Genoa, barely discernible on the walls of some of the tiny *vicoli* that head off into the maze of the city's medieval centre from the port and the Via di Sottoripa. Stencilled on the stone is a faded warning to occupying American soldiers not to go past that point, because of the dangers they might face on those tight, tangled alleyways. There is no doubt that they would face some dangers: its *vicoli* were home to countless desperate and unsavoury characters and any blundering GIs might prove an easy target. But there were also dangers posed by consorting with women of ill repute who filled the backstreets of port cities, and the American authorities were particularly worried about venereal disease as the actual war fighting ground to a halt.

The Nazis might also have benefited from such caution. One of the ghosts that is said to haunt the city is of a German soldier who ignored all advice while stationed in Genoa in 1943 and headed off into the rabbit warren of *vicoli* in search of prostitutes. He was never seen alive again. His ghost is apparently spotted occasionally, stumbling along in his search for whores. He cannot have been looking very hard.

19

GOLDEN YEARS ON THE RIVIERA

"I'm the idol of the ladies; Champagne Charlie is my name."
Graeme Souness T-shirt on sale at *SoulSamp*

It was 1984, and Italy had a fair amount to smile about. So did two British footballers, enjoying the sun and sea at Portofino, as they bobbed around on a boat in front of that stunning multi-coloured row of houses. Their hair was tousled and slightly bleached (surely from the sun rather than the bottle), and one of them sported a chunky gold chain that was the perfect accompaniment to his luxurious moustache. For Graeme Souness and Trevor Francis, life was good, and playing on the Italian Riviera for Sampdoria was a long way away from playing in an England still suffering its grey and rocky hangover from the decline of the seventies.

The 1980s were not entirely plain sailing for Italy, but many things seemed to be going right. By 1975 the post-war emigration of labour to northern Europe was reversing, and there were more returnees than emigrants. Although in 1976 the Italian economy shrank for the first time since the Second World War, the whole of Europe was suffering setbacks, and the situation in traditional heavyweights like Britain was teetering on the brink of disaster. The "Third Italy" of small businesses (especially in regions like Veneto) was on the rise, and in 1986 Italy achieved the *sorpasso*, overtaking the United Kingdom to become the fifth largest economy in the world (Italians felt that the next on the list, France, was in its sights, but this was never achieved). One needs to know both how quickly Italy grew in the post-war period and also how the trajectory that led to the *sorpasso* has since faltered, if one is to understand the Italy and – of course – the Genoa of today.

By the 1980s Italian football was also showing distinct signs of virility as it built up to its great moment in the sun with the 1990 World Cup. It had glamour and skill, just as British football was deep into its cul-de-sac of hoofball tactics and off-pitch thuggery. And it had money, which was bringing some of the world's biggest stars to *Serie A*, including Diego Maradona at Napoli, Michel Platini at Juventus and Marco van Basten at AC Milan. Sampdoria also looked abroad, and dug up classy players like Scotland's Graeme Souness and England's Trevor Francis. It was a good time to be at Samp, but it was not just a place to pick up a nice sunshine-laced pay-off at the end of a playing career. After a spectacularly trophyless history, Sampdoria was going places. The driving force was the club president, Paolo Montovani, and its Yugoslav manager, Vujadin Boškov. Over the next few years, fans of Genoa CFC could only watch and grind their teeth.

The team that Boškov and Montovani created was skilful and close-knit to the point of defiance. As well as a distinguished sprinkling of international talent, at its heart was a formidable crop of young Italian players such as Roberto Mancini and Gianluca Vialli. The arrival of the prodigious teenager Mancini in 1982 was a statement of the ambition that Mantovani brought to Sampdoria. He was fiery, and on several occasions the young man had to be separated from the established England international Trevor Francis in training.

The club then shocked its fans by starting to win things. It picked up three *Coppa Italias* in the 1980s, and slowly began to move up the *Serie A* table. Ominously, the bigger clubs started sniffing around the best players. Italian football is a clannish place, and the established powers were the place to be for titles and recognition. "You would hardly call us or our chairman part of Italian football's aristocracy", Vialli noted, looking back at the period in his book *The Italian Job*. Mancini himself blames his limited international career on his loyalty to the *blucerchiati*:[1] "It was my fault. My fault that I played for Samp. Just as it was Vialli's fault and Pietro Vierchowod's fault that they were also with Samp and not with a 'big club'." Despite this, the club's senior players made a pact over dinner in 1989 to resist the draw of more glamorous clubs until they had achieved something with Sampdoria.

The players stuck together, and a group of them became known as the "Seven Dwarfs" because they were always seen socialising with each other (Mancini was Cucciolo, the character known as Dopey in the English version). The team won the Cup Winners' Cup in 1990, the year that Italy hosted the World Cup and the city opened the Stadio Luigi Ferraris for its two teams in Marassi. Unlike the stadiums in other Italian cities, festering in the exurbs like home decoration superstores, the terracotta-coloured Luigi Ferraris is very much part of Genoa.

The real pay-off was a year later. The team was clearly the best in *Serie A*, and secured the *Scudetto* in style before the final match. In that last game of the season (against Lazio) the players once again showed their togetherness and exuberance by taking to the pitch with bleached hair: not something that would ever be seen at Italy's more aristocratic clubs. A year later Sampdoria were beaten by Barcelona in the final of the European Cup at Wembley, and gradually the team began to be dismantled. When Mancini left, he took with him a tattoo of the club badge on his ankle, and fifteen years of memories: "this team is my life [...] I will never forget Sampdoria. I may have won less than I possibly could, but the love is worth more than success. I have given so much, but I got even more back." To this day, Mancini's good looks remain burned on the retinas of many thousands of Genoa's women.

***

These glory years for Sampdoria and for Italy grew directly out of the post-Second World War period. It was a time of explosive economic growth in Italy, a country that had longed to stand shoulder to shoulder with the other major countries in Western Europe. There was a lot of underdeveloped capacity that was freed up: fascist controls and protectionist measures were relaxed, and entrepreneurship was let off the leash; there was a large pool of new workers, often agricultural workers from the *Mezzogiorno*, ready to fill the new factories;[2] foreign technologies shunned by Mussolini were adopted; and Italy's advantage in craft skills was easily translated into industrial production. The opening up of education also played a part: as late as 1951 only one in nine Italian children stayed in school past the age of thirteen.[3]

By 1950 its industrial production had recovered to pre-war levels, and continued to grow at an annual growth rate of over 5 per cent (at times Italy's growth rate was third in the world, behind only Japan and South Korea). Inflation was low, thanks to the strong supply of new workers keeping wages low. Living standards increased faster in the twenty years after the war than they had done in the previous century. Between 1950 and 1970 the infant mortality rate fell from 64 per cent to just under 30 per cent.

As soon as the money started coming in, Italian consumers also provided strong domestic demand for everything from domestic appliances to scooters. Car production was a strength: 100,000 were built in 1953; half a million in 1960; one million in 1963; one and a half million in 1967.[4] As electricity connections spread, so did television ownership: Italy was Europe's largest manufacturer, and in 1970 Italian households were more likely to have a TV than a telephone. Nationwide television also helped reinforce that often flimsy concept of Italianness – even in the early 1950s only around 20 per cent of families communicated exclusively in Italian.

Italy also became Europe's largest manufacturer of white goods. In 1951 it produced 18,500 fridges; two decades later it was making 5.25 million – almost as many as the US and the rest of Europe combined. This had a massive impact on daily life in an often very hot country. On a trip down the *funiculare* from Righi we listened to an older lady (born in 1925) reminisce about how life had changed. My wife asked her what the most remarkable changes were. "Ice," she answered. "It's got to be ice. If you were really rich they delivered it to your door. Otherwise you had to collect it in a nylon sheet and carry it home. Now we have fridges, and you can store anything." What is commonplace now must have seemed like a revolution back then: in 1957 12 per cent of West Germans had fridges, but not even 2 per cent of Italians. By 1974 94 per cent of Italians had fridges, the highest ownership level in Europe.[5]

Much of the growth was centred on the old "industrial triangle" of Milan, Turin and Genoa. Not only was Genoa's port shipping the Fiats, the Olivettis and the Pirellis, but its own industrial powerhouses like the Ansaldo shipyard were enjoying the good times. Northern industries were reluctant to set up shop in the *Mezzogiorno*, where organised crime continued to flourish, along with a reputation for backwardness. Many southerners headed north to work in the new factories, and the less establishment football teams (Juventus rather than Torino in Turin, and Sampdoria rather than Genoa CFC) picked up many supporters among the new arrivals.[6] Migrating often meant having to pick up the local dialect. Mauro Olivieri, the son of a local steel worker, told me that many of his father's newly-arrived Sicilian colleagues had to learn Genoese, as that was what everybody spoke at work. (Back home they continued to speak Sicilian to their wives. As late as the 1970s Genoese was still the working language of the city.)

This internal migration also left a physical mark on the recipient cities. Just as the Italians are famed for their elegant city centres, they have developed something of a cloth ear when it comes to the aesthetics of their suburbs. Many are grim and featureless, interspersed with modernist concrete experiments that began to go wrong from the moment the new residents moved in. In Genoa, however, at least the residents could often comfort themselves with a spectacular view (at least when the city grew up the slopes of the hills and mountains; when it grew along the river valleys between the slopes they often ended up becoming acquainted with floods). The city's most striking suburb is the Quartiere INA-Casa di Forte Quezzi, which was a 1968 brutalist solution for both southern workers and Genoese who were displaced by city centre construction projects (it came just after the mighty *sopraelevata* itself). From down near the city centre it looks like a forbidding extension of Genoa's fortifications, its massive concrete and glass dimensions following the contours of one of the hills above all other buildings. But the closer you get, the more disturbing it is, especially for those who live there (although the view is one of the most spectacular in Italy).

***

There is a pleasing symmetry between Sampdoria's fortunes and the post-war rebirth of Italy. The club was only created after the war ended, and its stylish peak was reached just at that point when Italy hosted the World Cup and *Serie A* was the envy of the world. There is also something deeply Genoese about the team and its humble, unfashionable roots: if Genoa CFC is the pedigree dog, Sampdoria is the mongrel. Fittingly it was formed from the merger of two different clubs, Andrea Doria and Sampierdarenese (the current club merges both their names and their colours), but the story goes back further.

Andrea Doria, as befits a team named after the city's great admiral, has a long history, reaching back into the nineteenth century. When Genoa CFC opened Italy's first proper stadium in the Marassi district in 1911 (featuring seats, and changing rooms for both teams and the referee), Andrea Doria had its own little ground just next door. La Caienna was named after a French prison camp and the supporters were right up against the pitch. It was the poor relation, and in 1913 Genoa CFC poached two of its best players. Unfortunately for the bigger club, the players tried to cash their illegal 1,000 lire signing-on cheques at a bank with an Andrea Doria-supporting bank teller, who promptly informed the authorities.

Sampierdarenese was another small team, with a base in the working-class Sampierdarena suburb. Sampierdarena used to be a fishing village just to the west of Genoa's port, and is named after the dialect for St Peter of the Sands (San Pietro d'Arena). With the arrival of the railways it became a centre for heavy industry such as shipbuilding, and was the heart of the area known as the "Manchester of Italy" for its manufacturing. Its football section was founded in 1899 but it did not challenge for anything meaningful until after the First World War, when it bought out a league team, Pro Liguria of Bolzaneto.

The first union between the two teams came at the end of the 1926-7 season, thanks to the fascists, who were inveterate tinkerers in the world of *calcio*. The new club went under the suitably fascist name of La Dominante, and after an almost-*dominante* 3rd place finish in their first *Serie B* season, they then managed a distinctly non-*dominante* bottom-placed finish and relegation. The marriage was over and the two former clubs went their own ways. A few years later Sampierdarenese tried the merger route once again, joining with Corniglianese and Rivarolese to make Associazione Liguria Calcio. The full merger of Andrea Doria and Sampierdarenese, however, only came after the end of the Second World War. They took on that curious name "Sampdoria", and that iconic shirt (the blue was from Andrea Doria, and the white/red/black/white hooped middle from Sampierdarenese).

They also picked up a curious club badge, as sported by Roberto Mancini on his ankle. At a distance it looks like an untidy cedar tree or a werewolf wearing a tam-o'-shanter. In fact the silhouette is of a typically Genoese roughly-bearded sailor, the *lupo di mare* ("wolf of the sea") called Baciccia, a dialect corruption of John the Baptist (Giovanni Battista). Jammed unapologetically in his mouth is a pipe – in 2009 an anti-smoking group failed in their slightly ludicrous campaign to get it removed from the badge.[7]

As with the team that stormed the league back in 1991, Sampdoria has developed a reputation for doing things differently, and a certain sense of style. When Christian Karembeu played for the club, the players protested against French nuclear tests in the Pacific (he was born in New Caledonia). They also wore "Peace No War" T-shirts in solidarity with their Yugoslav team-mate Nenad Sakić during the NATO bombing of Yugoslavia.

The club's sense of style is best seen at a small shop a few metres down the Vico del Fieno, a typical Genoese *carrugio* with an uncertain gradient, grubby uneven cobbles, and a drunk's slight meander. While Genoa CFC has its museum, full of black and white images of the men who introduced *calcio* to Italy and picked up an armful of titles, Sampdoria has *SoulSamp*.

The shop is not stylish in a precious catwalk way, but through a glorious, almost English, cross-fertilisation of style and the street. (Sampdoria fans can be credited with beginning the *ultrà* movement in 1971, fusing football, youth culture and politics.)[8] As John Ashdown wrote in the *Guardian*, "Sampdoria fans are a lucky bunch. When they buy a replica shirt they become wearers of one of football's Great Kits", and that kit is based around that simple but utterly pleasing combination of colours: blue, white, red, black, white, then blue again.[9] It is an iconic combination that sits alongside, or above, the most recognisable kits in the world – Arsenal, Ajax, Celtic, Flamengo, River Plate and Boca Juniors. With Genoa CFC you suspect that the ideal piece of merchandise would be a discreetly ornate enamelled stickpin featuring a griffin and the Cross of St George; for Sampdoria it is a T-shirt in the iconic club colours, and that is where *SoulSamp* comes in.

The T-shirts borrow heavily from a fashion-conscious *ultrà* culture and from that golden period in the late 1980s and 1990s when Sampdoria took on Italy's elite on its own terms, and won. Although it is Genoa CFC that cultivates its English links, it is the upstart neighbours that had British players, and they feature heavily on *SoulSamp* T-shirts: Graeme Souness ("The ball is mine", as well as "I'm the idol of the ladies; Champagne Charlie is my name"), Trevor Francis ("Trevormania"), and Des Walker ("You'll never beat Des Walker"). There are mod scooters in Samp colours, "Merseysamp", "Soulsamp fish and chips", "Northern SoulSamp" and a *Get Carter* era Michael Caine ("Going to the match, lads?").

Ultrà culture is not confined to Sampdoria: the city also hosted the first "summit" meeting of *ultrà* groups in 1995. This followed the killing of a Genoa CFC fan, Claudio Spagnolo, by the AC Milan fan Simone Brasaglia, during fighting before a match. Spagnolo's death led to a full-scale riot, with cars overturned and Molotov cocktails thrown. Throughout Italy 40,000 matches at all levels of football were cancelled. The "summit" meeting was a not-entirely convincing attempt by *ultrà* groups to draw a line between themselves and what they called "violent mavericks". The rather more benign and stylish side of the *ultrà* movement can be seen in the shirts of *SoulSamp*.

As is often the case with football clubs, they say something important about the nature of their home city and its people. In Genoa's case, the combination of Genoa CFC with its glorious past and Samp with its style and underdog grit is particularly fitting, just as the city has its UNESCO-listed Palazzi dei Rolli and then the chaotic exuberance of the *vicoli* tumbling down into the port.

The tension between the two Genoese clubs also speaks to the tension at the heart of the city. It is not a simple divide like the Glaswegian one between a Catholic club and a Protestant club, but something less tangible. Although Genoa CFC has a more establishment feel to it, and Sampdoria has an association with the industrial suburbs, there is no clear-cut geographical distinction. One friend suggests that the difference now is about mentality: Genoa fans are defensive and backward looking, and can be quite parochial in their focus on the rivalry with Sampdoria; Samp fans are more outward looking, but rather than pretend they are a big club (like a tramp in a top hat) they relish the role of the underdog. In this sense they are two sides to the same Genoese coin, and an indispensable part of the city that they represent.

20

STRUNG OUT ALONG A BRUTAL COASTLINE

"turisti di merda" *graffito near Vernazza*

It had been raining hard for several days, but that was hardly untypical for October in Liguria. At around 2 o'clock a couple of tourists came into Michele Lilley's shop to escape the rain. Michele told them that if they wanted to escape Vernazza before the rail tunnel flooded, they should try to get the 2.20 train. Vernazza, like all the Cinque Terre villages, relies heavily upon the railway for its connection to the outside world. The five villages cling to the rocks of the Ligurian coastline in various states of colourful effrontery to gravity, strung out above the surf and laced together by long rail tunnels that allow trains to burst out, gasping for breath, at each station. In the summer the villages are thick with tourists, spilling out of the doors of the carriages with their cameras clicking and their wallets leaching euros. In October, especially when the rain is falling hard, it is different, and Michele thought it was time to call it a day and close up her shop.

"Outside I saw everyone with brooms, scrubbing the street, clearing the debris that was being washed down by the rain," said Michele. Vernazza is crammed into a gully at the base of Liguria's ever-present mountains. Where the gully hits the sea a giant lump of rock forms a natural harbour and a perfect site for a fortification. The main street is the floor of the gully, running steeply through the village, with multi-coloured houses stacked vertically on both sides and the cylindrical tower of the Castello Doria high above. When it rains hard, the water flows down the main street like a stream, bringing whatever debris it has dislodged down with it. But on 25 October 2011, the stones and twigs that the villagers were sweeping away from the flagstones of Via Roma were soon replaced by rocks, statues and plants in heavy pots. This was different, and the men and women with their brushes gave up and retreated indoors.

Michele realised that there was a strong chance that her shop, the Bottega d'Arte Cinqueterre, would be flooded, as it opened directly onto the Via Roma. She started to square things away, putting cardboard on the floor to combat the water that had begun to bubble up under the door. When she looked out of the window she saw the water rising. The torrent was now carrying rubbish bins and scooters past her door. Trees were being sucked down in the muddy water, then disappearing underneath the brown froth. There was now no chance of crossing the street, and Michele knew she was trapped inside her small *cantina*. "It became apparent I could die," she told me, with barely a hint of drama.

The next time she looked outside, just a few minutes later, the water level had mysteriously started to go down. A van, caught up in the torrent, had jammed against something, and was temporarily blocking the flow. She opened the door and saw emergency workers yelling at people to get to safety. "But I shut the door, and the water level rose again straight away. I missed the opportunity. I don't know why." It was a decision that might have cost Michele her life. As soon as she realised her mistake she looked for other options. "Could I climb out and onto the awning above the doorway?" She looked out across the street and saw tourists on an upper level trying to escape, and remembered that there was a door to a stairwell just a couple of metres from her own door. That stairwell was her only chance.

"I got out, and clung on against the water for what seemed like an age." The water was almost up to her waist and moving very fast. Gripping onto a drainpipe and the stones of the wall, she pulled herself against the flow and up to the door. It was stuck, but she managed to break it open. The water poured in after her as she climbed the steps, rising and rising. A few doors away, the owner of a *gelateria* stayed too long in his shop and drowned.

An older couple, Vittoria and Nino, lived upstairs above Michele's shop. While Nino stared out of the window onto the fast-flowing river that Via Roma had become, Vittoria was determined to show their bedraggled and sodden guest around the apartment, as though it was a normal social visit. They had not grasped just how serious the situation was becoming. Outside, the water was now flowing over the top of the Chapel of Santa Marta, and was about to reach first-floor balconies and windows. Michele persuaded the elderly couple that they had to leave, and Nino set about preparing a bag full of food and water, and a bottle of wine. Vittoria at first did not want to go, but when water began to gurgle through the door to their first-floor apartment, she agreed.

They managed to climb up the stairwell and reach the fourth floor, but doors were locked: it was out of season and many residents were out of town, rental apartments closed up for the winter. They could see a binman on the other side of the internal courtyard, and made a plan to break windows and climb across the gap to him on a ladder, four floors up.

"I was feeling very vulnerable," says Michele. "And then we heard a strange whistling noise." The whistling was the sound of gas escaping from the enormous steel ball that was used to store Vernazza's gas supply. The ball had been wrenched free, and had been carried by the torrent over the railway tracks and down Via Roma. Further down Via Roma one man was struggling to hang on to the awning above his shop, with his family trying to help him up to a window. They were forced to take cover while the steel ball banged and clanged against houses like a giant pinball machine. When they returned the man had been swept away.

Michele tried to calm the frail Vittoria by zipping her up in her jacket and telling her that they absolutely had to go. "I told her, 'You're going now!'" They figured that they could get out over the rooftops. The plan worked, and Michele remembers the scene in the little *carrugi* below. "It was like Alice in Wonderland. Somebody was walking along normally with an umbrella in the rain." The narrow *carrugi* was a different world from the chaos and destruction just one street away. Michele got down, and walked home. The village's children were being kept in school, and she found her daughter. Michele had survived.

***

Imagine God collecting all the different elements of Liguria in a bucket, giving them a good shake and adding water, before baking in an oven. If he adds just a bit too much yacht to his mixture he ends up with Portofino. Too many *fin de siècle* traffic jams and the end product is Sanremo. But if he gets the ingredients just right, he ends up with the Cinque Terre – and the best of the five little villages is Vernazza.

Behind Vernazza the mountains rise like the wall of a dam. In front, there is the open Mediterranean. The villages of the Cinque Terre are in the most isolated part of Liguria, itself the most remote and inaccessible part of Italy. Vernazza is little more than a gully and that massive lump of rock, encrusted by multi-coloured houses that jostle for space like prisoners in an El Salvador jail. The Castello Doria is made from flat slabs of grey stone, its cylindrical tower gazing out across the sea to where the winter sun spends the day skirting the horizon. The rock underfoot is formed from twisted contortions of sedimentary pancakes, giving the whole precarious construct a barely warranted air of geological permanence. To the west, headlands jut out beyond the cliff face, around to the neighbouring village of Monterosso and a further mammoth chunk of mountain that plunges into the water. To the east of Vernazza the water is open, circles of swarming gulls marking the spots where shoals of small fish break the surface. Sections of mountainside have been defiantly carved into terraces, hemmed in by maritime pines, triffidian succulents and prickly pears.

Even before the mudslide of October 2011, Vernazza was used to fighting against the world. Heavy stones are cemented onto roofs to prevent the wind finding purchase on a loose corner. The cultivated terraces speak of carving out a meagre living in an inhospitable spot. The swell rises and swirls around the rocks of the harbour mole, promising that maybe not now, but soon, a winter storm will rise up and turn fishing into a mortal experience. Sudden storms are a regular part of off-season life in these mountains. One morning after a night of heavy rain and the sudden illuminations of lightning strikes, I saw a rowing boat bobbing about in the harbour, three-quarters submerged, with just the tip of its upturned prow breaking the water. Although the storm had gone, waves continued to crash over the harbour mole, reminding everyone who was really in control.

It is not just the weather. The Castello Doria that provides such a focal point for the tourist trade's calendars and painted trinkets had a more important previous life: it was a look-out point for slave raiders, the Muslim pirates looking to feed demand for human labour in the markets of North Africa. In modern times the villages, so long at the very end of the earth, have had to withstand the more stifling but less hazardous arrival of massive numbers of tourists.

The outsiders have brought compromises, but they have also brought wealth. On the trail leading up above the church and on towards Monterossa are the spray-painted words *turisti di merda – shitty tourists* – but it is the money from outsiders that has allowed the village to rebuild itself after the deluge of October 2011.

***

I met Michele Lilley in Levanto, the town immediately to the west of the Cinque Terre. We drank coffee and tea outside a cafe at a table, while locals thumped on the windows, inside and out, waving hello to their friends and neighbours. Michele was originally from California, but fell in love with both Vernazza and a local man. It is a seductive combination that has claimed others. Her account of her own escape from the disaster that hit Vernazza was fluent and practised, but retained all of the drama and intensity of that day when her life, her family and the village where she had built her life were almost all washed out to sea. "The whole event happened in an arc of only forty minutes," said Michele. Rebuilding would take much, much longer.

Vernazza itself was completely cut off. The rail line was completely blocked and the narrow road that snaked up out of the gully into the mountains was destroyed. The local community centre was converted into a refuge for locals and tourists. Michele was able to take in two German and four French tourists, and they shared the meal she had prepared earlier that day: five chicken legs, two tomatoes, a bottle of wine, and whatever the tourists dug out of their backpacks. There was no gas, no electricity, no cell phone coverage.

At day break a helicopter arrived, and a rope was thrown across Via Roma to connect the two sides of the village, allowing vital supplies such as medicines to get across. "The saving grace was that the sea was calm," said Michele. That meant that water and food could be brought in, although the harbour itself was ruined, and completely full of mud and debris. "It seemed like a war zone, just as my mother-in-law had described the war years when they were bombed out. But straight away people got to work clearing out rocks. The *piazza* is our living room." Boats evacuated the tourists, the elderly and the young families. At first forty men stayed behind, with the others returning every day to help the clearing up effort.

Another American woman, Diane Prahl, had not heard the disaster when it happened. She lives up in a tower high above the village, and with the weather so loud and so filthy she had not realised anything was wrong. When she walked down to the village the next morning she found that the debris had reached over the top of the concrete bridge that carries the rail tracks between its tunnels.

Diane was impressed by the rescue effort, with soldiers from different regions of Italy coming in to help, in bursts of several days each: Sicilians with their strong southern accents, followed by soldiers from the mountains in the north, with feathers in their caps. Supplies were airlifted in: "Cigarettes, wine, pasta," she remembers. "Can you imagine any other country doing that?" The soldiers cooked for the locals every evening in a large tent, after they had all spent the day digging through the piles of mud and wreckage that clogged the centre of the village and the harbour. They drank wine and talked and sang late into the night.

There was help from neighbouring towns too. Michele remembers that a construction company sent machinery from Levanto, and stayed for six months, while the rail tunnel was dug out by men wearing oxygen masks. Other villages up in the hills were also affected, but did not get as much help as Vernazza. "We were lucky," says Michele, although she acknowledges that the economy of the entire region now revolves around the visitors to the Cinque Terre villages. "Vernazza is the economic driver – that's why it was uneven." The lack of official government help that everybody mentions was felt most keenly in the villages up in the hills, without tourist euros to fall back on.

Clearly, money from the *turisti di merda* is the reason why Vernazza has been able to get back on its feet so quickly. As the village pharmacist noted, they were able to start spending straight away in Vernazza, because people had money and knew that if they cleaned up the tourists would come back. He contrasted the Cinque Terre with L'Aquila in Abruzzo, which is still struggling to recover from the earthquake that killed over 300 people in 2009. Relying on the national or regional government for assistance requires a lot of time, and faith that may not be rewarded.

The fame of Vernazza has also brought high-profile involvement. Richard Rogers, the world-famous architect, has put together a plan that will redesign and restore the village's communal spaces. He and his wife had spent a lot of time in Vernazza over the years, and their son Bo was staying there when the disaster struck. The building he was in was badly damaged, but he managed to climb out and was evacuated on the same boat as Michele. Bo eventually made it to the house of a friend in Pisa. While he was there he suffered a seizure while in the bath and died.

More than two years on the reconstruction efforts are continuing. An Albanian flag flies from one small shack, up a side gully and not far from where half a house has been torn away by flood water, leaving little more than the white tiles and fittings of a kitchen wall, naked in the open air. The Albanian workers who live in the shack are helping to rebuild and create obstacles in stream beds to slow down any future inundation. As I write this in late 2013, some of the vertiginous tourist trails that straggle across cliff faces, connecting the Cinque Terre and providing visitors with effortlessly stunning photographs, remain closed.

On the beach just to the east of Vernazza, a small earth-mover was going about its Sisyphean task of piling up surf-soaked stones into a ridge against the rapacious white spume, which does its utmost to rip apart anything in its path. The beach itself was largely formed from assorted debris that was washed down during the floods, and the environmental impact is uncertain. Just offshore, beneath the cliff that forms one side of Vernazza's giant rock, was a favoured spot for local fishermen.

Michele contributed to the rebuilding by co-founding Save Vernazza, which raises awareness and funds, and channels some of the tourists up into the hills, where they eat and work with local farmers. They restore terraces, clean up, and do the prep work for dry stone walls. "If we don't prepare the ground up there we won't be around for long – it'll all slip down." The project, she says, was born out of love for Vernazza, and that it was time to give something back.

The focus on the hills above Vernazza is crucial. For decades Italy has been blighted by unregulated and often illegal development. Liguria, with its steep, vulnerable slopes and tempting locations with stunning sea views, has suffered more than most. The World Wildlife Fund believed that unchecked construction was a major factor in the disaster that hit Vernazza, Monterosso and the Cinque Terre.[1] There was also neglect: terraces and other traditional labour-intensive methods of stabilising the slopes had been abandoned in favour of chasing the tourist euro. Other parts of the coast have also been hit by sudden flash floods. In November 2011 six people were killed in Genoa itself when the River Bisagno overflowed with mud and water after storms. Cars were washed away, apartments were flooded, and the rescue services struggled to evacuate locals. More died in the city in late 2014 as the Bisagno once again burst its banks following torrential rain.

In Liguria the rivers and streams are more likely to be called *torrente* than *fiume*, and they demand respect. Unfortunately modern Italy has a well-recognised but much-ignored blight of unregulated development, and the developers pay little respect to geography. Between 1956 and 2000 the amount of land that has been urbanised in Liguria has doubled. This does not in itself sound like a lot, but so little of Liguria is suitable for urbanisation that even this represents a strain on the region's natural geography. The numbers of second homes – especially for wealthy northerners from Milan and Turin – exacerbates matters, with large chunks of the seaside shuttered for much of the year and the locals crammed into apartments without those glorious sea views. Everywhere, as above the Cinque Terre, the hard work of keeping marginal agricultural land productive on vertiginous slopes has been abandoned in favour of jobs in air-conditioned offices and hotels.

Liguria has always been remote and rugged, and life here has been precarious for centuries. The harsh land was also the source of the region's wealth: it created the character that drove its population out to sea to explore, make fortunes and compete with the more fortunate. Although the land continued to constrict growth into the modern era, preventing Genoa from developing a large industrial hinterland to go with its excellent port, that forbidding coast is still its greatest asset. Without it the coast would be yet another endless Italian strip of private beaches and bars blaring out witless pop music. The Italian curse of private beaches, with blocks of colour-coded deckchairs laid out in tight grids like regiments in an eighteenth-century battlefield, has thankfully only limited purchase on the Ligurian coast.[2] The endless outcrops and bays have put paid to that, also creating a stunning coastline that is more dramatic and picturesque than most. Those who have marvelled at the beauty of Portofino and the Cinque Terre have geography to thank. The old ladies watching the sun setting behind La Lanterna from high up the Genoese amphitheatre know it. Byron, Nietzsche and Dickens all knew it. The Piedmontese and Lombardians who fly down the mountain passes in their Audis to their holiday homes know that the whole coast would lose its sense of spectacle if it was a flat, marshy plain. Hikers up in the mountains near where I went mushrooming, spotting the blue Mediterranean peeking out between distant hilltops, also know it. But such geography demands respect, and however sybaritic the holidaymakers or however profitable it is to leave those carefully tended slopes behind to chase the tourist dollar, if Ligurians forget it then disasters such as the one that befell Vernazze in 2011 will happen again and again.

21

THE DERBY DELLA LANTERNA

"Genoa for us"[1] (Paolo Conte)

In some cities a local derby match between two fierce rivals is an occasion for displaying the worst side of that city; in Genoa it is quite the opposite. My first *Derby della Lanterna* took place in teeming rain, in conditions wetter than a mermaid's pocket. It was technically a Genoa CFC home match, but beyond Samp's *gradinata sud* and Genoa CFC's *gradinata nord*, the posher seats were pretty mixed – more like an English rugby match than football.

Both teams were lower-mid table in *Serie A*, so there was little danger of being overwhelmed by quality on the pitch. Off it, however, was a different story. It is a derby well-known for the clever choreography of the *ultràs*, and both sides played to their strengths. For Genoa that meant something of a historical pastiche: an enormous 20-metre-high cut-out of the Porta Soprana, complete with the figure of Balilla – a vaguely ludicrous superhero version of a griffin – chucking his stone at the Austrians, and two huge flanking knights in armour, heading off to the crusades with St George's crosses on their shields. Just before kick-off the rest of the *gradinata nord* formed a tinselly multi-coloured background, and the stand where I was sitting was entirely draped in large blue and red banners that included a composite team photo of some of Genoa CFC's most famous old stars. This meant that half the stand missed the kick-off as the organisers fumbled around taking the banners down. Meanwhile the jaunty club song blared out of the loudspeakers and black and white memories of the club's good old days flashed up on the screens.

While Genoa CFC indulged in its slightly kitsch nostalgia trip, complete with the date "1893" in large numerals and nine shields for those nine championships, Sampdoria responded with flags and colours. For Samp, that simple blue-white-red-black-white-blue combination was all they needed. Bundles of giant flags were handed out by the *ultràs*, and when the moment came, they simply unfurled them and swooshed them around as one, singing from the bottom of their lungs and jumping up and down. Fireworks were set off by both sets of fans throughout, the loudest sounding like planet-sized bass drums thumped periodically by hidden giants. It was a true spectacle, and the type of thing that had utterly bewitched English football fans of my generation when they first caught sight of it on *Football Italia*. A freezing Tuesday night crammed into Ayresome Park, as my nostrils filled with the aroma of Bovril, pies and donkey-jacketed steelworkers, could never compete for glamour.

From where I sat, squashed between my father-in-law and Samp-supporting teenage twins, there was also a disconcerting lack of menace. Italian football is not short of drunken idiots who threaten players and use knives on each other. But whether in the rain-sodden crowds outside, or in the middle tier of the *distinti* along the eastern edge of the pitch, fans of the Genoese rivals sat next to each other with barely a hint of friction. Even when the big-boned blonde Maxi Lopez slotted the only goal of the game past the Genoa CFC keeper, prompting a heavy scattering of Samp fans to leap into the air in delight, there was nothing other than a bit of scowling among the Genoa CFC majority. The closest to any physical confrontation that I witnessed was a playful nudge on the back of a Sampdoria scarf-wearing fan as he had a pee, prompting a half-chuckled *Genoa facia di merda*. One father, queuing for his half-time espresso, paraded his two sons decked out in the respective kits of each team, and it did not seem out of place.

The whole match showcased the best of Genoa today. There was the nod to history, to style, to a great past and a middling present that still meant something even if neither team was up there with Juventus and the other current Great Powers. The stadium was intimate, attractive and functional, and resolutely part of the city itself. The hotheads focused on their North Korean-level choreography and their loud explosions, rather than anything more vicious. The result mattered, but not enough to punch somebody. Victorious Samp fans drove their scooters around in packs afterwards, honking their horns gleefully. It was a family occasion in the great Italian tradition. In fact, the biggest fuss over the match was its original scheduling for 12.30 on a Sunday lunchtime: both sets of fans protested and said they would boycott the match (my suspicion is that it clashed with the Sunday lunchtime ritual of visiting grandma), and then 48 hours before kick-off the authorities decided to give in and move it to Monday night. Draped across a mammoth "You'll never walk alone" banner in the *gradinata nord* was a homemade tribute to an 80-something Genoa CFC stalwart who had recently died. I drank in the atmosphere, glanced up at the twinkling of lights from buildings on the slopes above the stadium, tried to remember to watch the action on the pitch, and felt proud that my son was half-Genoese.

***

If the atmosphere at the *Derby della Lanterna* was the symbolic high point of my time in Genoa, a visit to a *vinoteca* with my wife (while *nonna* fed our baby son back at the flat) might have been the low point. There was nothing wrong with the *vinoteca* itself – generous glasses of good wine to wash down a series of plates of free grub, all in a cosy building buried deep in Genoa's winding *vicoli*. What made it the low point was the waiter. He was young and friendly, almost garrulous. Where were we from? Did we live here? How old was our son? Had Genoa changed since my wife left, almost two decades earlier? But then the tone changed. Did we know London? How easy was it to find work? Was it really the land of opportunity? (He was more convinced than we were.) Was the weather really so awful? When we finished and headed out to find our son again, he wished us well and jokingly said he would see us back in London, where he was soon to be heading.

The saddest thing about Genoa is that so many of its young do not appear to see a genuine future there.[2] The waiter was not the only person who believed he was going to have to look abroad for the opportunities he craved. This is, of course, not just a Genoese problem, as the statistics bear out. The purchasing power per person in Italy in 2020 is projected to be 87 per cent of what it was in 1970. From 1960 to 1990 (that year of the World Cup and just before Sampdoria's triumph), Italy was the third fastest growing country in the world; over the last two decades it has been the third slowest. The money spent on pensions has steadily risen while the amount spent on education has fallen lower and lower; Italy's performance on the educational PISA tests is generally dismal. Meanwhile Italy's structural problems, such as its massive, expensive and inefficient public bureaucracy, continue to defy reform. The best example of how its sclerotic legal system functions (or fails to) came with a snippet of news in October 2013, when Sophia Loren finally won a legal case over how much tax she had to pay in 1974 (60 or 70 per cent).[3] The relative golden years of the *sorpasso* now seem a long way in the past, and Italy, even more than the rest of Europe, has a fight on its hands. With Liguria's demographics the most catastrophic in the country, its fight will be harder than most.

The winter of 2013 and 2014 saw many Italians taking to the streets in the name of the fight, although many of those who periodically paralysed the centre of Genoa were more concerned with preserving the employment privileges they had won over many decades than any sense of general justice and dynamism (the transport workers were especially vocal). A movement called the Pitchforks tried a home-grown version of Occupy with a few tents in the shadow of a statue of Garibaldi, but the focus of the anger was hard to pinpoint and the camp fizzled out after a few weeks.[4]

As with Balilla and Mazzini, Genoa is still seen as fertile ground for rebels. The country's most notable current rebel, Beppe Grillo, is from the city. His recipe for solving Italy's problems – harnessing anger and satire in a demand to tear up the entire system – was enough to land more than a quarter of the vote in the 2013 general election. Grillo continues to shadow the formal political system with his 5 Star movement, although it is uncertain exactly how the latent power he has tapped into can be turned into genuine change.

Beppe Grillo certainly is no Andrea Doria, a visionary who did not simply identify the problems in a system, but was able to do something about it. Perhaps I am being unkind – few politicians, especially those who have yanked up their own movement to be a considerable force on the national stage, have the advantage of a fleet of galleys at their command. Maybe that is the next step for Mr Grillo. It will certainly take something dramatic to shake Italy's elites out of their torpor.

I asked one of Genoa's leading businessmen – the shipping magnate Augusto Cosulich – what he thought of Genoa's future. His answer would not chime with the more populist demands of the pitchfork-wielding hotheads: "The workers need to pay taxes; the politicians need to stop corruption and work with the business people. My duty as a businessman is to create opportunity. I have 200 people in Genoa – they are my asset. It is up to us." His company, however, looks across the water for its opportunities, and only 30 per cent is still based in Italy; the rest is spread across the US, Brazil, Turkey and Britain. Despite this globalised outlook he remains personally committed to Genoa. "I could not live in a city without the sea. The sea is part of Genoa. The city is our amphitheatre; the sea is our stage."

This latter observation is one that many Genoese cling to. Simon Kuper of the *Financial Times* made a similar point at the height of the financial crisis after sipping a €1 *macchiato* in Turin and reflecting that "such a cheap moment of happiness, obtainable in its pure form only in Italy, gets you wondering: are things really so bad in Europe?"[5] Genoa will always have its mountains, its sea, its dramatic coastline, its pesto, its *Derby della Lanterna*. "One day young Europeans will get jobs again," Kuper continued, slightly optimistically, "and we'll just be a delightful backwater with excellent *macchiato*. I can think of several worse places to live." On the other hand, if reality really was this seductive, why is Beppe Grillo so angry?

This, however, is not a book about the troubles besetting Genoa or Italy, or whether semi-comfortable caffeinated irrelevance is a viable option. There are enough books of this type around already, and many are very good indeed. This book is about a city that grew from nothing into an enormously influential merchant pirate superpower, and then slowly faded into a long but still remarkable dotage. It is also about a city that does not fit in with the admittedly glorious theme-park Italy of Rome, Florence and (*Boo! Hiss!*) Venice, and does not get the credit that its extraordinary history deserves. Other cities seem to dwell on the past almost too much, while Genoa could do with recognising its own past rather more. Unlike some parts of Italy it is hardly in danger of becoming a museum; work is too much part of the Genoese make-up. Read about Venice's glory years, the blooming of the great trade with the Orient, the fall of Constantinople, the Barbary Corsairs, the Black Death, Italian football, the *Risorgimento*, the tides of emigration across the Atlantic, and Genoa is often little more than a footnote. This is wrong, and I hope this book has done something to redress the balance. Read this, go there, take the *funiculare* up to Righi, and look down on that port from the top of the Genoese amphitheatre, with the two wings of mountains arcing out into the Mediterranean to the east and to the west, and enjoy.

NOTES

2. NOWHERE TO TURN BUT THE SEA

1. Sardinia had suffered nine significant attacks by Muslim raiders, stretching back to at least 721.
2. All examples from Epstein, p56.
3. This example is from Epstein, pp108-9.
4. The word "biscuit" means "twice baked", because this made them hard enough to keep on a ship, and easy to store.

3. THE DOWNTRODDEN

1. The Commenda was a Christian institution, although, as we have seen, Jewish and Muslim travellers and pilgrims were also likely to be found on Genoese vessels travelling to and from the Holy Land.
2. It is yet another reason to sit on the right-hand side of a plane into Genoa. Once you spot it you have around twenty seconds before touchdown.
3. Records show that the removal of this natural windbreak substantially lowered wintertime temperatures in the old city of Genoa itself.
4. In paintings he looks a more gaunt and pained figure, perhaps like the heroin-addicted bass guitarist in a 1970s prog-rock band.
5. *Oblazione* denotes a donation; *Legato* denotes a payment from a will or legacy.

4. THE LIGURIAN MENU

1. Genoa Cricket and Football Club is one of Genoa's two football teams, and the oldest club in Italy. See Chapter 15.

2. And as pesto deserves a category of its own, I've given it a chapter of its own – Chapter 15.

3. The Romeo Viganotti company logo, however, is totally Genoese: it combines Christopher Columbus, one of his ships, and La Lanterna.

5. LA SUPERBA AGAINST LA SERENISSIMA

1. Modern Zadar.

2. To take control of both Crete and Corfu, Venice had to expel Genoese pirates.

3. The Genoese commander at Meloria was Lamba Doria's older brother, Oberto Doria.

6. THE PLAGUE

1. Genoa was to control much of the southern Crimean coast into the fifteenth century.

2. The Arab writer Ibn al-Wardi talks of the plague starting in the "Land of Darkness".

3. The translation is from Ole J. Benedictow, in his comprehensive study *The Black Death*, p50.

4. De Mussis translations are from W. J. Simpson.

5. Benedictow argues that any of these bodies would not have been contagious for long, with fleas leaving the bodies as soon as their temperature fell. However, the Mongols would probably have let the bodies fester before catapulting them in, as the contemporary understanding of the disease would have led them to believe that this actually made them more infectious.

6. Thanks to the plague the fleets were smaller and there were manpower problems. The Venetians employed many Dalmatians on their galleys.

7. FROM FRANCESCO THE SPITEFUL TO THE FLOWERSELLER OF SEBORGA

1. http://www.riviera24.it/articoli/2010/05/24/86346/no-text -3207305003896286689 accessed 4/1/14.

2. See Chapter 13 for more on the *Risorgimento* and its impact on Italy.

3. See Chapter 13.

4. A British agent, Lord William Bentinck, was instrumental in the brief restoration of the Republic of Genoa in 1814. For more of the background to this whole period, flick through to Chapter 13.

8. WHEN IS A PIRATE NOT A PIRATE?

1. Epstein, pp120-1.
2. The Barbarossa brothers were known by several different names. Aruj was also known at various times as Oruç Reis, Baba Aruj and Arrudye. Khzir's names included Hizir, Hayreddin and Khdir. Barbarossa, meaning "Red Beard", probably came from a corruption of Baba Oruç. Neither should be confused with the Holy Roman Emperor, Frederick Barbarossa, who brushed against Genoese history in the mid to late twelfth century (and subsequently gave his name to the doomed Nazi invasion of the Soviet Union in 1941).
3. The *condottieri* were in essence late medieval and renaissance-era mercenaries, and were often employed by the papacy and Italian city states. At the time (and through into the Napoleonic period) standing armies were rare, and so the *condottieri* provided instant military (and naval) muscle on tap.

9. THE STEVE JOBS OF THE MEDITERRANEAN

1. "*...un personaggio ambiguo, servitore di molti padroni, opportunista. Impresario di guerra in proprio, talvolta corsaro, talvolta principe rinascimentale, pragmatico, ma anche capace di congiure, e di clamorosi voltafaccia*", from Campodonico, p6.
2. The name will also be familiar from the Turkish football giant, Galatasaray. Rather pleasingly, at the time of writing the club was managed by Sampdoria hero Roberto Mancini, with Samp star Attilio Lombardo his assistant.
3. Another impact of the labour shortages that persisted after the Black Death was that the large crews needed for galleys became harder to assemble – unless, of course, you used slaves and prisoners of war.
4. See the next chapter.
5. I was lucky enough to have access to a small room in the cloister for a few months, where I was able to conduct research, curse Italian Wi-fi, and get nervous about the prospect of meeting one fearsome Doria ghost or another on the crooked slate and marble staircase that led back out into the fresh air.
6. The name Palazzo Doria is not exactly unusual; the larger and more powerful families built numerous *palazzi* over the years, sometimes in conjunction with other families when they became united in marriage. There are Palazzo Dorias dating from medieval times all the way through to the era of

the Palazzi dei Rolli (see Chapter 11).

7.   Many notables built *palazzi* just outside the city walls, escaping both the stench of a febrile and densely packed port, and strict rules on food and drink.

10. LEPANTO AND THE END OF THE MEDITERRANEAN ERA

1.   Gian Andrea Doria and the Genoese contingent had been forced to anchor well behind the rest of the Christian fleet, thanks to the inevitable friction with the Venetians and the danger that two of the main Christian contingents would rather fight each other than anybody else. This may have led to a crucial Ottoman underestimation of Don John's forces.

2.   The newer maritime powers also started encroaching on the Mediterranean. Two English ships docked in Genoa in 1411, and in 1457 Robert Sturmy set off for the Levant with three ships, picking up some pepper and other spices that he hoped could be grown back in England. On his return he was attacked by Genoese "pirates" near Malta. Northern Europeans naturally accused Genoa of trying to restrict access to the Mediterranean, and the mayor of Southampton ordered the arrest of any Genoese to be found in the city.

3.   One pragmatic solution to the funding of a church was to build it – literally – above a run of shops, which then generated the profits to finance the church. The Chiesa di San Pietro, nestling just above what is now a crammed hardware shop, is the result.

4.   That period of Habsburg control had lasted since 1522.

11. A CITY OF ADVENTURERS

1.   Cabot's birthplace is not known for certain, but scandalously (from a Genoese point of view) at one point he lived in Venice long enough to become a citizen.

2.   Epstein, pp310-11.

12. THE GRAND TOURISTS

1.   To be fair, mosquitoes seem to be the unspoken ubiquitous curse of Italy, and Liguria actually has far fewer of them than most other parts of the country.

2.   The most important Treaty of Rapallo was signed in 1922, with Moscow and Berlin renewing diplomatic links. Only two years later the Italians and Yugoslavs (then the Kingdom of the Serbs, Croats and Slovenes) signed their own Treaty of Rapallo. In 1917 the Italians met the British and French, and between the three of them they decided to reinforce the Italian front after the disaster of Caporetto. That grim battle was also responsible for the detention of Second Lieutenant Giuseppe Chioni (see Chapter 14).

13. NAPOLEON AND THE FRENCH INFLUENCE

1.   The anthem is a very Genoese affair. Goffredo Mameli wrote the lyrics there in 1847, and Michele Novaro – also from Genoa – worked out the tune. It was inspired by the desire for Italian unification and, just as during Balilla's time, opposition to the Austrian occupiers. It was only chosen as the (provisional) anthem in 1946, and officially confirmed in 2012. In memory of the 20-year-old lyricist it is sometimes called the *Inno di Mameli* (Mameli's hymn).

2.   Balilla's good name was also co-opted by the Fascists, as we shall see in Chapter 18.

3.   Genoa consolidated its influence over Corsica after defeating Pisa at the Battle of Meloria in 1284. The island was formally annexed by Genoa in 1347. The Corsican language was a mixture of Genoese and Tuscan.

4.   Despite its catastrophic financial position, Genoa still held out hopes of getting Corsica back at some point in the future. A clause was inserted in the treaty that allowed Genoa the option of buying the island back from France. The only practical use for the clause was to help Genoa deal with its shame at having to pawn its last vestiges of empire.

5.   Fully *An account of Corsica, the journal of a tour to that island, and memoirs of Pascal Paoli*. Paoli was the leading Corsican patriot, who drew up the island's constitution during the years of *de facto* independence from Genoa. After Corsica was sold to France he led the resistance until his forces were defeated and he was exiled to Britain. He was very well received in Britain, in large part thanks to Boswell's book.

14. UNIFICATION AND EMIGRATION

1.   Among the movements inspired by La Giovine Italia was "Young India", the inspiration for Nathuram Godse, who went on to assassinate Gandhi in 1948.

2.   One result of his life on the run was that his devoted mother saw very little of him. In a very Italian touch, a note under a portrait of Maria Mazzini in the museum of his life in Genoa states that after 1831 she was only able to hug her son once, in 1848.

3.   I am being slightly disingenuous – to be fair he does get a museum in his name, and a splendid tomb. I stand by the broader point, though, that Mazzini's memory is less recognised than it should be, both at home and abroad.

4.   Mack Smith, p16.

5.   Quoted in Mangione and Morriale, p52.

15. THE GREEN FIST OF PESTO

1. *Soldati e prigionieri italiani nella Grande Guerra* by Giovanna Procacci, quoted in Dickie, p253.
2. Ibid., p254.
3. The chefs were also told not to cook rabbit, which is a feature of most Ligurian menus away from the coast. This may have been because of the association with domestic pets in North America and Britain.
4. The verb *pestare* means to beat up.
5. Dickie, p331.

16. THE ENGLISH GIFT OF FOOTBALL

1. See George, pp119-74, for a riveting and horrifying account of the impact of modern Somali piracy.
2. This does not mean that football was completely new to Italy. Games of varying complexity and levels of bloodshed have been played on the Italian peninsula for centuries, notably *calcio storico* in Florence. The quote at the start of this chapter is from a 1580 description of the game by Giovanni Maria de'Bardi.

18. SURVIVING MUSSOLINI

1. Ginetta was a resident of the Albergo dei Poveri (see Chapter 8). She related her life story in *La memoria, la mia storia* by Marino Muratore.
2. There is a plaque commemorating the dead on the side of the Porta Soprana.
3. http://www.ilsecoloxix.it/p/italia/2013/09/15/AQOZ6vO-nazisti_silenzio_della.shtml accessed on 4th May 2014.

19. GOLDEN YEARS ON THE RIVIERA

1. "Blue-circled" – the Italian tradition is for nicknames to describe the colours of the teams.
2. In 1950 around 40 per cent of the working population was employed in agriculture. By 1977 this figure had fallen to 16 per cent. Between 1949 and 1960 agriculture's share of GDP fell from 27.5 per cent to 13 pe rcent.
3. Judt, p227.
4. Although Italian cars, like British ones, often suffered from quality control problems. As Tony Judt puts it: "Italians could certainly design cars... What Italian car manufacturers appeared unable to do with any consistency was build the cars that their draughtsmen had imagined."

5.   In the UK the figure was 82 per cent; in France it was 88 per cent.

6.   Between 1955 and 1971 an estimated 9 million Italians moved from one region to another, including my own in-laws.

7.   http://digilander.libero.it/neter_khnum/baciccia01.jpg

8.   This is disputed. For instance AC Milan's Fossa dei Leoni group date back to 1968, although they did not use the term ultràs.

9.   http://www.theguardian.com/football/blog/2013/dec/13/joy-of-six-weird-wonderful-club-crests

20. STRUNG OUT ALONG A BRUTAL COASTLINE

1.   See http://www.wwf.it/il_pianeta/lo_stato_di_salute_del_pianeta/acqua/?1504/Inaugurato-il-cantiere-per-il-sentiero-post-alluvione (accessed 17-1-14).

2.   In Genoa's eastern suburbs there is both a private beach for dog owners (Spiaggia Bau) and one owned by the armed forces.

21. THE DERBY DELLA LANTERNA

1.   Or as his fabulous song has it, *Genova per noi*.

2.   This, of course, is not just a Genoese or Italian problem. I come from the north-east of England, and I have always felt aggrieved at how many of its children have to leave to find their living.

3.   http://www.theguardian.com/film/2013/oct/24/sophia-loren-tax-victory-40-years accessed 25 October 2013; Sophia Loren won the case.

4.   As well as impromptu camps, the protesters blocked motorways elsewhere in Italy. We were caught in one snarl-up on a slip road near Vicenza, with the police standing 100 metres back from a mob who had taken it upon themselves to block the road. The motorists who were stuck there gave little sense that they sympathised with the aims of the protesters.

5.   http://www.ft.com/cms/s/2/15c4d902-b1e6-11e2-9315-00144feabdc0.html#axzz32Dw6OJEs accessed on 20-5-14

BIBLIOGRAPHY

Genoa 'La Superba' – select bibliography (NB many of the older works are available online at archive.org, Project Gutenberg or Google Books).

Abulafia, David, *The Great Sea: A Human History of the Mediterranean* (Allen Lane, 2011)

Antonelli, Quinto and Gianfranco Bettega (eds), *Giuseppe Chioni e Giosué Fiorentino – La Fame e la Memoria: Ricettari della Grande Guerra, Celle Lager 1917-1918* (Agorà Libreria Editrice, 2008)

Bevilacqua, Piero, Andreina De Clementi, Emilio Franzina (eds), *Storia dell'Emigrazione Italiana: Partenze* (Donzelli Editore, 2001)

Boswell, James, *An Account of Corsica, the Journal of a Tour to that Island, and Memoirs of Pascal Paoli* (1768 Glasgow edn)

Braudel, Fernand, *The Mediterranean and the Mediterranean World in the Age of Philip II: Volume I* (1966 revised edition, translated 1972, this edition University of California Press, 1995)

Brennan, Stuart, *Roberto Mancini: the Man Behind Manchester City's Greatest-Ever Season* (Carlton Books Ltd, 2012)

Belgrano, Luigi Tommaso and Cesare Imperiale (eds), *Annali Genovesi di Caf faro e de' suoi Continuatori* (Genova, Tipografia del R Instituto Sordo-Muti, 1901)

Benedictow, Ole J., *The Black Death 1346-1353: the Complete History* (The Boydell Press, 2004)

Carden, Robert Walter, *The City of Genoa* (Methuen and Co, 1908)

Campodonico, Pierangelo, *Andrea Doria* (Tormena Editore, 1997)

Casaccia, Giovanni, *Vocabolario Genovese-Italiano* (Genoa, 1851)

Chambers, James, *The Devil's Horsemen: the Mongol Invasion of Europe* (Phoe nix Press, 2001)

Chioni, Giuseppe with Luigi Marazza, *Arte Culinaria*, 1918 – unpublished (Archivio Ligure della Scrittura Popolare, Genoa)

D'Albertis, Anna, *Marinaio Gentiluomo: La Vita Avventurosa di Enrico d'Albertis, un Modern Viaggiatore di Altri Tempi* (Il Golfo, 2008)

D'Albertis, Luigi, *New Guinea: What I did and What I Saw* (Volumes 1 and 2) (Sampson Low, Marston, Searle, and Rivington, 1880)

De Amicis, Edmondo, *Sull'Oceano* (trans. *On Blue Water*) (G.P. Putnam's Sons, 1897)

De Palma, Maria Camilla, *Castello D'Albertis: Museo delle Culture del Mondo* (Silvana Editoriale, 2008)

Dickens, Charles, *Pictures from Italy* (Transcribed for free Kindle download by David Price from Chapman & Hall edition, 1913)

Dickie, John, *Delizia! The Epic History of Italians and their Food* (Sceptre, 2008)

Dwyer, Philip, *Napoleon (Volume I): The Path to Power 1769-1799* (Blooms bury Paperbacks, 2014)

Epstein, Steven A., *Genoa and the Genoese: 958-1528* (The University of North Carolina Press, 1996)

Foot, John, *Calcio: a History of Italian Football* (Harper Perennial, 2007)

Garibaldi, Giuseppe, *My Life* translation by Stephen Parkin (Hesperus Classics 2004)

George, Rose, *Deep Sea and Foreign Going: Inside Shipping, the Invisible Industry that Brings You 90% of Everything* (Portobello, 2013)

Gilmour, David, *The Pursuit of Italy: A History of a Land, its Regions and their Peoples* (Allen Lane, 2011)

Gioffré, Domenico, *Il Mercato degli Schiavi a Genova nel Secolo XV* (Genova, 1971)

Guilianotti, Richard, *Football: A Sociology of the Global Game* (Polity Press, 1999)

Hall, Martin and Jonathan Phillips (translators) *Caffaro, Genoa and the Twelfth-Century Crusades* (Ashgate Publishing, 2013)

Currey, E. Hamilton, *Sea-Wolves of the Mediterranean* (John Murray, 1910, available at http://www.gutenberg.org/ebooks/13689)

Hoffer, William, *Saved! The Story of the Andrea Doria – the Greatest Sea Rescue in History* (Pan Books, 1979)

Hooper, John, *Alien Landing: Beppe Grillo and the Advent of Dotcom Politics* (Kindle Single, 2013)

Kirk, Thomas Allison, *Genoa and the Sea: Policy and Power in an Early Modern Maritime Republic 1559-1684* (The Johns Hopkins University Press, 2005)

Konstam, Angus, *Lepanto 1571: The Greatest Naval Battle of the Renaissance* (Osprey Publishing, 2003)

Konstam, Angus, *Renaissance War Galley: 1470-1590* (Osprey Publishing, 2002)

LaGumina, Salvatore et al, *The Italian American Experience: An Encyclopedia* (Garland Publishing, 2000)

Livingstone, Marilyn and Morgen Witzel, *The Road to Crécy: The English Invasion of France 1346* (Pearson Education Limited, 2005)

Mack Smith, Denis, *Modern Italy: A Political History* (Yale University Press, 1997)

Mangione, Jerre and Ben Morreale, *La Storia: Five Centuries of the Italian American Experience* (Harper Perennial, 1993)

Monelli, Paolo, *Il Ghiottone Errante: Viaggio Gastronomico Attraverso l'Italia* (Touring Club Italiano, 2005)

Munro, A.O., *Practical Guide to Genoa and the Rivieras* (Pagano, 1903)

Muratore, Marino and gli ospiti dell'ASP Brignole, *La Memoria, la mia Storia* (ASP Emanuele Brignole, 2008)

Norwich, John Julius, *The Middle Sea: A History of the Mediterranean* (Chatto and Windus, 2006)

Nicolle, David, *Failure of an Elite – The Genoese at Crécy* July 1 2000, available at http://www.ospreypublishing.com/articles/medieval_world/failure_of_an_elite_the_genoese_at_crecy/

————— *Italian Medieval Armies 1000-1300* (Osprey Publishing, 2002)

Polo, Marco, Henri Cordier and Henry Yule, *The Travels of Marco Polo – Complete [Illustrated]* Kindle Edition (MacMay, 2008)

Polo, Marco, *The Travels of Marco Polo,* greatly amended and enlarged from valuable early manuscripts recently published by the French Society of Geography and in Italy by the Count Baldelli Boni, by Hugh Murray (Oliver and Boyd, 1845)

Runciman, Steven, *The Fall of Constantinople 1453* (Cambridge University Press, 1990)

Smollett, Tobias, *Travels Through France and Italy* (1766)

Steinacher, Gerald, *Nazis on the Run: How Hitler's Henchmen Fled Justice* (Oxford University Press, 2011)

Vialli, Gianluca with Gabriele Marcotti, *The Italian Job: A Journey to the Heart of Two Great Footballing Cultures* (Bantam Press, 2006)

Waley, Daniel, *The Italian City-Republics* (3rd ed) (Longman, 1988)

Whitehouse, Rosie, *Liguria* (Bradt Guides, 2013)

Dal Porto al Mondo: Uno Sguardo Multimediale su Genova e la Grande Emigrazione (Centro Internazionale di studi sull'Emigrazione Italiana, 2004)

La Via delle Americhe: l'Emigrazione Ligure tra Evento e Racconto (Sagep Editrice, 1989)

Il Comune di Genova – Bollettino Municipale (31 August 1922)

INDEX

INDEX